'*The Handbook of Therapeutic Care* is a wonderfully practical and readable guide for all of us dedicated to creating pathways to health for children exposed to chronic trauma and abuse – children who are stuck in an inner world filled with helplessness, chaos and danger. Despite the multiplicity of voices of (outstanding) contributors, this handbook provides a unified synthesis of practices that help us understand the pressures from the past on current behavior, and presents a comprehensive and well-tested model to provide sensory, relational and emotional repair for children and young people who carry the legacy of danger, abandonment, and unpredictability. This is the integration we have been waiting for.'

– *Bessel A. van der Kolk MD, Medical Director, the Trauma Center, Professor of Psychiatry, Boston University School of Medicine, Author: NYT best seller:* The Body Keeps the Score: Brain, Mind, and Body in the Healing of Trauma

'Finally, a book that successfully addresses all of the complex bio-psycho-social-developmental consequences of early trauma! Therapeutic Care treats the embodied and encultured mind at each stage of life in a way that leverages the way the brain evolved to heal - in security and safety. Highly recommended.'

– *Louis Cozolino Ph.D., Professor of Psychology, Author of* The Neuroscience of Human Relationships

The Handbook of THERAPEUTIC CARE for CHILDREN

of related interest

The A-Z of Therapeutic Parenting
Strategies and Solutions
Sarah Naish
ISBN 978 1 78592 376 0
eISBN 978 1 78450 732 9

Revealing the Inner World of Traumatised Children and Young People
An Attachment-Informed Model for Assessing Emotional Needs and Treatment
Christine Bradley with Francia Kinchington
Foreword by Judith Trowell
ISBN 978 1 78592 019 6
eISBN 978 1 78450 265 2

A Therapeutic Treasure Box for Working with Children and Adolescents with Developmental Trauma
Creative Techniques and Activities
Dr. Karen Treisman
ISBN 978 1 78592 263 3
eISBN 978 1 78450 553 0

Creative Therapies for Complex Trauma
Helping Children and Families in Foster Care, Kinship Care or Adoption
Edited by Anthea Hendry and Joy Hasler
Foreword by Colwyn Trevarthen
ISBN 978 1 78592 005 9
eISBN 978 1 78450 242 3

Creating Loving Attachments
Parenting with PACE to Nurture Confidence and Security in the Troubled Child
Kim S. Golding and Daniel A. Hughes
ISBN 978 1 84905 227 6
eISBN 978 0 85700 470 3

Innovative Therapeutic Life Story Work
Developing Trauma-Informed Practice for Working with Children, Adolescents and Young Adults
Edited by Richard Rose
Foreword by Deborah D. Gray
ISBN 978 1 78592 185 8
eISBN 978 1 78450 468 7

The Handbook of THERAPEUTIC CARE for CHILDREN

Evidence-Informed Approaches to Working with Traumatized Children and Adolescents in Foster, Kinship and Adoptive Care

Edited by **JANISE MITCHELL**, **JOE TUCCI** and **ED TRONICK**

Foreword by Stephen W. Porges

Jessica Kingsley *Publishers*
London and Philadelphia

First published in 2020
by Jessica Kingsley Publishers
73 Collier Street
London N1 9BE, UK
and
400 Market Street, Suite 400
Philadelphia, PA 19106, USA

www.jkp.com

Library of Congress Cataloging in Publication Data
A CIP catalog record for this book is available from the Library of Congress

British Library Cataloguing in Publication Data
A CIP catalogue record for this book is available from the British Library

ISBN 978 1 78592 751 5
eISBN 978 1 78450 554 7

Printed and bound in Great Britain

Contents

Foreword

Feeling Safe is the Treatment

STEPHEN W. PORGES, PHD

Mitchell, Tucci, and Tronick have assembled a paradigm-shifting volume that informs us about the unique vulnerabilities of children exposed to trauma and abuse. The book is organized around an evolving treatment model developed by staff, affiliates, and collaborators of the Australian Childhood Foundation (ACF). During the past decade, ACF implemented a bold and innovative strategy to inform clinicians, scientists, and educators about the breakthrough treatment for trauma and cutting-edge research that conceptualized the neural pathways through which traumatic events are transformed into debilitating mental and physical health. This strategy focused on engaging world-renowned innovators in the field of traumatology.

Initially, ACF invited pioneering clinicians and scientists to inform their staff and to conduct workshops for clinicians and educators in Australia. This evolved into a biennial trauma summit in which world-leading researchers, clinicians, and advocates in traumatology met in Melbourne and shared their knowledge and insights with more than 2500 conference participants. As clinicians and educators were informed through these structured vehicles (i.e. workshops and summit), ACF incorporated this knowledge into a model of improved treatment for children with trauma histories, who were dependent on foster, kinship, and adoptive care. This Handbook is a product of the synergistic collaborations between ACF and the clinicians and scientists who have been welcomed into the ACF community.

By targeting the volume to children who, following trauma and abuse, have been placed in foster, kinship, and adoptive care, the four major points of the Handbook are unveiled. First, due to the greater physical and 'neural' vulnerability of the young child relative to a full-grown adult, trauma and abuse result in a trajectory with frequently poorer outcomes. Second, trauma experiences have the potential to retune the child's nervous system from a normal state of welcoming and trust to a chronic state of defense devoid of the feelings of safety that the nervous system requires to thrive and develop. Third, treatment models for these vulnerable children need to reconceptualize the child's chronic defensiveness as a neurobiologically driven adaptive response that lowers thresholds to be aggressive and raises the threshold to detect and respond to cues of safety. Fourth, a unique model of care, *therapeutic child care*, is presented, which attempts to facilitate the positive development of children with trauma histories, who have been removed from their biological families and placed in foster, kinship, and adoptive care. These are the children who, by being locked in a chronic state of defense, are the least welcoming to well-intentioned approaches of support and the least receptive to cues of safety and trust.

As we study the impact of trauma and abuse, we learn through the absence of specific emotional reactions and social behaviors what it is to be a successful, adaptive, and social human. In the study of adult survivors, we see the loss of function in 'real time'. Almost immediately after the traumatic insult, we can see the massive impact of the trauma on the individual. We see trauma 'retune' a survivor from loving and trusting others into a withdrawn individual who distances from previous social relationships, finds it difficult to trust friends, and loses a sense of purpose and a desire to live. These changes occur rapidly as the body changes neural state in response to a violation of trust and an expectancy to be safe. This sequence provides a window to see the unfolding of phylogenetically newer neural circuits that evolved to enable connectedness and co-regulation with others. With this unfolding following trauma, reflecting a disinhibition of evolutionarily ancient defense mechanisms, we are informed that the critical and most devastating transformative biobehavioral feature is a loss of feeling safe and a capacity to connect and share moments of intimacy with others. This trajectory, illustrating the loss of affiliative function and trust, provides therapeutic clues of the importance of reintroducing cues of safety to down-regulate states of defense and to provide opportunities to engage and co-regulate.

In the case of child survivors of trauma and abuse, the opportunity to feel safe is frequently limited or non-existent during early child development. These children are often abruptly removed from the care of their biological parents and assigned by government agencies into foster, kinship, or adoptive care settings that, at least initially, do not provide a resource base of connectedness and co-regulation with family that would be consistent with biological (i.e. evolutionary) expectation. By being born into severely dysregulated families, these children never have had the opportunity to experience a prolonged period of safety consistent with their bodily needs for health, growth, and restoration. Without feeling safe, the child's nervous system becomes highly reactive to violations of contingent reciprocity and incapable of the self-regulation necessary for spontaneous repairs.

The impact of disruptions of normal child–parent connectedness may be visualized through the Tronick still-face model (Tronick *et al.*, 1978). This brief laboratory manipulation requires the mother, after social engaging and interacting with the infant, to abruptly freeze her face in a blank expression for a couple of minutes. This disengagement serves as a violation of the expectancy for reciprocal interaction and co-regulation with the mother. Often this disruption results in the child crying or going into a tantrum. The disruption is short-lived, when the mother is required to repair the disruption by re-engaging and calming the infant. As a model of transitory disruptions and repairs, the still-face paradigm provides insight into the adaptive flexibility of the child's nervous system. It is a model of the normal ruptures and rapid repairs that occur in healthy family units. However, in homes of abuse, repairs are infrequent and infant bouts of crying and tantrums often trigger physical and emotional abuse.

Using the still-face paradigm as a model of 'normal' ruptures and repairs, researchers have been able to track the potency of maternal cues (e.g. facial expressions, intonations of voice, and gestures) on the infant's behavior and autonomic state. The still-face paradigm provides a model to observe the adaptive importance of the caregiver's engagement in the regulation of the infant's physiological state to optimize health, growth, and restoration. However, violations without repairs, which characterize the environments of the children removed from the care of their biological parents, functionally retune the child's nervous system into a state of chronic defensiveness.

This is in contrast to more optimal developmental environments, which reframe transitory disruptors into opportunities for repairs. A predictable cycle of disruption followed by repairs functions as a neural exercise increasing the effectiveness and efficiency of the repairs. This sequence improves the child's resilience. These sequences enable self-regulation to emerge from predictable opportunities for co-regulation. As the social interaction between the caregiver and infant becomes a predictable mode for co-regulation, a trust emerges that enables transitory violations, which are followed by repairs, to become a neural platform for humor (e.g. peek-a-boo) and play.

In contrast to the normal sequence during which a parent actively co-regulates the infant and the infant trusts the intentions and consequences of the parent's behavior, children from severely abusive homes start their vulnerable and dependent lives in volatile contexts dominated by cues of danger and threat. These cues are sufficient to chronically trigger the child's neurophysiology into states of defense. *Therapeutic Care* is proposed to treat this vulnerable group. Critical to an understanding of this paradigm shift in treatment is an understanding that the chronic defensive states observed in children who come from these backgrounds reflect an adaptive 'biological' survival strategy that is relatively independent of intention and conscious awareness. Rather than expressing an intention to be aggressive, oppositional, and defensive, due their early abusive history, their nervous systems are tuned to be hypervigilant and hyper-defensive. Without being able to efficiently calm their physiological state and to down-regulate their defenses, these children provide few opportunities to co-regulate with another that in turn could provide opportunities to establish trusting relationships with caregivers, therapists, educators, or peers.

Polyvagal Theory (Porges, 2011) forms a component of this new model by emphasizing the important role that physiological state plays in mediating the effectiveness of an intervention. Within a clinical treatment model, Polyvagal Theory emphasizes that physiological state functions as an intervening variable either opening or closing the portal for trust and co-regulation. Consistent with ACF's goal, Therapeutic Care incorporates a respect for the child's physiological state and how that state changes thresholds that will either facilitate the child feeling safe and trusting others or become defensive and biasing the nervous system to detect risk (i.e. neuroception), even when there is no real risk in the environment.

At the core of the new model is a strategy to build relationships of safety with the child. Thus, although moving the child from abusive biological parents removes threat, it is not the equivalent of providing the child with the neurobiological state that promotes feelings of safety. The importance of safety, and especially fostering feelings of safety, becomes the theme of the new paradigm and is central to several of the Handbook's chapters, and was introduced by two of the co-editors in an earlier publication (Tucci, Weller and Mitchell, 2018).

As I read the Handbook, I was reminded that trauma and abuse need to be understood from a biological perspective and not solely from behavioral, sociological, and psychosocial perspectives. A biological perspective informs us that the survival repertoire of an abused child, being physically small and neurologically immature, is limited to more primitive defense systems dependent on the fight and flight (i.e. mobilization) and dissociation/death feigning (i.e. immobilization) strategies. These strategies tend to be reactive and reflexive, rather than being voluntary and intentional. The defensive strategies functionally are dependent on physiological states that preclude moments of feeling safe and trust. The 'retuned' nervous system of the abused child makes it difficult to reverse the antisocial tendencies and to rehabilitate the child into a more typical social context of trust and co-regulation. Thus, as proposed in the Handbook, a new treatment model is needed that acknowledges the abused child's need to 'feel' safe.

There is a contrast between the importance of how 'feeling' safe optimizes development and how good intentions of educators, family members, therapists, advocates, and government agencies may misinterpret the biological need for safety and infer that the removal of threat is the panacea. Institutionalization of removing threat as the sole priority has resulted in the displacement of children from families and familiar communities.

In Australia, the *Stolen Generation* resulted from an intention by institutions that did not match the biological needs of the child born to Indigenous peoples. In Australia, we can see the impact of marginalization and disenfranchisement on mental and physical health and all aspects of child development. From a Western scientific perspective, we see the effects in 'real time'. Although similar strategies injured First Nations cultures in both the United States and Canada, the initial legislation that promoted the separation of child from family and culture occurred several decades before the policy was implemented in Australia; the understanding gained from these traumatic separations did not lead to enduring lessons. We are now at a historical time when we need, as stated in the Handbook, cultural humility.

Decades of research have documented what ancient societies intuitively knew about fostering and optimizing development in children. These societies knew and respected the importance of delivering cues of safety through family and community. During the past 100 years, anthropologists have rediscovered the important role that family and community has in enabling a child to feel safe.

Within our contemporary society (and science), we tend to minimize feelings and focus on cognitions and language. Perhaps, as modern Indo-European languages evolved from oral communication to written transcriptions, the syntax was optimized to describe objects and observations. This enabled scientific discoveries to be shared and allowed structured prose and poetry to proliferate. As the syntax and grammar of these languages became formalized, the languages became poor vehicles for the expression and sharing of feelings. However, on the positive side, modern European written languages have an obvious benefit of sharing unambiguous descriptions of events and objects.

When it comes to expressing our feelings, we tend to use primitive vocalizations such as screams and not words. When suffering pain, physicians do not ask for words that convey qualitative or quantitative differences in the experiences. Instead, physicians ask the patient to rate the pain on a scale from 1 to 10. It comes as no surprise that feelings of safety have only recently been brought into discussions of mental health treatment. Common use of English does not provide a syntax that distinguishes between feeling an external object and feelings experienced inside one's body.

The Handbook unambiguously emphasizes that the Therapeutic Care of abused and traumatized children requires a new paradigm that emphasizes the role that 'feeling' safe has in treatment. We learn that cues of safety are distinct from the words used to communicate. Cues of safety are conveyed through neurobiological channels that do not require cognitive processing (e.g. neuroception). These cues are frequently conveyed by intonation of voice (not words), spontaneous facial expressions, and welcoming hand gestures and body posture. In emphasizing this point, it encourages therapists to explore the cues of safety that have the capacity to open brief time windows during which the child's physiological state becomes calm. It will be during these brief moments that the astute therapist can build sufficient trust to dampen feelings of defense. As these moments expand in duration, the relationship starts to have the capacity to co-regulate, with the potential to repair disruptions.

The Handbook provides an important step in providing an integrated treatment model, Therapeutic Care, that is consistent with the observations of therapists, the experiences of children, and the science that has evolved to explain the neural pathways through which trauma disrupts function. It will be through treatment models such as Therapeutic Care that children who have experienced abuse and trauma early in life will have an opportunity to 'feel safe' and be enabled to spontaneously re-engage with the world of trust, co-regulation, and relationships.

References

Porges, S.W. (2011). *The Polyvagal Theory: Neurophysiological Foundations of Emotions, Attachment, Communication, and Self-Regulation*. New York, NY: W.W. Norton and Company.

Tronick, E., Als, H., Adamson, L., Wise, S., and Brazelton, T.B. (1978). The infant's response to entrapment between contradictory messages in face-to-face interaction. *Journal of American Academy of Child Psychology*, 17(1), 1–13.

Tucci, J., Weller, A., and Mitchell, J. (2018). Realizing 'Deep' Safety for Children Who Have Experienced Abuse: Application of Polyvagal Theory in Therapeutic Work with Traumatized Children and Young People. In S.W. Porges and D. Dana (eds), *Clinical Applications of the Polyvagal Theory: The Emergence of Polyvagal-Informed Therapies*. New York, NY: W.W. Norton and Company.

Acknowledgements

Many people have made the seeming impossible challenge of completing this book not just a possibility, but a reality. As a six-year-old child accompanying my mother to work in her role as a relief cottage mother in a 'home' for eight 'Wards of the State' (yes, you were allowed to do that way back when!), so my interest in children and young people living in out-of-home care began. Little was I to know it would shape my career and my life.

My mum, who died a number of years ago, was and always will be an inspiration to me. Her 'heart' was ever present in her care and support of the 'cottage kids'. She reminds me to this day of the importance of connection, belonging and hope.

My children, Kate and Matthew, have shown great love and support to me always. I am forever grateful for all that they have taught me.

Thank you to all the contributors to this book who have been generous with their time and commitment. Finally, thank you to my amazing colleagues at the Australian Childhood Foundation whose commitment to children drives such creativity in the work we do. You are inspiring.

Janise Mitchell

I have learned about relationships from the wisdom of my family, the children I have worked with and the wonderful therapists, trainers and consultants at the Australian Childhood Foundation. My dad was a lovely man who showed me how deep respect is a quality of immense value. My mum, Rose, Carmen and their families have been a source of constant love and affection. Angie, Mikey, Liam, Kate and Matthew are a font of fun and mirth. And, of course, Mim, Ruby and Oscar bring humour and warmth to my life, and undeniable patience. Thank you.

Joe Tucci

I want to thank my wife – therapist and author – Marilyn Davillier for her wonderful residential care of me.

Ed Tronick

1

The Need for a New Paradigm in the Care and Support of Children in Foster, Kinship and Adoptive Care

JOE TUCCI, JANISE MITCHELL AND ED TRONICK

> *During a time of great pain and crisis in my life, my great grannie came to me and gave me a gift. She sent me a dream... I asked 'What do we do now?' And the answer came 'We come here, and we sit with each other. We tell our stories. We grieve together. And we dance and we sing together. If we do this, as we listen to each other's stories, in our grieving, in our singing, in our dancing, we give power to each other for the healing to begin...'*
>
> Judy Atkinson, Prologue to *Trauma Trails: Recreating Song Lines* (2002)

In the dream offered by her ancestors, Professor Judy Atkinson experiences relationships across generations as a timeless living resource. As a strong Aboriginal woman of Jiman and Bundjalung descent, Atkinson's research into the traumatic effects of colonising power on the Indigenous peoples of Australia is both a haunting personal reflection of loss and a confronting analysis of the historical legacy of oppression and racial violence. In tracing the trauma trails of her people and suggesting a way for obliterated song lines of strength and courage to be recreated, she offers up the insight that the essence of survival lies in the effort of community to hold relationships that collectively nurture even the smallest act of an individual to resist the forms of violation they are forced to endure.

For those engaged in the practice of supporting others to recover from the effects of interpersonal violence and abuse, it is a simple truth that relationships have an inherent power to heal trauma. Relationships offer the opportunity for hurt to be understood, shared and ultimately, as Bonnie Badenoch suggests, 'digested' (2018). Tronick (1989) and Schore (2012) have described the change process of therapy as emanating from a relationship between therapist and client through which the client is able to experience stressful and dysregulated states in affectively tolerable doses, allowing them to become integrated and repaired. Perhaps described differently, the views of many authors in the trauma field coalesce around the pivotal nature of the therapeutic relationship between therapist and individual and/or family in recovery (Bromberg, 2011; Cozolino, 2002; Hughes, 2007; Siegel, 1999; Stern, 2004; Wilkinson, 2010;).

All of these therapist/authors locate themselves within the tradition of psychotherapy with an inherent tendency to privilege the relational dyad between the therapist and client as the generator of healing. Of course, this is not surprising. They come from long-standing systems of practice organised around the needs of individuals who have suffered trauma in their past and who come to seek relief post these experiences. Often, they arrive at much later points in time, as adults who were abused during their childhoods. Or they come because they are overwhelmed with issues in the present that they do not understand and are slowly supported to engage with the genesis of these experiences being related to a history of trauma. It is at these moments that therapists and individuals form profound relationships that cover the terrain of powerful emotions as they emerge in the present but are sourced with references to their past. The therapeutic dyad works at multiple levels concurrently – physiologically, emotionally, metaphorically, narratively.

This is not the context, at all, for children who come to be placed with carers who are not the carers who have hurt or violated them. These children in out-of-home care (foster care, kinship care, adoptive care) face a number of challenges. Their needs are in the present. Their experience of trauma is in the very recent past. Their relational world has undergone painful upheaval.

Many of them have experienced neglect, sexual abuse, physical abuse and/or family violence. Frequently, they have experienced these forms of violation in combination. As a result, the connective flow of their neurobiology has been forced to adapt under pressure to enable them to survive their ordeal. They engage in repetitive patterns of behaviour, feelings and thoughts that swirl through them out of their control. Organised around protecting them from threat, their inner experiences of others hold them suspended in relational substrates that perpetuate instability and rejection. Their internal states seek comfort and attuned responses that have never arrived. They are stuck in endless loops of expectancy that further aggravate the toxic levels of stress in their neural networks, making them disengage from the present moment. It makes it very difficult for them to access resources that relationships in the here-and-now offer them.

Many have also experienced multiple forms of loss. They do not live in their family home any longer. Some have been removed from their cultural context and their connection to traditional practices and the experience of country. They are not always able to stay in the same school, with familiar teachers and friends who they know and who know them. They carry with them the weight of unexplainable grief that coagulates their senses, forever dampening the experiences of joy and fun. They wait with anticipation for an event like a birthday or a holiday only to find an emptiness permeating them from the inside.

Their routines change beyond their control. They leave behind everything they have known. They are forced to start again. If they have had to move a number of times, they will find it difficult to settle into a new place and make friends again, learn new rules at school and remember the names of their new teachers. They will expect to move again. They deeply know that relationships do not last. Even if they can, it will be painful to become too attached to anything or anyone. They fear familiarity because it breeds the expectation of a continuity that in their experience is rarely realised. Change itself is more predictable than stability.

Many of their developmental needs have remained unmet for some time. The co-organisation of meaning-making between infant and carers, as noted in the pioneering work by Tronick (2017), has been absent. In the face of disorganised internal systems of the adults around them, from an early age these children have been often left in a void lacking the congruency of synchronous response to their needs generously given, warmly experienced by the child and carer alike. Instead, the rupture-and-repair cycle is left in an open loop. Spontaneous episodes of play, as they occur, are subordinated in favour of tension and confusion. Children's offers to engage are met with harshness or indifference. The stimulation required by the growing brain is not available. Children's cries are unattended. Their sense of wonder in the nascent experiences of the colour of life are sources of frustration for the adults. There is no delight or shared curiosity. Children's developmental push for fun and creativity is experienced as a drag on the already pushed-to-the-limit resources of their carers. Children come to play by themselves away from the opportunity for criticism. They learn to keep their impulses to connect away from the glare of the relationships which may redefine them as burdensome, extreme and selfish. Children sense it. Sometimes they can even articulate it. They come to know that, of all the possible ways to anticipate relationships, the form that previous interactions have taken shapes what they will expect from now on (Badenoch, 2018).

When child protection authorities remove them from the abuse and violence, they move into relationships that offer them care and embodied reciprocity. And yet they continue to act as if they were still stuck in the environments that were filled with danger. Often their behaviour is misinterpreted. They are not testing relationships to see if they will be loved. They are not pushing people away or avoiding intimacy. They are doing what they have always done. Their internal neural networks play out anticipatory relational dynamics with predictable monotony. Indeed, their behaviour is more of an echo of the past than it is a portal to what is happening in the here-and-now. The new relationships have the opportunity to reconfigure these expectancies, but only with patience, only with the intent to hear and listen to children's own purpose for the way they are and how they believe life to be.

They have not been listened to. Often, they have known that verbalising an utterance would lead to more violence. They may have refused to speak. They may have tried to communicate a protest and been actively silenced. Their words may have been manipulated and used against them. They have been told that their opinions do not count. Their views have not been sought. Even without it being obvious, they have been left to believe that there was no point expecting them to be worthy of being noticed or being considered. Their needs have been less than visible. These children are not fully acknowledged in the gaze of the relationships they crave.

They have come to feel that they are paid attention to only when it is for the purpose of the other. There is little unconditional attention paid to them without some other agenda. Their systems have not been accompanied and encouraged as Badenoch (2018) suggests they should.

They are not able to influence or exert control over decisions about them. In their family, their body has not been their own. It has been taken over by those with intentions to hurt them, and in the case of sexual abuse, for the adult's own gratification. Who these children can love, what they can find funny, where they can play, when they can sleep or eat, who they can see, what explanations they can give have all been determined by the adults with the power in their family. Sometimes they have had to act in a dramatic way for anyone to notice their influence – they have overdosed, or run away, or set something on fire. They have hurt themselves deliberately – scratching their face, burning their arms with matches, taking medication meant for other conditions to stay asleep. They have drunk alcohol, sniffed paint, injected drugs sold to them in exchange for sex. Every behaviour a statement aimed at broadcasting their need for support and for protection. None of these experiences have given them the sense of personal agency they see in their peers for whom life has felt normal. Their internal systems drive or reflect the environments of impoverished resources to enable them to slowly find and express how they want their life to be, who they want to live with, what they can do to feel safer. These children have not had the opportunity to rehearse thinking and planning – they have reacted to events, to circumstances, to their experience from deeply embedded circuitry using sensory and implicit memory inputs that are bound to repeat past engrained patterns of defences and self-protection.

The narratives which emerge about them sit perched upon the underlying physiological states of their neural networks. Heightened activated states of arousal are experienced and stored in their body (Briere, 1992, 2004; Ogden, 2015; Ogden, Minton and Pain, 2006; Porges, 2011, 2014; van der Kolk, 2014), recruiting muscles to act in ways that are set by the parameters of the relationships they are in. They slump when they feel the oppression that accompanies the brutal enforcement of power in their family. The familiarity of their internal bio-behavioural rhythms is plagued with inconsistency.

They clench, they jerk, they cower, they disconnect, they tremble as the circuitry enlisted to mediate the intensity of the toxic consequences of the violence sets off cascades of micro-physiological changes all over their brains and bodies. The whispered descriptions in their mind surface into stories that affirm them as damaged, as throwaway, as unworthy. They believe that they are stupid, crazy, insignificant, incapable. They come to know themselves in the reflective accounts of others around them – they are terrible friends, they are dangerous, they fight all the time, they steal, they are disrespectful, they do not listen, they do not follow rules, they cannot learn, they need to be medicated, they are a risk to themselves, they will hurt others. The stories precede them into new relationships. They are written into case files. They become the version of the truth that takes hold and can be extremely difficult to dislodge.

New carers hear these biographical sketches and brace themselves for what will follow – they prepare for the worst, trying the best they can to keep themselves open to the possibility of change. But others in the child's network are more pessimistic. They believe in punishment, in treatment, in ensuring that the child's behaviour does not escalate even further. The warnings for new schools are to keep a tight rein on the young person's behaviour, to watch for what they bring with them, to tolerate no more than average testing of boundaries and limits. Some even insist on medication before they are considered. These systems have been burnt before, too – they have learned from cruel experience how easy it is for these children to be dumped with them and forgotten. The stress caused by multiple incidents amplifying over time with each unsupported child who disrupts the school, or the sports game, or the camp, or the excursion.

Without a collective orientation and active resourcing, the networks of relationships around these young people follow the previous sub-plots through to their previous conclusions. They, like the children themselves, are systems with patterned dynamics that are difficult to shift, especially when the intensity of the energy released by the crises prompted by these children sets off alarm bells for staff, other service users, other families. These children represent risk, hazards, danger. They need monitoring. They need to be controlled. The softness and kindness required by these children can be present but often only in short bursts. Individuals within these systems put effort into compassionate forms of understanding in attempts to keep the system open enough to receive and hold the distress of these young people – only to experience the rebuff of colleagues when these children's behaviour inevitably escalates. And in the process the children are left without defenders, patrons to make it a little easier for them to be comprehended, for them to be responded to tenderly and sensitively.

These children have not been safe for a long time and no longer feel safe. Their embodied memories of people and places surge with associations with intolerable pain, threat and danger. Any slivers of warmth, nurture and reassurance they have had sit as unintegrated experiences diminished in influence and potency. As Tucci, Weller and Mitchell (2018) have described:

> When abuse involves force and violence, it compels children's mobilization system to stay activated. Terror fills their hearts. They are not sure when the next time their father will come home drunk on a rampage against them or their mother. They are not sure the next time they will be hit with a pipe or a hose because they did not finish their dinner. They cannot predict when they will be pushed onto the bed and raped. Their home, their room, the family kitchen hold the sensory elements that evoke cascades of overwhelming danger. Every exchange with the adult who has abused them triggers fear. They must be ready to defend themselves, their bodies in a constant state of preparedness for action. Mobilization becomes the steady state for a child. At least, until such threat is so overwhelming that there is little hope of changing it, stopping it, running far enough away from it. And then children collapse. They immobilize to survive. They disconnect. Their physiology moves to conserve whatever resources it still has. They become small, lose their voice. Their bodies and minds give up on safety. (p.94)

Indeed, as they enter into new relationships away from those who have hurt them to those who intend to care for them, these children find the transitions unbearable as their internal systems designed to experience safety are paralysed. At a very real level, the ability to survive for these children depends on their capacity to evaluate accurately if a person or a situation is safe or dangerous. Porges (2011) coined the term 'neuroception' as the function of the neural networks that make these determinations. These brain–body systems are embedded deeply in mammalian physiology as a result of the evolutionary shifts caused as the violence of our own species becoming as likely, if not more likely, to be as life-threatening as the behaviour and action of other species. The interdependency of humans is both their greatest strength and their very vulnerability.

With repeated evidence that those who are supposed to care for you can also violate you or leave you unattended to fend for yourself, the neuroceptive capacity of these children in out-of-home care wisely works to keep them cautious and apprehensive of others who step into the role of carer. They have seen it before. They have heard it before. They know that words and gestures that carry intonations of trustworthiness may not be backed up. They have been proven to be empty and often hurtful. As a result, their internal drivers send them to the fringes of relationships, guarding against the moment that they will turn against them.

And in this sense, they are doubly betrayed. Not only have their relationships in the past hurt them, but they have also ill-prepared them to be able to use the resources offered by safe relationships to heal. The very relational safety their systems crave can be beyond their reach.

These children are not waiting for relationships to work in the future for them. Their needs are so severe that they cannot afford to be supported only within one therapeutic dyad. They depend on relationships across the multiple contexts that they inhabit. *They need relationships to work for them in real time.* The impact of their experiences is so severe that they need multiple relationships to work for them, to help support the healing their brains and bodies are so desperate for. They need relationships to be sensitive to their needs in a consistent way across settings and over time.

This is the context in which the new paradigm of Therapeutic Care has surfaced. It is a recognition that traumatised children benefit from experiencing relationships around them that embrace therapeutic intent and hold therapeutic capacity. This does not mean that children should only have relationships with trained therapists. Far from it. These children need and use relationships that all children have – with adults who care for them directly, with adults who are teachers, with adults who are coaches, with the parents of their friends and with adults who act in the roles of uncles, aunts and grandparents. They also need to have and use relationships with other children and young people – siblings, friends, cousins, school friends, team mates, friends on social media. It means that for healing to occur, some of these relationships need to be purposeful and oriented to being used as resources in transformation.

Of course, therapists play an important role, too. In this process, the therapist adds the therapeutic effort (Tucci and Mitchell, 2019) locating themselves 'in between' children, their relationship community, their past, their present, their restraints, their strengths. Therapists find ways to coax new co-organised meanings from children and their relationships. They stitch and braid narratives from those that are available into cohesive truths that speak of connections between children and their carers, their schools, their families. They frame children's behaviour as an appeal to belong, to find grounded safety, to experience the developmental push to imagine and be different, to explore the sensory allegories that awaken with enlivened engagement of another. They recruit the collective commitment to understanding the meaning of behaviour. They keep open the relational heart of the adults in order to minimise their tendency to respond in kind to the confusion and blocks from embedded implicit patterns of survival of the young people. Therapists also map the curvature of the system's way of responding to the child, searching for points where new paths can be traced to offer the potential for different relational rhythms and the outcomes that may flow. They ensure that the networks of relationships involved in the lives of children in out-of-home care assess, consider and plan to meet the needs of children over their developmental lifespan. Just like a family does, the collective of key relationships projects into the future, examining how the children will change and grow and what needs to be in place to nurture their interests, their talents, their education, their own goals and ambitions.

Therapists also engage with children in relational therapeutic processes that introduce co-created opportunities to experience deep visceral safety while feeling the tentative beginnings of the developmental resources that have been resting dormant, waiting for the terror to dissipate. Therapist and child, therapist and child and carer, therapist and child and school teacher, move in coordinated ways to explore how implicit memories take shape in the enactments of the present. As they do, they overlay them with the sensory input of attuned curiosity, celebration, heart-to-heart exchanges that fill the deep void left by past unattended needs. These reciprocal exchanges between children and their relationship network, mediated by the therapist, also activate the cascading experiences of pleasure of carers and others in the acts of loving, connecting and caring.

In Therapeutic Care, therapists (who are given an expanded role as change leaders and systems enablers and renamed Therapeutic Specialists) and the relationship network around these young people recognise and work from the view that children's healing occurs in a milieu of relational transformation over time. It integrates therapeutic intent into the daily practices of care for children. In this definitional form, Therapeutic Care is the collective endeavour of relationship networks around children to engage in moments of relational repair that resonate back in the sensory memories of children to re-shift patterns of neurobiological activation that serve to keep the child's experience of trauma continuous and alive in the present. Children are resuscitated into new forms of being, relating and knowing experienced in embraces of care with lifelong resonance.

Therapeutic Care increasingly finds expression in forms of programs that have evolved from a range of different starting points but all with the same purpose: to reconstruct out-of-home care as active intervention seeking to deliver foundational experiences to children that apply the healing properties of safety, attunement, trust, predictability and stability (Boyd, Brylske and Wall, 2013; Bryant, 2004; B. Cairns, 2004; K. Cairns, 2002; Chamberlain *et al.*, 2008; Durham *et al.*, 2005; Fisher and Chamberlain, 2000; Fisher, Chamberlain and Leve, 2009; Fisher and Gillian, 2012; Foster Family-based Treatment Association, 2013; Frederico *et al.*, 2017; Hahn *et al.*, 2004; Hudson, Nutter and Galaway, 1994; Johnson, Pryce and Martinovich, 2011; Kessler *et al.*, 2008; MacDonald and Turner, 2008; Philpot and Thomas, 2009; Roberts, 2007; Rubenstein *et al.*, 1978; Smith, Chamberlain and Eddy, 2010; Snodgrass, 1989; Staines, Farmer and Selwyn, 2011; Webb, 1988).

Over the past 20 years, we (Mitchell and Tucci) have had the experience of conceiving and nurturing a Therapeutic Care program that has shown promising results in two evaluations (Gatwiri *et al.*, 2018; McPherson *et al.*, 2018; SuccessWorks, 2005). It is these efforts related to this long-term endeavour that have prompted this collection of writing. During this time, the need to improve outcomes for children and young people living in out-of-home care has evolved as a distinct clarion call for reform. Child protection systems around the world have moved, at different paces, towards realising more effective relational environments for children, enhanced levels of support for carers and ways to resource the therapeutic role of the network of professionals and important adults around children in foster, kinship and adoptive forms of care.

The ambition of the Handbook is to offer a synthesis and interpretation of the key elements that constitute Therapeutic Care as an emerging paradigm of practice that works to meet the past, present and future needs of children and young people in these contexts. Each chapter represents knowledge that practitioners in Therapeutic Care should be familiar with and use in their roles. At the end of each chapter, we have drawn out the key implications from the content and offered a reflective practice commentary for practitioners to consider.

Therapeutic Care is the programmatic translation of a knowledge base founded in the neuroscience of development, attachment and trauma. It offers ways to empower all relationships around children to hold therapeutic intent in the everyday of children's lived experiences of family, culture and contexts in which children find themselves playing and learning. Despite more than two decades of thinking, conceptualising and testing, the benefits for children who have suffered undeniable pain and neglect offered by the relational approaches that underpin Therapeutic Care are only now being gradually recognised. It is at this juncture in its narrative that this Handbook has emerged.

References

Atkinson, J. (2002). *Trauma Trails: Recreating Song Lines. The Transgenerational Effects of Trauma in Indigenous Australia.* North Melbourne: Spinifex.

Badenoch, B. (2018). *The Heart of Trauma: Healing the Embodied Brain in the Context of Relationships.* New York, NY: W.W. Norton and Company.

Boyd, L.W., Brylske, P. and Wall, E. (2013). *Beyond Safety and Permanency: Promoting Social and Emotional Well-being for Youth in Treatment Foster Care.* Hackensack, NJ: Foster Family-based Treatment Association.

Briere, J. (1992). *Child Abuse Trauma: Theory and Treatment of the Lasting Effects.* Newbury Park, CA: SAGE Publications.

Briere, J. (2004). Treating the long term effects of childhood maltreatment: A brief overview. *Psychotherapy in Australia*, 10, 12–18.

Bromberg, P. (2011). *The Shadow of the Tsunami and the Growth of the Relational Mind.* New York, NY: Routledge.

Bryant, B. (2004). *Treatment Foster Care: A Cost-Effective Strategy for Treatment of Children with Emotional, Behavioural or Medical Needs.* Hackensack, NJ: Foster Family-based Treatment Association.

Cairns, B. (2004). *Fostering Attachments: Long-Term Outcomes in Family Group Care.* London: BAAF.

Cairns, K. (2002). *Attachment, Trauma and Resilience: Therapeutic Caring for Children.* London: BAAF.

Chamberlain, P., Price, J., Leve, L., Laurent, H., Landsverk, J. and Reid, J. (2008). Prevention of behaviour problems for children in foster care: Outcomes and mediation effects. *Prevention Science*, 9, 17–27.

Cozolino, L. (2002). *The Neuroscience of Psychotherapy: Building and Rebuilding the Human Brain.* New York, NY: W.W. Norton and Company.

Durham, D., MacDonald, S., Palmer, S. and Sullivan, K. (2005). Growing the Tri-CAS Treatment Foster Care Program: A fifteen year retrospective. *OACAS Journal*, 49(3), 10–18.

Fisher, P. and Chamberlain, P. (2000). Multidimensional treatment foster care: A program for intensive parenting, family support, and skill building. *Journal of Emotional and Behavioural Disorders*, 8(3), 155–165.

Fisher, P., Chamberlain, P. and Leve, L. (2009). Improving the lives of foster children through evidenced-based interventions. *Vulnerable Children and Youth Studies*, 4(2), 122–127.

Fisher, P. and Gilliam, K. (2012). Multidimensional treatment foster care: An alternative to residential treatment for high risk children and adolescents. *Psychosocial Intervention*, 21(2), 195–203.

Foster Family-based Treatment Association (2013). *Program Standards for Treatment Foster Care*, 4th Edition. Hackensack, NJ: Foster Family-based Treatment Association.

Frederico, M., Long, M., McNamara, P., McPherson, L. and Rose, R. (2017). Improving outcomes for children in out-of-home care: The role of therapeutic foster care. *Child and Family Social Work*, 22, 1064–1074.

Gatwiri, K., McPherson, L., Macnamara, N., Mitchell, J. and Tucci, J. (2018). From adversity to stability to integration: How one Australian program is making a difference in therapeutic foster care. *Journal of Child and Adolescent Trauma*, 9 November 2018.

Hahn, R.A., Lowy, J., Bilukha, O., Snyder, S. *et al.* (2004). Therapeutic foster care for the prevention of violence. *Morbidity and Mortality Weekly Report*, 53(10), 1–8.

Hudson, J., Nutter, R.W. and Galaway, B. (1994). Treatment foster care programs: A review of evaluation research and suggested directions. *Social Work Research*, 18(4), 198–210.

Hughes, D.A. (2007). *Attachment-Focused Family Therapy.* New York, NY: W.W. Norton and Company.

Johnson, S., Pryce, J. and Martinovich, Z. (2011). The role of therapeutic mentoring in enhancing outcomes for youth in foster care. *Child Welfare*, 90(5), 51–69.

Kessler, R., Pecora, P., Williams, J., Hiripi, E. *et al.* (2008). Effects of enhanced foster care on the long-term physical and mental health of foster care alumni. *Archives of General Psychiatry*, 65(6), 625–633.

MacDonald, G. and Turner, W. (2008). Treatment foster care for improving outcomes in children and young people. *Cochrane Database Systematic Review*, 23(1).

McPherson, L., Gatwiri, K., Tucci, J., Mitchell, J. and Macnamara, N. (2018). A paradigm shift in responding to children who have experienced trauma: The Australian Treatment and Care for Kids Program. *Children and Youth Services Review*, 94, 524–535.

Ogden, P. (2015). Proximity, defence and boundaries with children and care-givers: A sensorimotor psychotherapy perspective. *Children Australia*, 40(2), 139–146.

Ogden, P., Minton, K. and Pain, C. (2006). *Trauma and the Body – A Sensorimotor Approach to Psychotherapy*. New York, NY: W.W. Norton and Company.

Philpot, T. and Thomas, M. (2009). *Fostering a Child's Recovery: Family Placement for Traumatized Children*. London: Jessica Kingsley Publishers.

Porges, S.W. (2011). *The Polyvagal Theory: Neurophysiological Foundations of Emotions, Attachment, Communication, and Self-regulation*. New York, NY: W.W. Norton and Company.

Porges, S.W. (2014). *The Pocket Guide to the Polyvagal Theory – The Transformative Power of Feeling Safe*. New York, NY: W.W. Norton and Company.

Roberts, R. (2007). A new approach to meeting the needs of looked after children experiencing difficulties: The multidimensional treatment foster care in England project. *AMACH Occasional Papers*, 26, 59–68.

Rubenstein, J.S., Armentrout, J.A., Levin, S. and Herald, D. (1978). The parent–therapist program: Alternate care for emotionally disturbed children. *American Journal of Orthopsychiatry*, 48, 654–662.

Schore, A.N. (2012). *The Science of the Art of Psychotherapy*. New York, NY: W.W. Norton and Company.

Siegel, D.J. (1999). *The Developing Mind: Towards a Neurobiology of Interpersonal Experience*. New York, NY: Guilford Press.

Smith, D., Chamberlain, P. and Eddy, J. (2010). Preliminary support for multidimensional treatment foster care in reducing substance abuse in delinquent boys. *Journal of Child and Adolescent Substance Abuse*, 19, 343–358.

Snodgrass, R. (1989). Treatment foster care: A proposed definition. *Community Alternatives: International Journal of Family Care*, 1(2), 79–82.

Staines, J., Farmer, E. and Selwyn, J. (2011). Implementing a therapeutic team parenting approach to fostering: The experiences of one independent foster-care agency. *British Journal of Social Work*, 41, 314–332.

Stern, D.N. (2004). *The Present Moment in Psychotherapy and Everyday Life*. New York, NY: W.W. Norton and Company.

SuccessWorks (2005). *Evaluation of the Treatment and Care for Kids (TrACK) Program*. Melbourne: SuccessWorks. Accessed on 21/12/2018 at https://professionals.childhood.org.au/app/uploads/2018/09/TrACK-Report-Evaluation-SW.pdf.

Tronick, E. (1989). Emotions and emotional communication in infants. *American Psychologist*, 44(2), 112–119.

Tronick, E. (2017). The caregiver–infant dyad as a buffer or transducer of resource enhancing or depleting factors that shape psychobiological development. *Australian and New Zealand Journal of Family Therapy*, 38(4), 561–572.

Tucci, J. and Mitchell, J. (2019). Therapeutic Services for Traumatised Children and Young People – Healing in the Everyday Experience of Relationships. In R. Benjamin, J. Haliburn and S. King (eds), *Humanising Mental Health Care in Australia – Introducing a Trauma-informed Approach*. Oxford: Routledge.

Tucci, J., Weller, A. and Mitchell, J. (2018). Realizing 'Deep' Safety for Children Who Have Experienced Abuse: Application of Polyvagal Theory in Therapeutic Work with Traumatized Children and Young People. In S.W. Porges and D. Dana (eds), *Clinical Applications of the Polyvagal Theory: The Emergence of Polyvagal-Informed Therapies*. New York, NY: W.W. Norton and Company.

Van der Kolk, B.A. (2014). *The Body Keeps the Score: Brain, Mind and Body in the Healing of Trauma*. New York, NY. Viking.

Webb, D.B. (1988). Specialized foster care as an alternative therapeutic out-of-home placement model. *Journal of Clinical Child Psychology*, 17(1), 34–43.

Wilkinson, M. (2010). *Changing Minds in Therapy: Emotion, Attachment, Trauma and Neurobiology*. New York, NY: W.W. Norton and Company.

2

What are the Key Elements of Therapeutic Care?

JANISE MITCHELL, JOE TUCCI AND NOEL MACNAMARA

As it continues to evolve as a form of practice, Therapeutic Care draws together a number of important resources in order to achieve its programmatic objectives and theoretical intentions. In this chapter, each of these elements is described in detail. Some trace their history to long-standing traditions of therapy, whereas others have emerged more recently as reinterpretations of knowledge that has had a peripheral association with the welfare of children in out-of-home care. All of them are at once familiar and slightly refashioned, guided by principles that seek to focus specifically on the needs of traumatised children and young people.

At the heart of Therapeutic Care is an understanding of the neuroscience of development, attachment and trauma. It finds its genealogy in the pioneering work of Allan Schore, Dan Siegel, Bruce Perry, Bessel van der Kolk, Jan Panksepp, Pat Ogden and Steven Porges. It has also been invested with the meaning of those who have studied the development of children through an early relational lens, most notably Ed Tronick, Colwyn Trevarthen and, of course, John Bowlby. More recently, cultural voices from the perspective of Indigenous peoples from around the world have been shaping the need to consider the wisdom of relationships that lie in the collective mind of communities and their connection to heritage, country and tradition, including Judy Atkinson, Michael Yellowbird and Cindy Blackstock. And in its implementation, Therapeutic Care has amplified the clarity and significance of the work of Dan Hughes and his colleagues, most notably Jon Baylin and Kim Golding.

This body of knowledge is in the process of transforming the therapeutic, child welfare, child protection and out-of-home care fields, specifically and more broadly reshaping so many others including mental health, drug and alcohol, homelessness and justice programs.

Complementary to this knowledge base, as it takes shape, Therapeutic Care is underscored by the children's rights movement and, in particular, the rights of children in out-of-home care. These rights enshrine the needs of children to access family, culture and education, to be safe and feel safe, and to actively participate in decisions that affect their lives.

This knowledge and value base intertwine in Therapeutic Care and are elucidated by the following practice principles.

Therapeutic Care recognises that trauma related to abuse and violence has a differential impact on each child and young person, leading to a unique configuration of impact and downstream consequences

Children and young people who have experienced or continue to experience trauma frequently experience developmental delays across a broad spectrum, including cognitive, language, motor and social skills. As a result, they display very complex disturbances, with a range of different presentations. They often show a combination of appropriate developmental behaviours as well as patterns of activation trapped from their past as a result of their efforts to survive the violation and protect themselves from its ongoing impact. Perry, for example, has demonstrated that experiences of trauma in early stages of development affect the organisation of the brainstem and effectively destabilise the maturation of the neural networks that follows (Perry and Hambrick, 2008). In this sense, children's development itself constricts around the stage that children were in at the time the trauma was most intensely experienced. In day-to-day life, the implicit memory systems of the brainstem of children, so far away from their conscious awareness, meets the constraints imposed by the violence or neglect. Children find ways to compensate by setting up complex behavioural routines that express the gap in their developmental progression. They avoid, they cry, they rage, they withdraw. All because somewhere inside them their systems are not up to the demands required of them in their present context. Components of the present context also serve to rouse past activated pathways that only need the slightest of recognition for them to roar back into their body. They need repetitive opportunities to engage with rhythm, and/or playful activities invoking their coordination and balance, and/or reliable interactions that pull them towards motor exploration of relationships that help to regulate them.

However, it is not accurate to describe these children's systems as exclusively reared in the interpersonal interactions filled with trauma. Many of these children have not been totally deprived of relational and other developmental resources. They have had some fragments of timely relational experiences that have delighted them, responded to them with genuine curiosity, actively engaged them in games, held them gently. These experiences of others have also been stored in the implicit memory systems associated with activated states that have been in harmony with their developmental momentum. Children can sometimes express these activations when the context allows. Children are in continuous movement between the states that cripple them and those which bring them back to life. The unique configurations of strengths and needs are important to acknowledge and work with. It is, as Badenoch (2018) claims, the depth of what can occur when an individual is received with respect for the deep wisdom of their brains and bodies to resist trauma and find a way to live with its effects.

Therapeutic Care views children from a developmental perspective, noting their challenges and appreciating their strengths. Children are more than a cluster of symptoms which need treatment (Tucci, 2016). Their unique history braids their interaction with people, the impact of events and the messages they have received about the world and themselves into ways of understanding them and their needs. This is the starting and return point for the practice of Therapeutic Care.

Therapeutic Care practice privileges children's needs as the basis of all of its decisions

Children in care have multiple needs. They have a need for safety and protection. They have a need for stability. They have educational and relational needs. They have developmental needs. They have cultural needs. All of these needs are expected to be met in the present by the adults in the child's networks – carers, teachers, therapists, coaches, extended family figures, friends. Often, given the urgency with which the decisions to place them in alternative care arrangements are made in order to ensure their protection, these needs are viewed through a prism of the here-and-now. It is the way that child protection systems typically function. The present, the most urgent, needs dictate what will happen next.

In many circumstances, it is the child's behaviour that directs decision-making. Traumatised children's behaviour can be challenging and complex. The child protection system, which is set up from inception to be reactive, responds to these behaviours quickly as a blunt instrument of care and control. Often, it fails to appreciate the subtlety of children's range of behavioural expressions.

Therapeutic Care privileges children's needs as they connect through time. It recognises that, at its heart, trauma leaves children's developmental needs unfulfilled and compromised. Its intervention takes the form of supporting carers and others in the child's relational network to understand the myriad of children's communication as failures in the past to repair overwhelming intrapsychic, neurophysiological, interpersonal and cultural ruptures caused by violence and abuse. These unmet needs from the past combine into strong thematic axioms along which run powerful repetitive patterns of interaction, drawing in the activated circuitry of those around them. Meeting children's needs in the present, when they remain unmet from their past, seals the reverberating gap left in their neural networks with a new line of filler that satisfies a little of the implicit memories of those needs which are so vividly aroused in their moment-by-moment lived experience.

Constructed through time, these needs become the plot lines of the narratives that explain, reimagine and reconfigure the ways in which these children are perceived, responded to and ultimately cared for. Therapeutic Care builds revived stories over time, weaving back into them what has been omitted or purposefully edited in order for previous responses to children made by the system to make sense and flow with logic. The assessments undertaken in Therapeutic Care are not only about the bio-psycho-social functioning of children over time. They gather this information with the specific purpose to portray their lives as holding different truths

– more hopeful views of children that are more compassionate and able to recruit the commitment of important others to act on their behalf to serve their interests.

These stories are therapeutic interventions themselves. They position children as in need of authentically reparative care, in need of love and in need of concurrent resourcing for who they are right now, what has happened to them and who they can become.

Therapeutic Care understands that children's behaviour communicates the efforts made by their internal systems to protect them from the traumatic experiences of violation

With children's needs the defining core of the practice that follows, Therapeutic Care recognises that children and young people's behaviours are enactments of their implicit neurophysiological systems. This is true for all of their behaviour – the challenging, the positive, the close, the withdrawn, the aggressive, the loving. These enactments take place at the boundary between all that occurs in their current environment and the implicit memory states that are awakened in the minutiae of time intervals through which their life is experienced.

There is no state for children in which the past does not seek to find its place. The past is not only what happened during the periods of violence or neglect. It is a continuous flow of experience that scrapes, grinds and mixes the last five minutes, the last few hours, the last week with longer-held memories from infancy to now.

> A foster child comes home after disappointing his teacher by not handing in his homework that he had forgotten all about. The teacher had been calm and asked him to do it again that night. She had tried to be matter-of-fact and avoid penalising him. The child likes the teacher and felt the rupture that his failure to complete his homework had caused between them, expressed in his gaze aversion and red cheeks emanating from embarrassment. As he walked home, he was bouncing his tennis ball trying to find his usual rhythm. But he could not get it quite right and his ball hit a stone and bounced into traffic. He knew he could not chase it and he had to leave it as it disappeared among the cars on the busy road. He had not eaten his lunch that day because the bread was soggy and

he did not like soggy bread. It was a hot day. As he opened the door of his house, he pushed it a little too hard and it made a louder noise than usual against the wall behind it. The sound made him pause. He threw his bag down and looked for his foster mum in the kitchen where she always was. But she was hanging out some clothes to dry outside.

In all this time, the sensory input through his systems flowed through implicit memory filters from last week when he had forgotten to put out the bins and had been reminded by his foster dad; from three months earlier when he had felt he had let his team down for getting out at cricket failing to make a score; from the time when he was a child at primary school and had been screamed at for losing his reader by both his parents. At every turn, his body is reacting to current and previous states of activation – his heart rate, his breathing, his sound acuity, his hungry belly, the strength of his flush when feeling ashamed. These small fusions are enactments in real time – open circuits seeking responses in the here-and-now but with a concurrent purpose for what has been not been responded to earlier at any of those moments.

Therapeutic Care understands that, in this frame, children's expressions through their behaviour reflect implicit sensory states which are fluid, changing, circulating in and through an endless number of previously stored sensations, cognitions, emotions, motor routines. These activated filters of memory states orient children to how to best organise all of this internalised data. It is the relational responses from the past and which are active in the present that coordinate the way that fits best for the context they find themselves in. It is the contingent difference between the past and the *now* that offers children the opportunity for healing, or, put this way, is a differently organised flow of implicit memory states that ends (only for that enactment) in the *now* with the possibility of an emerging pattern of relationally co-organised live states being more stably reproduced in ever-expanding numbers of contexts.

Therapeutic Care holds as its central tenet that children come to heal from trauma when the relationship network around them is resourced with therapeutic intent.

Carers, teachers, siblings, friends, coaches, extended family are able to and do offer spaces in the now that respect the inherent life-surging states children have experienced whenever they have occurred. These are experiences which act like a tuning fork for children in out-of-home care. The ways in which children are responded to in their interactions with these others set off a relational resonance that is sensed by children, vibrating the implicit memory filters in an effort to align with the state they are in at the time. In the here-and-now experience, the interactions of the relationship invites past memories of relationships to be re-influenced by the one in the *now*. If that relationship in the *now* vibrates with pain or activated states of threat and danger, then these past relationship filters amplify and consolidate further – as a lesson to the child to expect nothing different ever.

If the relationship in the *now* vibrates with softness, fun, play and attentiveness, matching the elements of the child's state with responses that soothe, comfort or accompany, then these past relationship filters find harmony with experiences held in implicit memory systems of strength, affirmation and receptiveness – coaxing children with the possibility of further exchanges that will bring delight, learning and attunement to learn the lesson that openness to more adaptation is safe.

Many in these children's relationship networks will always do what they do without much opportunity to be influenced. However, Therapeutic Care adopts the position that some of these relationships can be resourced to hold therapeutic intent and be deliberate about the nature of the relational responses that children in out-of-home care are offered. It is through these relationships that Therapeutic Care applies what Tucci and Mitchell (2019) have described as 'therapeutic effort'. Such effort is the combined input of the practitioners who support these children and their relationship network to interpret their needs, plan, rehearse and execute consistent responses to these children's needs in the *now*; facilitate their narratives to emerge which re-deposit their histories of survival states; and re-engage them with their cultural heritage that would, if not for their experience of trauma, provide them with the resources of identity that speak about their health and strengths.

The intentionality of Therapeutic Care does not leave healing to chance. It structures these relationships to be able to maintain a clear focus and single purpose to support the needs of children in care. It provides a shared knowledge base and language to understand children. It delivers routine methodologies for convening collaborative discussions between key figures in children's relationship networks. It titrates the decision-making of child protection authorities into manageable processes so that the network can have the time and the information needed to properly consider all eventualities in their deliberations. It brings into sharp focus children's ongoing lived experiences and orients the system to become more child-serving.

Therapeutic Care adopts a lifespan approach to planning for children and young people as they grow and change

Therapeutic Care recognises that child protection systems are inherently oriented towards making decisions about children according to legislative and policy-based planning cycles which generally emphasise the immediate and short-term needs of children. For example, the requirements to make an annual plan for children compels a focus on where children should live, whether it is safe for children to be reunified with parents, how to prevent placement breakdowns and where the child should attend school. In addition, child protection systems are frequently overburdened with high demands and inadequate resources. As such, the system is more likely to prioritise what it must do in the time it can allocate in order to meet compliance expectations. Therapeutic Care engages the system in order to affirm its role in ensuring the here-and-now needs of children, but it also supports it to consider the children's relational needs over time.

Therapeutic Care considers which relationships, pre-existing or those that may need to be developed, will scaffold children's development into their future. Therapeutic Care considers which relationships will be important to children in the long term over the course of their lives and why. It orients the system to make it possible for some relationships which may not be safe for children now to be rectified so that they can become more available as time goes on and the children's needs change. It does not consider relationships as snapshot portraits only with currency now. It supports networks to find or build and relationships which over time can share experiences with children so that they benefit from the belonging that a common history brings to them. All children need relationships which sustain them over time. These are the relationships that can be accessed for different reasons at different times as children need. These are the relationships that witness the emerging identity of children in out-of-home care and accompany them as they grow and change. Therapeutic Care holds the hope that relationships stand for all children, ensuring that they continue over their lifetime, beyond their formal care period and into adulthood.

Therapeutic Care also allows for children to have opportunities to connect with the adults in their family who hurt them if it is possible. Therapeutic Care can resource these adults who have been abusive or neglectful to these children to make changes, prove themselves over time and be facilitated to rejoin the relational network around children in an appropriate way that attempts to predictively ameliorate relational crises that may emerge in the future. Therapeutic Care holds the position that all relationships for children have the potential to offer therapeutic impact, while recognising that the perpetuation of abusive dynamics cannot be tolerated for children who are in the process of recalibrating their internal systems to a deep and sustained sense of relational safety and security.

Therapeutic Care ensures that the extended family of children is not lost to them. Too often, the network of children in out-of-home care is overly dominated by professional relationships which by definition are time-limited. The extended family provides an alternative network of informal relationships which children can remain connected to that will scaffold their development and be there during major transition points in their development. Therapeutic Care treats the extended family as an undervalued resource that needs to be incorporated as an intrinsic part of the relational network of children in out-of-home care.

Therapeutic Care honours the strengths of cultural heritage as resources for children and their relationship networks

The cultural heritage of children is viewed by Therapeutic Care as integral to and foundational for the well-being of children in care. Children's culture is not separate to the relationships around them, their sense of belonging, or their identity. Their culture is experienced in and through their relationships with family and community, their stories, traditions and practices. In Australian Aboriginal and Torres Strait Islander communities, for example, culture determines not only the ways that relationships between people are structured, how knowledge is communicated and the deep resonating connections that Aboriginal and Torres Strait Islander families and communities have to land, sea and their Dreaming stories. Within extended kinship systems every adult and child has a place, a role in the family group that comes with obligations and responsibilities for the care, teaching and support of others. Culture, development and well-being are intertwined in children's lives. Often denied and disrupted by the echoing consequences of colonial oppression and intergenerational trauma, culture provides important protective factors and opportunities for healing.

Therapeutic Care recognises the deep reservoir of cultural knowledges, practices and beliefs that innervate the life of communities and the relationships they hold. It actively seeks out individuals within the cultural communities to care for these children directly, or, at the very least, be connected with in some way so that they may live within rather than visit their culture, as is too commonly the case. Practitioners act with cultural humility, slowly and respectfully learning about the ways that children's cultural heritage is part of their experiences to date and how to ensure that they access experiences that support the relational experiences that are steeped in that culture.

Therapeutic Care adopts the view that children's experiences of deep visceral safety is both an outcome and a form of intervention

Therapeutic Care primarily establishes and maintains an organised interpersonal milieu which recognises that children's deep experiences of relational safety are both a major goal of intervention and a major resource in the healing process (Tucci, Weller and Mitchell, 2018). It adopts the view that the experience of safety is not the equivalent of removing threat and danger (Porges, 2014). Relationships which heal are trustworthy and enduring. They are attuned to the children's flow of implicit activated memory states. They stabilise and they help organise regulation of activated states in children.

> They allow new meanings to emerge which are based in the grounded visceral experience of comfort. They brace and allow resistance to old neural activation to take hold, reinforcing them gently and allowing them to grow. They recruit our phylogenetically new systems to connect and stay connected. They help to create new memories of care and trust. They support the generation of narratives that make the world feel less dangerous and help children feel more capable. (Tucci, Weller and Mitchell, 2018, p.96)

This experience of deep safety for children occurs when children and caring adults share moments in which their respective internal safety–threat systems meet and embrace. It revolves around the continual cycles of relational matched–mismatch–matched states that are commonplace to every relationship between humans (Tronick, 1989, 2006, 2017; Tronick and Beeghly, 2011; Tronick and Cohn, 1989; Tronick and DiCorcia, 2015; Tronick and Gianino, 1986), and in particular between adult carers and children. It is through the predictability of the matching – the inevitability of the biological expectancy that mismatched states are repaired – that deep experiences of safety are lured back into the experience of children, recruiting the neural circuitry responsible for thriving along the way.

As Tucci, Weller and Mitchell (2018, p.102) have noted:

> Children learn to tolerate the boundary of activation so that their physiology can be coaxed back into the safe zone of proximity and relational connectedness. Children come to feel themselves as being safe through their experience in relationship with a caring and protective adult. They become more open and less fixed. They use their own social engagement system to approach the adult and seek mutually satisfying interactions. They play and experience curiosity. They test the reliability of the safety being offered. They reach out and begin to hold on to safety for what it offers them. They change. They begin slowly to shed the habitual patterns of activation that have defined by their trauma-based responses to the world. Their heart opens itself to the adult's affection.

Therapeutic Care is active in ensuring that children and young people who have experienced abuse and neglect are not further disempowered by the way practice is implemented

Therapeutic Care is fundamentally a form of practice that seeks to enact the basic human rights of children and young people as articulated in the UN Convention on the Rights of the Child (United Nations, 1990). Nationally, in Australia, government and non-government organisations have also adopted a set of rights for children and young people living in out-of-home care. These frameworks make explicit the core entitlements of children and young people to protection, family, culture and privacy and to participate in decision-making which affects their lives.

Therapeutic Care translates these rights into meaningful actions that support its intended outcomes. It ensures that it promotes and references the language used to describe young people's behaviour, motivation or functioning that does not disempower them. It challenges constructs which fail to account for the impact of violence or neglect and its expression in behaviour that can be perceived as problematic by the individuals and the systems with which children and young people come into contact. It resists diagnostic criteria that define children and young people's identity on the basis of the trouble they cause or experience. For example, instead of adopting diagnoses such as oppositional defiant disorder or reactive attachment disorder (both of which locate the responsibility for the condition with the child or young person), the narratives that are aligned with the identity of children are fully explained with connections between behaviour and trauma articulated at every turn. Additionally, any language practices that label children and young people in ways that hold them responsible for their abuse are opposed (Tucci and Mitchell, 2017, 2018).

Therapeutic Care recognises that sensitivity to the developmental capacities and stages of young people is in itself a respectful orientation to practices of assessment and intervention. It does not expect children and young people, especially those affected by trauma, to achieve more than they are capable of at any given time and does not penalise them for not doing so. It respects the unique configuration of developmental capacities and vulnerabilities that each child and young person brings with them into any interaction or exchange.

Therapeutic Care fosters the authentic participation of children and young people in decision-making processes that are about them

Consistent with a human rights framework, Therapeutic Care enables young people to be empowered, to be respected and heard. Children and young people in out-of-home care are agents in their own lives. Like all children, they need support to identify, rehearse and engage with qualities as they emerge in relationships which also notice them and facilitate their growth. Children who have experienced deep violation or neglect have missed out on the affirmation of being seen and held in relationships for whom it is important that the child's emergent self is made visible and celebrated. Therapeutic Care acts to remediate this experience and reposition children in the hierarchy of relationships so that the very practice it undertakes is based on a bedrock of listening to children's distinct perspective and narrative about their lives. Therapeutic Care implements into its routines ways to support children to communicate their opinions, thoughts and own ambitions for themselves into decision-making forums.

Through its practice, Therapeutic Care communicates to children and young people that their views, beliefs and ideas hold an intrinsic value. They are provided with ways to rehearse sharing in problem-solving and decision-making processes in supported contexts. Then, when the time comes for them to be more independently responsible for these decisions, they are more likely to be better prepared. This is what all families do for and with their children.

Therapeutic Care empowers relationships to be therapeutic

Relationships that are the closest to children have the most capacity to take responsibility for the most significant proportion of therapeutic effort (Tucci and Mitchell, 2019). The direct carers of these children hold a special place in Therapeutic Care. They are in interaction with children in the daily activities of living which enables them to act as the relational resources these children require. Therapeutic Care typically provides carers with the knowledge and the support they need to be empowered to undertake this role.

There is a great deal at stake for carers and children as they live together. Carers invest themselves in the relationship with these children. They make up a special room for them. They buy the ingredients for the child's favourite meals. They learn about the child's routines. They find out which football team the child follows. They prepare their own children for the arrival – much like a newborn sibling. They learn about the child's cultural heritage and what might be expected of them. They open up their hearts to receive the child and all of their pain. This is an investment that they are aware of but they do not always appreciate its significance. They want the child to belong. They do not want to be hurt, or hurt anyone themselves.

Children have so much on the line too. They want to be loved. They need to be looked after. They need to find people who they feel will commit to them. They crave stability. Their internal systems seek out resolution. With every change, every placement breakdown, their hearts become a little more brittle, a little less forgiving to change, to possibilities. They do not want to be hurt again.

Therapeutic Care finds in this reciprocal relational embodiment the way to have the therapeutic impact required for these children – and, of course, the carers. It empowers all relationships to be therapeutic, but it particularly resources carers in their role. It achieves this through sequenced strategies that promote carers to know, understand and engage with the *mind of the child in relationship with them* and in so doing it supports children to experience the *collective mind of the relationship between them and the carers and the caring family unit*. This, of course, is based in the mentalising work of Peter Fonagy and colleagues (Allen, Fonagy and Bateman, 2008; Fearon *et al.*, 2006; Fonagy and Adshead, 2012; Fonagy *et al.*, 2002), who have described it as an imaginative process whereby those in relationships with each other ascribe intention and meaning to human behaviour. Through making reference to the emotions, feelings, thoughts, intentions and desires of another, it creates an understanding of each other in the lived experiences of relationships.

Therapeutic Care practice renders the opaque nature of the internal states of the child, the carer and the others in the child's relational network more transparent. It achieves this through a sequence of strategies that starts with training carers and the relational network around the child about the neurobiology of trauma, attachment and child development. This knowledge base lays the foundation for the adults to understand the internal systems of traumatised children in out-of-home care. It integrates their own intuition and experience with children in their own family or in their community with the outcomes of research that builds an orientation to undertaking more of a therapeutic parenting role (Cairns, 2002; Hughes, 2007; Hughes and Baylin, 2012). It also softens the terrain of expectations, aiming to dislodge set views that may have developed about how children should behave, what they need, how to respond to them and how children should respond in return.

Training, of course, is not enough on its own. Access to knowledge does not necessarily translate into changed behaviour. Therapeutic Care, then, supports carers in real time to apply this knowledge in practice in day-to-day moments of care. Therapeutic Specialists utilise patterns of trauma enactments as opportunities to reflect on their meaning with carers and resource them to respond intentionally with sensitivity, openness and care. These experiences offer children's activated circuitry the repair and reattunement they need. Often the support is provided at the time when children come home from school, get ready for bed, wake up in the morning – many of the transition points in a normal day when the change of state is likely to occur because of the nature of the routine itself. Therapeutic Care recognises how the flux of a normal day can in and of itself prompt activation of implicit memory systems that awaken in children and need a response.

Next, Therapeutic Care does not set a time limit on how long the intervention and support are provided to carers and others connected to children. The intensity of the support may differ over time, moving up and down as children's needs vary across their development. Therapeutic Care works across developmental transitions. As children move from preschool to primary school or between primary school and secondary school, they encounter periods of upheaval which can be accompanied by increases in stress on relationships around children. It is at these points that there often needs to be an increase in therapeutic effort, attending to particular needs that may arise for children in the context of their past.

At the same time, Therapeutic Care recognises that if carers have a background of their own relational disruption or trauma, it may act as a source of constraint in their actions to meet the needs of the child as they share growing aligned activated states. Carers themselves need to experience the same deep visceral sense of safety that children need. Having experienced it themselves, carers are in a better position to know how to offer it and pass it to the children in their care. This is why Therapeutic Care intervention supports carers so that they are able to sense and locate safety and danger in their own lives, tracing their history and allowing it to resonate in their lived experience. With sensitivity, carers are engaged in reflective practice that links their awareness of embodied safety to an understanding of their own internal states (Tucci, Weller and Mitchell, 2018). They perceive more fully the source of their volition and intentions in their own behaviour. They gradually find in their relationships with the practitioners of Therapeutic Care the trust they need for even the most painful implicit memories to be integrated.

With an openness to their own internal states, carers now have the basis upon which to mentalise the mind of the children and the relationship itself. The relationship becomes the embodied shared agent of their co-organised neural activation. They see how their actions elicit reactions in children. They gain insight into the lineage of children's behaviour and begin to hold an understanding of how the relational environment can so vividly shape how children's implicit activation system dissolves into safety or escalates due to experiences of threat and danger that are perceived even if they are not real. Children in this relational environment begin to feel their activated states matched in the *now*. They sense their physiological systems being invited to activate differently, to follow new paths that are being co-created with the carer together in a deeply embodied way, with safety at its core.

Therapeutic Care spreads the approach to supporting carers to as many of the adult relationships in the network of the children as can be reached. Empowered relationships ripple in concentric circles around the child, reinforcing and amplifying the safety and comfort that are now the primary qualities of the child's experience in relational exchanges. The therapeutic impact takes hold as the child stops needing the threat-activated circuitry in favour of safety-satiated internal systems that are oriented towards mind and body restoration and resuming their developmental progression.

Therapeutic Care conceptualises the physical and sensory environments that children inhabit as therapeutic

Therapeutic Care acknowledges that traumatised children have a fundamental need to experience safety not only within their relationships but also in their environments. As such, it pays particular attention to reconstituting the physical and sensory qualities to reduce the physiological burden that children carry with them as they live with the uncertainty of inputs that can awaken implicit traumatised states. Past experiences of their environments are often characterised by chaos and confusion, requiring children to be constantly wary of possible signs of threat. In chronic states of hypervigilance, with all their attentional resources and energy focused on survival, children are unable to thrive. Therapeutic Care undertakes sensory assessments of children to develop plans that are used to organise consistent physical spaces at home, school and other places that children frequent. It attends to sounds, textures, smells, lighting and other physical properties of the environment as a strategy for decreasing the stress load on children's nervous systems.

It appreciates that the physical space through which children can interact can support children if it is structured and clearly marked. Practitioners in Therapeutic Care, as do early childhood educators, appreciate how marking out zones in a room or a home for different functions allows children to orient themselves to what to do where. The arranging of space also creates physical boundaries to be experienced which can also act as tangible replicas of interpersonal boundaries, exposing children to experiences of negotiation, flexibility and co-organisation.

Therapeutic Care also invests effort into evaluating and strengthening the predictability of children's day-to-day experiences – in particular eating, sleeping, school and play routines. Temporal maps enable children to know what to expect when, when their transition points are in a day or week or month, who will be involved and how they will be supported throughout. Plans about time, just as diaries resource adults, make the world a little easier for children to navigate. Conversely, for these children where predictability is a theme anchored in tension, changing or ignoring a routine after it has been established without warning and support can unearth activated internal states that terrify them or cause distress.

Therapeutic Care holds a focus on optimising the environments that foster for children a felt experience of safety.

Therapeutic Care expands the role of therapists to become relational brokers, network enablers and system advocates for children in out-of-home care

The role of the therapist is extended beyond the traditional scope of dyadic or family engagement in the practice of Therapeutic Care. It invites therapists to take on functions as facilitators of safety, relationship and resource brokers, network enablers and system advocates. As mentioned in the first chapter, this is the reason for their role title being changed to Therapeutic Specialists – a term that was first introduced into the lexicon of our broader field in 2000 by Mitchell (Mitchell, 2008; SuccessWorks, 2005) in the formulation of the original Treatment and Care for Kids (TrACK) Therapeutic Foster Care Program in Melbourne, Australia.

First and foremost, Therapeutic Specialists provide therapeutic leadership across all the critical relationships around the child in order to develop a shared understanding of the needs of children as the basis for developing congruent and collaborative trauma-informed responses which are consistent across the settings in which children live, learn and play. They broker these relationships, moulding them into a collective that works to keep the whole child in perspective. They help to establish trust and open lines of communication between these relationships and deal with the dynamics that can arise between individuals, organisations and systems. They support safety in these networks to emerge as qualities between people who engage each other for children. They develop the goodwill that will allow tension or immobilisation to be addressed and dissipate.

Therapeutic Specialists also walk alongside the carers and other really close relationships to the child. They offer carers the intersubjective resource (Hughes, 2007, 2015, 2017; Hughes and Baylin, 2012) that enables them to stay open to the relationships with children, which can in themselves be stressful if not traumatising to the carer. Therapeutic Specialists provide the neurobiological brace that carers can rely on in the face of the activated states of the children and their implications back into the implicit memory systems of the carer, who may be carrying reverberating experiences of loss, disruption and even direct experiences of violence and abuse. Therapeutic Specialists hold their relationship with carers as working templates for the relationship that children need from the carer and other close relationships.

Therapeutic Specialists undertake a comprehensive gathering of information about the history of experiences of specific children in out-of-home care and compile it into a formal assessment that is used as the basis for therapeutic plans involving the children, the carers and the relationship network around children. In this assessment process, children, carers, family members (where possible) and professionals in the network around children are provided with the opportunity to provide input. Therapeutic Specialists ensure that the narrative that is retold about children includes their strengths, their wishes, their descriptions of their lived experiences. The assessment and documentation process is a meaning-making endeavour that generates deep insight into the needs of children that remain unattended to because of their violation or neglect. It also enables children to be viewed compassionately in ways that inject delight and hope into the relational experiences that children and others have of each other.

Therapeutic Specialists use this integrated narrative about children to interpret their behaviour so that the impact of their history is always incorporated into explanations and descriptions about them. Therapeutic Specialists use their knowledge about trauma and evidence-informed intervention to offer the necessary adjustments to relational exchanges and the environmental routines that facilitate children's capacity to use these relationships to shift their reoccurring patterns of activated states.

When it is warranted, Therapeutic Specialists engage directly with children to enable them to have another relationship which offers opportunities for the co-organisation of regulated states, co-construction of meaning about past experiences and shared activities which awaken developmental momentum. Therapeutic Specialists use naturally occurring opportunities as well as formal therapeutic sessions to process traumatised states using a variety of modalities. Therapeutic Specialists provide another regular, consistent and compensatory relational template that children are exposed to over time and context.

Therapeutic Specialists support carers and the whole of the relational network as needed to take a step back from the intensity of caring, educating or being with these children in order to reflect the meaning of events in the present and their links to children's past. This reflective practice orients the network of relationships around children to remain engaged with a higher form of understanding of their 'relational mind'. Such reflective practice draws on a collective mentalising that enables carers and others in the children's network to remain open to possibilities of change and creativity.

Therapeutic Specialists carry a significant load in resourcing the therapeutic impact that all of these relationships around children can achieve when they are aligned, informed and supported.

Therapeutic Care is resourced by coordinated collective decision-making that serves the needs and interests of children

Therapeutic Care intervenes to refocus decision-making about children so that it not only incorporates the traditional emphasis on reducing future risk of experiencing further abuse and harm, but also centralises ways to organise the execution of plans that address children's needs from the past in the context of their present relational environment. This shift means that systems of protection, care and therapy are more closely aligned and integrated. It ensures that there are shared objectives driving decision-making.

Therapeutic Care uses vehicles such as Care Teams to organise important relationships to coordinate the actions and responses of services and individuals in the here-and-now. Often led by Therapeutic Specialists, Care Teams work by enlisting a shared view and understanding of children's needs. They use the understanding about children that has been informed by the comprehensive assessment of Therapeutic Specialists to co-opt and use a common language to explain and interpret children's behaviour and needs. Care Teams allow agreement between individuals who engage children in different contexts about strategies for these children that are replicated or at least consistent across those contexts. In so doing, children are given the experiences of safety that are built into predictable structures and routines applied consistently at home, school and during their involvement in recreation or other similar activities.

Care Teams also provide the reinforcement to those individuals when children's behaviour arising from their own internally activated states triggers stress in the systems around them. It is at these times that the individuals in a child's relational network need additional support to stay the course with the strategies that have been jointly developed and agreed to collectively. It helps to ensure that all these people continue to know why they are doing what they are doing in response to these children, even when there is a significant crisis or event that tempts a wholesale reappraisal of the understanding of children, often leading to more controls being called for.

Care Teams keep the child in the centre of their frame. They look for the successes that occur with children, even when they are almost imperceptible, and celebrate them with children and others in the relational network around them. They also reflect on how those successes were born and examine how these lessons may be able to be applied into a different setting or with a different relationship. The changes that occur within relationships that lead to improvements in children's lived experiences are amplified.

Finally, Care Teams are based on a partnership approach that challenges the definition of family for children which can blind child protection to the involvement of family as a legitimate and effective part of processes that shape the experiences of children in out-of-home care. Care Teams work to find and involve relationships of significance in children's lives even when they are in out-of-home care. It facilitates adults who are family and safe for children to move closer and become a resource in the here-and-now and/or as children's development seeks them out.

The orientation to a collective mechanism for planning and executing therapeutic response plans for children in out-of-home care is part of the paradigm shift provided by Therapeutic Care. It possesses inherent properties of collaboration and congruence which are increasingly valued by child protection systems that have been forever plagued by interagency failures.

Conclusion

Therapeutic Care represents a significant paradigm shift in the practices of supporting change and healing for children in foster, kinship and adoptive care. Its relational focus integrates a focus on children in the here-and-now. It is concerned with their needs, their entitlements and their voice. It is informed by the consilience of knowledge (Siegel, 2015) distilled from a range of disciplines and practice areas encompassing interpersonal neurobiology, trauma, therapeutic intervention, child protection and children's rights.

The movement it represents is the realisation that children's experience of trauma needs an immediacy of response that is integrated into the everyday of being looked after. To do otherwise is to offer only partial and fragmented responses to children's needs. Therapeutic Care integrates evidence, coordinates systems and co-organises relationships to do the therapeutic heavy lifting for children who are in desperate need of care, comfort and love.

References

Allen, J.G., Fonagy, P. and Bateman, A.W. (2008). *Mentalizing in Clinical Practice.* Arlington, VA: American Psychiatric Publishing.

Badenoch, B. (2018). *The Heart of Trauma: Healing the Embodied Brain in the Context of Relationships.* New York, NY: W.W. Norton and Company.

Cairns, K. (2002). *Attachment, Trauma and Resilience: Therapeutic Caring for Children.* London: BAAF.

Fearon, P., Target, M., Sargent, J., Williams, L.L. *et al.* (2006). Short-Term Mentalization and Relational Therapy (SMART): An Integrative Family Therapy for Children and Adolescents. In J.G. Allen and P. Fonagy (eds), *Handbook of Mentalization-Based Treatment.* West Sussex, UK: John Wiley and Sons.

Fonagy, P. and Adshead, G. (2012). How mentalisation changes the mind. *Advances in Psychiatric Treatment,* 18(5), 353–362.

Fonagy, P., Gergeley, G., Jurist, E. and Target, M. (2002). *Affect Regulation, Mentalization, and the Development of the Self.* New York, NY: Other Press.

Hughes, D.A. (2007). *Attachment-Focused Family Therapy.* New York, NY: W.W. Norton and Company.

Hughes, D.A. (2015). The complex journey of traumatised children: Discovering safety in order to experience comfort, joy and self-discovery. *Children Australia,* 40(2), 147–151.

Hughes, D.A. (2017). Dyadic Developmental Psychotherapy (DDP): An attachment-focused family treatment for developmental trauma. *Australian and New Zealand Journal of Family Therapy,* 38(4), 595–605.

Hughes, D.A. and Baylin, J. (2012). *Brain-Based Parenting: The Neuroscience of Caregiving for Healthy Attachment.* New York, NY: W.W. Norton and Company.

Mitchell, J. (2008). A case study in attempted reform in out of home care: A preliminary examination of the introduction of the Circle Therapeutic Foster Care Program in Victoria. Unpublished Masters Thesis, Monash University, Victoria.

Perry, B.D. and Hambrick, E.O. (2008). The neurosequential model of therapeutics. Accessed on 28/12/2018 at https://childtrauma.org/wp-content/uploads/2013/08/NMT_Article_08.pdf.

Porges, S.W. (2014). *The Pocket Guide to the Polyvagal Theory: The Transformative Power of Feeling Safe.* New York, NY: W.W. Norton and Company.

Siegel, D. (2015). Interpersonal neurobiology as a lens into the development of wellbeing and resilience. *Children Australia,* 40(2), 160–164.

SuccessWorks (2005). *Evaluation of the Treatment and Care for Kids (TrACK) Program.* Melbourne: SuccessWorks. Accessed on 28/12/2018 at https://professionals.childhood.org.au/app/uploads/2018/09/TrACK-Report-Evaluation-SW.pdf.

Tronick, E. (1989). Emotions and emotional communication in infants. *The American Psychologist*, 44(2), 112–119.

Tronick, E. (2006). The inherent stress of normal daily life and social interaction leads to the development of coping and resilience, and variation in resilience in infants and young children: Comments on the papers of Suomi and Klebanov and Brooks-Gunn. *Annals of the New York Academy of Sciences*, 1094, 83–104.

Tronick, E. (2017). The caregiver–infant dyad as a buffer or transducer of resource enhancing or depleting factors that shape psychobiological development. *Australian and New Zealand Journal of Family Therapy*, 38, 561–572.

Tronick, E. and Beeghly, M. (2011). Infants' meaning-making and the development of mental health problems. *The American Psychologist*, 66(2), 107–119.

Tronick, E. and Cohn, J.F. (1989). Infant–mother face-to-face interaction: Age and gender differences in coordination and the occurrence of miscoordination. *Child Development*, 60(1), 85–92.

Tronick, E. and DiCorcia, J.A. (2015). The Everyday Stress Resilience Hypothesis: A reparatory sensitivity and the development of coping and resilience. *Children Australia*, 40(2), 124–138.

Tronick, E. and Gianino, A. (1986). Interactive mismatch and repair: Challenges to the coping infant. *Zero to Three*, 6(3), 1–6.

Tucci, J. (2016). What comes after trauma-informed practice? *Prosody*, 12 December. Accessed on 28/12/2018 at https://professionals.childhood.org.au/prosody/2016/12/what-next.

Tucci, J. and Mitchell, J. (2017). *Building a Practice Framework to Break Cycles of Significant Disadvantage through the Youth and Homelessness Services Provided by MercyCare*. Melbourne: Australian Childhood Foundation and MercyCare.

Tucci, J. and Mitchell, J. (2018). *Preparing Young People for Their Future: A Framework for Practice. A Collaboration between Anglicare NT and the Australian Childhood Foundation*. Melbourne: Australian Childhood Foundation and Anglicare NT.

Tucci, J. and Mitchell, J. (2019). Therapeutic Services for Traumatised Children and Young People – Healing in the Everyday Experience of Relationships. In R. Benjamin, J. Haliburn and S. King (eds), *Humanising Mental Health Care in Australia*. London: Routledge.

Tucci, J., Weller, A. and Mitchell, J. (2018). Realizing 'Deep' Safety for Children Who Have Experienced Abuse: Application of Polyvagal Theory in Therapeutic Work with Traumatized Children and Young People. In S.W. Porges and D. Dana (eds), *Clinical Applications of the Polyvagal Theory: The Emergence of Polyvagal-Informed Therapies*. New York, NY: W.W. Norton and Company.

United Nations (1990). *Convention on the Rights of the Child*. Geneva: Office of the High Commissioner for Human Rights.

3

Understanding the Needs of Vulnerable Children

The Importance of Type and Timing of Maltreatment on Brain Development and Risks

MARTIN H. TEICHER AND ORGILMAA MUNKHBAATAR

Introduction

An essential factor associated with optimal child well-being is the provision of a safe and nurturing environment. This provision allows for the favorable development of cognitive and emotional skills and builds potential to grow into healthy, productive adults. As such, exposure to trauma endangers children, and extensive research has affirmed the vulnerability of brain development to stressful experiences.

In this chapter, we define trauma to encompass the long-standing impacts of experiences of childhood neglect and abuse as well as peer victimization. Childhood maltreatment presents a significant public health threat that deserves greater awareness and investigation into how our community can best prevent, pre-empt, and treat the trauma it inflicts. Through this chapter, we hope to elucidate the therapeutic implications of neuroscientific research and highlight how it may guide efforts to ensure children are treated according to their specific experiences of maltreatment. To do so we present a frame of reference in which brain alterations associated with maltreatment are not viewed as damage but instead as neuroplastic development adaptations selected in our evolutionary past to foster survival and reproductive success in what, based on experience, may be a malevolent world.

These alterations, however, may be maladaptive at the present time and exert untoward consequences throughout life.

The cost of maltreatment: Developing an understanding of the burden on the individual and their community

It is estimated that childhood maltreatment is one of the most significant causes of psychopathology, accounting for about 45% of the population attributable risk for childhood-onset psychiatric disorder (Green *et al.*, 2010). It is crucial that we strive to improve life opportunities and enable maltreatment survivors to live to their full potential. We believe that the integration of neuroscientific knowledge will help synthesize informed approaches on how to care for and support individuals who experienced childhood maltreatment.

Neuroimaging and the impact of maltreatment on the brain: A general overview of maltreatment and altered trajectories of brain development

The neuroimaging findings presented below assess differences in morphology and connectivity with regard to specific brain regions of interest. These studies dedicated to distinct regions further our understanding of the possible impact of childhood adversity on brain structure and function as well as provide insight into potential consequences, including changes in cognition, behavior, and associated psychiatric disorders.

Hippocampus

The hippocampus is a key limbic structure involved in the formation and retrieval of explicit memories, including autobiographical memories (Nadel, Campbell, and Ryan, 2007). It is also responsible, along with the parahippocampal gyrus, for our internal positioning system for the representation of places, routes, and corresponding experiences (Moser, Kropff, and Moser, 2008). Abnormalities in the hippocampus are reported in several different psychiatric disorders such as major depression, bipolar disorder, posttraumatic stress disorder (PTSD), schizophrenia, and borderline personality disorder (Geuze, Vermetten, and Bremner, 2005). Because the cellular anatomy of the hippocampus is strongly influenced by cortisol, a critically important stress hormone, it is predicted to be especially vulnerable to childhood maltreatment (Sapolsky, Krey, and McEwen, 1985). This is validated, as the vast majority of studies report that adults with histories of maltreatment have, on average, smaller hippocampi than non-maltreated individuals (Teicher and Samson, 2016; Teicher *et al.*, 2016). Further, longitudinal studies report attenuated development in maltreated children (Carrion, Weems, and Reiss, 2007; Rao *et al.*, 2010). These results are important, as diminished hippocampal volumes are associated with decreased ability to restructure emotional memories, which influences the contextualization of present experiences. Thus, affected individuals may ultimately repeat poor behaviors such as continued engagement with health-risk activities.

Research also suggests gender-specific differences in the vulnerability of the hippocampus to maltreatment. In one study 336 subjects were examined to assess important predictors of adult hippocampal volume to determine if a greater vulnerability was dependent on the severity of exposure to maltreatment throughout childhood or exposure at selective ages (Teicher *et al.*, 2018). Male hippocampal volume was noted to be best predicted by neglect up to seven years of age, with these experiences fostering inadequate hippocampal development. On the other hand, abuse at 10, 11, 15, and 16 years was determined to be the most important predictor of female hippocampal volume, with the abuse exposure associated with stress-related deficits. Exposure at sensitive ages was a better predictor of hippocampal volume than the number of types, severity, or duration of maltreatment. This distinction in the susceptibility of the hippocampus to maltreatment may be one of the most noteworthy gender differences in the developing brain.

It is critically important to note that although several different psychiatric disorders have been associated with reduced hippocampal volume (Geuze *et al.*, 2005), these earlier studies did not take into account maltreatment history. We and others have found that maltreatment is the key determinant and that depression, anxiety, and PTSD were no longer predictive of hippocampal volume once maltreatment was accounted for (Teicher *et al.*, 2018). In short, the psychiatric implications of reduced hippocampal volume are unclear.

What is perhaps clear is the association between hippocampal abnormalities and neurocognitive abilities. Deficits in short-term verbal and visual memory, distractibility, reduced inhibitory capacity, impaired sustained attention, and problems with mathematical aptitude and verbally mediated higher cognitive abilities have been reported in abused children and in adults with abuse histories (Cowell *et al.*, 2015; Navalta *et al.*, 2006), which may be due, at least in part, to impaired hippocampal function.

Amygdala

The amygdala is a limbic structure that is significantly involved in detecting and responding to salient stimuli such as facial expressions and potential threats (Derntl *et al.*, 2009) and the encoding of implicit emotional memories (LeDoux, 1993). Structural or functional abnormalities in the amygdala have been implicated in a wide array of psychiatric disorders, including drug addiction (Koob and Volkow, 2010); autism (Kleinhans *et al.*, 2010); PTSD, social phobias, and specific phobias (Shin and Liberzon, 2010); schizophrenia (Suslow *et al.*, 2013); unipolar and bipolar depression (Grotegerd *et al.*, 2014); and borderline personality disorder (Goodman *et al.*, 2014).

Increased amygdala response to emotional faces has been the most consistent functional imaging finding in maltreated individuals (Teicher *et al.*, 2016). A noteworthy exception was Taylor *et al.* (2006) who reported a hypoactive response to fearful/angry faces in adults raised in 'risky families' (characterized by harsh, chaotic, or conflict-ridden parenting). Effects of maltreatment on amygdala volume have been inconsistent. Most studies report a significant or non-significant reduction in volume, with a moderate number of studies reporting a significant increase. We have proposed that maltreatment in childhood may lead to increases in amygdala volume if they do not experience subsequent trauma. However, early exposure also sensitizes the amygdala so that exposure to subsequent traumas will then lead to a significant reduction in amygdala volume (Teicher and Samson, 2016).

We have recently discovered that there are two sensitive periods when exposure to maltreatment is most predictive of adult amygdala response to threatening experiences. The first period occurs at 3–6 years of age, and the most influential form of exposure is parental physical abuse or peer physical bullying. The second period occurs at 13–15 years of age, and the most important predictor is peer emotional abuse. The critical factor, however, appears to be the timing – early prepubertal versus postpubertal – more than type. Early exposure was associated with hypoactive response, whereas later exposure was associated with hyperactive response in adulthood. These differences make adaptive sense as young children may need a blunted amygdala response to perceived threat to remain attached to episodically abusive parents. In contrast, maltreated teenagers may benefit from enhanced ability to detect and respond to threat.

This finding of sensitive periods specifically associated with blunted response or accentuated response is important information as heightened response of the amygdala to threat has been associated with symptoms of anxiety and inhibition, as in PTSD (Badura-Brack *et al.*, 2018) and phobias (Klumpp *et al.*, 2010). In contrast, blunted response may lead to problems with disinhibition and impaired social judgement (Schumann, Bauman, and Amaral, 2011), such as in substance use (Glahn, Lovallo, and Fox, 2007) and conduct disorders (Lozier *et al.*, 2014). The presence of sensitive periods with opposite effects on amygdala function may help explain why maltreatment can lead to such a diverse array of clinical outcomes.

Corpus callosum

The corpus callosum is the largest nerve fibers tract in the brain and provides the vast majority of interconnections between left and right hemispheres. There are consistent reports of diminished area or integrity of the corpus callosum in maltreated children (De Bellis *et al.*, 1999, 2002; Teicher *et al.*, 2004). Diminished corpus callosal thickness has been found in children and adults with bipolar disorder (Baloch, Brambilla, and Soares, 2009) and in children with attention deficit hyperactivity disorder (ADHD) (Luders *et al.*, 2009). The resulting neurobiological changes have various potential adverse consequences, including affective lability and poor problem-solving (Luders *et al.*, 2007; Schutter and Harmon-Jones, 2013).

In addition, several studies suggest the influence of gender, as depicted by a twofold greater reduction in the corpus callosum area in boys than girls with exposure to maltreatment (De Bellis *et al.*, 1999; Teicher *et al.*, 2004). As with the hippocampus, the corpus callosum was most vulnerable to neglect in males (Teicher *et al.*, 2004).

Cerebral cortex

Maltreated children with PTSD and orphans who suffered early emotional deprivation have overall reductions in cortical gray and white matter (De Bellis *et al.*, 2002; Sheridan *et al.*, 2012). Studies focused on specific cortical regions evaluating differences in volume, thickness, and surface area show consistent findings of reduced size of the anterior cingulate cortex (Baker *et al.*, 2013). Furthermore, reduced volume and blood flow were noted in maltreated subjects with and without psychopathology in the dorsolateral prefrontal cortex (Edmiston *et al.*, 2011) and the orbitofrontal cortex (Gerritsen *et al.*, 2012). The sensitive period for total prefrontal gray matter volume was found to occur between 14 and 16 years of age (Andersen and Teicher, 2008). However, not all frontal regions develop late. Our retrospective sensitive period analysis indicates that the most important predictor of dorsal anterior cingulate cortex (dACC) volume was physical neglect at ages 2–6. These findings are in accord with the results of the Avon Longitudinal study in which a birth cohort was prospectively assessed for exposure to childhood adversity at eight, 21, 33, 47, 61, and 73 months of age, with neuroimaging obtained in participants at 18–21 years of age. They found that severity of early adversity at 0–6 years was specifically associated with reduction of gray matter volume of the ACC (Jensen *et al.*, 2015). These regions of the prefrontal cortex displaying consistent differences in maltreated individuals are involved in emotional regulation and decision-making. The changes in function and connectivity of these structures carry implications of disrupted inhibitory control of impulses, which is significant in linking maltreatment-related brain alterations as a mechanism for enhanced risk for addiction (Koob and Volkow, 2010).

Importance of the type of maltreatment on brain changes: Shifting our view of brain changes from damage to adaptive response

The primary perspective held by many researchers in the field is that abuse and neglect enhance stress responses in children and disrupt brain development, resulting in damage and enhanced risk for psychopathology. However, it seems highly unlikely that through all of the eons of evolution mammalian brains have not evolved to be resistant to the effects of early stress.

The alternative view is that the brain is shaped in an adaptive manner by early experience and that maltreatment fosters adaptive responses that promote survival and reproduction in an adverse environment. In this context, psychopathology in maltreated individuals may instead be the result of a mismatch between the environment the brain developed to survive in and the environment in which it finds itself during subsequent developmental stages. This narrative coincides with the enduring understanding of the potential of human beings to be remarkably resilient while still portraying traces of devastating experiences in our biology and capacity for well-being.

Translational studies examining the effects of early stress on the hippocampus provide the most compelling support for the idea that hippocampal abnormalities are neuroplastic adaptations rather than damage. Adult rats that experienced low levels of licking and grooming in infancy (as a potential model of neglect) had shorter dendritic branch length, lower spine density, and impaired long-term potentiation (LTP) in their hippocampus under basal conditions. However, when corticosterone (rodent equivalent of cortisol) levels were elevated, LTP in these animals exceeded controls and their memory was enhanced relative to controls when tested in a stressful contextual fear-conditioning paradigm (Champagne *et al.*, 2008). Hence, their hippocampus was modified to perform better than controls in a high-stress environment but performs more poorly in less stressful circumstances.

Abuse type-specific effects on the developing brain

Neuroimaging studies looking at the association between specific experiences of maltreatment and brain morphology establish the importance of evaluating the type of maltreatment when considering treatment options. These studies demonstrate that exposure to specific types of maltreatment may lead to changes in the sensory systems most involved in perceiving and conveying the experience.

Verbal abuse

Verbal abuse is typically defined as experiences with harsh and insulting language that criticize and humiliate the individual. In the neuroimaging studies considered here, verbal abuse was perpetrated by the parents and was associated with increased risk for psychopathology.

To explore the effects of parental verbal aggression on brain morphology, Choi and colleagues (2009) studied subjects whose maltreatment history included severe exposure to parental verbal abuse but no other form of maltreatment. The results revealed three white matter tracts with reduced fractional anisotropy (a measure of connectivity reflecting fiber density, axonal diameter, and myelination of the white matter which informs overall ability of the fiber to carry information between regions). These include the arcuate fascicles, body of the fornix, and cingulum bundle all on the left side. The arcuate fasciculus interconnects Broca's area and Wernicke's language centers, and there was a significant inverse correlation between fractional anisotropy in the arcuate fascicles and measures of verbal IQ and verbal comprehension.

These findings are further supported through a study by Tomoda *et al.* (2011) of young adults with a history of parental verbal abuse versus healthy controls. Evaluation of whole-brain images in these subjects demonstrated significant increases in gray matter volume in the superior temporal gyrus. The observed result provides additional evidence that the development of the auditory association cortex involved in language processing may be altered with exposure to verbal abuse. These findings are consistent with the neuroadaptive hypothesis that the type of maltreatment experienced by individuals can lead to specific alterations in the sensory systems that convey the aversive experiences. These alterations may protect individuals from the immediate stress of verbal abuse, but have a detrimental effect on verbal IQ and comprehension and increase risk for depression and anxiety disorders (Choi *et al.*, 2009).

Witnessing domestic violence

This specific type of adverse experience typically involves visual exposure to interparental violence and has been associated with negative outcomes such as depression, PTSD, and reduced cognitive abilities.

In their research, Choi and colleagues (2012) assessed the neurobiological consequence of visually witnessing multiple episodes of domestic violence during childhood in subjects with no history of physical or sexual abuse. Neuroimaging and subsequent analysis demonstrated that witnessing domestic violence affected the fractional anisotropy of the left inferior longitudinal fascicles. This finding is important as the left inferior longitudinal fascicles connect visual and limbic systems and help determine the emotional and memory response to things we see. These fractional anisotropy values were also correlated inversely with risk ratios of depression, anxiety, and neuropsychological measures of processing speed. The pathway was also found to be most vulnerable to witnessing interparental verbal aggression during the ages of 7–13 years.

Additionally, Tomoda *et al.* (2012) examined the impacts of witnessing domestic violence on childhood gray matter volume and cortical thickness. In this study, significant differences in gray matter density were found in the right lingual gyrus and occipital pole. Participants who witnessed domestic violence in their childhood had reduced thickness in the lingual gyrus, which is a component of the visual system involved in visual memory for shapes, faces, and letters. Maximal sensitivity to exposure to witnessing domestic violence was analyzed by the researchers to occur between the ages of 11 and 13 years.

In conclusion, visually witnessing domestic violence was found to be associated with specific alterations in the gray matter volume in visual cortex areas and in the pathway linking the visual and limbic systems. This has significant implications for therapeutic planning and can help address why some maltreated children with a history of witnessing domestic violence may have impaired ability in processing and incorporating visuospatial information.

Sexual abuse

Sexual abuse entails being forced or coerced to engage in undesired or age-inappropriate sexual activities, and victims of childhood sexual abuse often experience sexual aversion or dysfunction as an enduring clinical symptom.

Tomoda and colleagues (2009) examined gray matter volume in female subjects who were raised by non-abusive parents but suffered from extra-familial sexual abuse or sexual abuse by relatives not part of the household. Childhood sexual abuse in these subjects was associated with reduced gray matter volume bilaterally in the primary visual and visual association cortices. The degree of gray matter reduction was found to be directly related to the duration of sexual abuse before the age of 12 and correlated with measures of visual memory. Further analysis of subjects who had a history of sexual abuse also revealed reduced gray matter volume in the left middle occipital, left fusiform, and right lingual gyrus. These implicated regions are all involved in facial recognition and processing, further demonstrating the effect of childhood sexual abuse on the development of the visual cortex.

In addition, Heim and colleagues (2013) performed neuroimaging analyse on 51 medically healthy adult women to evaluate the cortical thickness in areas critical to the processing and perception of behavior implicated in the nature of the abuse. In this study, experiences of childhood sexual abuse were associated with specific thinning of the somatosensory cortex that processes touch and tactile sensations from the clitoris and surrounding genital area. In contrast, exposure to emotional abuse was associated with cortical thinning in the regions relevant to self-awareness and self-evaluation.

As with verbal abuse and witnessing domestic violence, the brain changes associated with sexual abuse may shield a child from overwhelming stress. However, because these adaptations may decrease the intensity of sexual experience, sexually abused individuals may avoid sexual activity because it is not pleasurable or alternatively engage in such activity for other purposes, such as prostitution. The specific neurobiological and associated behavioral changes tied to the experience of sexual abuse further our understanding of these individuals and their therapeutic needs.

Threat detection and response

The brain's threat detection and response system, which leads to amygdala activation and engagement in fight–flight reactions, has two major components. There is a direct subconscious pathway through the thalamus and the superior and inferior colliculi to the amygdala for rapid responses, and a conscious component in which sensory information is relayed to sensory cortical regions and then to the amygdala (Teicher *et al.*, 2016). The adaptations that occur following verbal abuse, witnessing of domestic violence, and sexual abuse modify the conscious component of the circuit and can attenuate conscious perception and awareness of the threat. However, these experiences leave the subconscious component intact so that maltreated individuals may continue to respond to these threats but without full conscious awareness (Teicher *et al.*, 2016).

Maltreatment, brain network architecture and the nature of susceptibility and resilience

Brain structure and function in resilient maltreated individuals without psychopathology

The studies enumerated above have identified a host of stress-susceptible brain regions that are affected by exposure to childhood maltreatment. However, although maltreatment has robust effects on brain structure, function, and connectivity, and is a critically important risk factor for psychopathology, it has not been possible to draw direct connections between brain regions affected and psychiatric outcomes. What complicates the linkage is the vast number of studies reporting maltreatment-associated abnormalities in mixed samples and occurrence even in studies of maltreated individuals with no evidence of psychopathology (see Teicher *et al.*, 2016 for specific citation).

These findings led us to conclude that maltreated individuals with better-than-expected outcomes were not unaffected but were effectively compensated. The critical question is, how do they manage, neurobiologically, to maintain mental health despite a host of abnormalities in stress-susceptible structures? Our suspicion was that to answer this question we needed to use an approach that would enable us to simultaneously consider the interconnections between the large number of regions that appear to be affected in maltreated individuals. Hence, we conducted the first large sample size studies of brain network architecture in maltreated participants.

nt, brain network architecture, atric vulnerability

dies have been most revealing. First, we found in an ex tion of cortical network architecture (based on the interconnections of 112 cortical regions) that regions comprising the highly interconnected communication backbone ('rich club') of the network were almost entirely different in maltreated and non-maltreated participants (Teicher *et al.*, 2014), indicating a marked shift in network organization. The communication backbone consisted primarily of frontal and temporal regions in non-maltreated controls and in occipital and temporal regions in maltreated individuals.

We also found important alterations in the centrality of specific brain regions, which indicates their connectedness and importance to the overall network. There was a markedly reduced degree of centrality in maltreated individuals in the left anterior cingulate cortex, temporal pole, and middle frontal gyrus. The anterior cingulate cortex participates in the regulation of emotions and monitors cognitive and motor responses during potential conflict situations. The temporal and middle frontal gyri play a role in aspects of social cognition such as person perception and mentalizing. Conversely, the brain networks of adults with histories of maltreatment demonstrated increased centrality in the anterior insula and precuneus. The precuneus is involved in self-centered mental imagery and self-referential thinking, while the anterior insula plays a critical role in interoception (perception of bodily sensations) and possibly self-awareness. Hence, maltreated individuals may be at increased risk for psychopathology due to reduced centrality of the anterior cingulate, temporal pole, and middle frontal gyrus (decreased ability to regulate emotions and to read others), coupled with increased centrality in the precuneus and anterior insula (increased emotional and internal perceptions and preoccupation with self).

More recently, we used diffusion tensor imaging and tractography to examine combined cortical–subcortical brain network architecture by determining presence or absence of interconnecting fiber streams between 90 brain regions (nodes). We discovered that maltreated individuals had a sparser whole-brain fiber stream network architecture with increased vulnerability to disruption

(Ohashi *et al.*, 2017) and then showed in an expanded data set (N=342) that maltreated individuals with and without psychopathology had the same array of abnormalities in global network architecture, including decreased global efficiency and degree and increased small-worldness and vulnerability to disruption (Ohashi *et al.*, in press).

Vulnerability to psychopathology in maltreated individuals can be understood from the perspective that brain network architecture needs to balance the opposing demands of integration and segregation in order to combine the presence of functionally specialized and segregated modules (highly interconnected regions working together to perform certain functions) with a robust number of connecting links. We found that maltreated individuals had sparser networks with increased small-worldness resulting from intact local modular architecture but lower connectivity between modules. The weaker degree of integration between modules in maltreated individuals is associated with increased vulnerability and puts them at risk for psychopathology by making it harder to compensate effectively for abnormalities that might occur within a module or node. We propose that neurobiological resilience occurs in maltreated individuals with both global network and specific nodal abnormalities but who are effectively compensated, which we theorized may result from partially isolating and limiting the impact of problematic nodes.

We provided an initial test of this hypothesis by predicting that asymptomatic maltreated individuals would have a lower degree of right amygdala centrality, as right amygdala hyperactivity to threatening stimuli is the most consistent functional abnormality in maltreated individuals (Teicher *et al.*, 2016). As predicted, right amygdala nodal efficiency (the ability of a node to propagate information to other nodes in the network) was significantly lower in asymptomatic maltreated individuals than in maltreated individuals with clinically significant psychiatric symptoms or in healthy unexposed controls.

Our next step was to use machine learning strategies to identify other brain regions with abnormal measures of nodal efficiency (Neff) in asymptomatic maltreated individuals. This approach confirmed the right amygdala abnormality and identified eight other nodes that followed the same pattern of reduced Neff in the asymptomatic participants. We then assessed whether this was a meaningful set of findings by using predictive analytics to assess how well information on global network architecture (5 measures) and Neff (9 measures) could identify whether an individual was maltreated or control and whether those designated as maltreated were symptomatic or asymptomatic. Overall, controls, asymptomatic participants, and symptomatic participants were identified with 75%, 80%, and 82% balanced cross-validated accuracy, respectively, versus 33% chance ($p < 10^{-7}$, N=310). This noteworthy degree of predictive accuracy suggests that this approach is likely to provide important insights into mechanisms enabling maltreated individuals to effectively compensate.

The nodes that distinguished maltreated individuals with and without psychopathology based on fiber stream network architecture consisted of: right amygdala, dorsal anterior cingulate cortex (dACC), and paracentral lobule; left frontal inferior pars triangularis; supplementary and pre-supplementary motor areas; and bilateral subcallosal cingulate gyrus and postcentral gyrus. Considerable evidence links the amygdala, dACC, and subcallosal cingulate with various forms of psychopathology. This is less true for the other regions, suggesting that our approach may have identified important regions that have been predominantly overlooked.

Our next step was to determine if Neff in these 'resilience nodes' moderated the relationship between maltreatment and specific sets of symptoms. Neff in the left pars triangularis moderated the association between maltreated (number of types) and current symptoms of anxiety ($p < 0.005$). There was a strong interactive effect. Individuals with low Neff appeared to be fully protected or compensated, whereas individuals with high Neff were very susceptible to maltreatment. Neff in the left pars triangularis also moderated the relationship between maltreatment and symptoms of depression and number of drug use issues. The pars triangularis contains a portion of Broca's area and could potentially play a role in the self-castigating 'voices' that maltreated individuals often perceive. Reducing Neff of the left pars triangularis may enable maltreated individuals to more effectively compensate. Similarly, Neff in the right amygdala moderated the association between maltreatment and somatization, anxiety and drinking concerns, whereas Neff in right dACC moderated the association between maltreatment and depression as well as recreational use of opioids. Reduced connectivity is probably not the sole mechanism leading to effective compensation. Herringa *et al.* (2016) showed that relatively resilient maltreated children (low internalizing scores) had enhanced prefrontal–amygdala connectivity. So resilience may result from reduced connectivity of a 'resilience node' to the global network or by enhanced top-down regulation-suppression of the 'resilience node'.

Brain network architecture and development of psychopathology

Our structural brain network model proposes that psychopathology occurs when one or more abnormally functioning brain regions (nodes) exert untoward influence on a vulnerable global network (Ohashi *et al.*, 2017). A critical question is whether nodal abnormalities precede or follow the development of global network vulnerabilities and how maltreatment-related differences in global network architecture emerge during development. A considerable amount is known about changes in network architecture during development (see Di Martino *et al.*, 2014 for review). Of note is the increasing connectivity and reorganization of hubs, particularly those constituting the 'rich club' (Baker *et al.*, 2015). Connectivity between subcortical hubs decreases over time in favor of an increasingly prominent role for frontal hubs (Baker *et al.*, 2015). This fits with our reported observation that maltreated individuals have significantly fewer fiber streams in the hub–hub (frontal–basal ganglia, frontal–thalamic, frontal–insula, frontal–parietal) and hub–feeder (frontal–occipital) interconnections (Ohashi *et al.*, 2017) that Baker *et al.* (2015) reported as increasing with age in a sample of 15–19-year-olds, and our findings showing a paucity of frontal hubs in the maltreated rich club (Teicher *et al.*, 2014). Our hypothesis is that maltreatment interferes with the development or myelination of these late-developing fiber streams, resulting in a progressive increase in vulnerability. We can confirm in our 18–25-year-old maltreated sample that vulnerability rapidly increases until 21–22 years of age.

The second question is, when do nodal abnormalities emerge in maltreated individuals? As indicated above, exposure to parental or peer physical abuse was an important predictor of amygdala response at 3–6 years of age, and this suggests that right amygdala nodal abnormalities may precede emergence of global network abnormalities in many instances. Similarly, we found that the dACC was most susceptible to physical neglect at ages 2–6. Hence, it is likely that some nodal abnormalities precede the peripubertal-to-adult shift in network vulnerability of maltreated individuals.

The third question is, when does the reduction of Neff in 'resilience nodes' take place in participants with resilient outcome trajectories? Our hypothesis is that this varies between individuals and would be reflected in their pattern of change in symptom scores during development. We propose that individuals with pre-existing low levels of Neff in certain 'resilience nodes' will appear protected and will show a 'minimal impact' resilience pattern during this time. Individuals with typical levels of Neff but who develop a compensatory reductive adaptation in Neff would display a more protracted 'emergent resilient' or 'recovery' pattern.

Brain network architecture: Implications for treatment

These network findings have critically important implications for understanding the effects of treatment. Prior to these findings we had assumed that effective treatment of psychiatric disorders in maltreated individuals would need to reverse at least some of the effects of maltreatment on brain development. The alternative idea that emerges from this work is that effective treatment of maltreated individuals works by bringing the nodal network architecture of susceptible individuals more into line with the abnormal but effectively compensated nodal architecture of resilient maltreated individuals. What this would entail would be a reduction in Neff (or top-down suppression) of one or more of these 'resilience nodes'. We envision that different types of treatment target different nodes.

We have a very small amount of preliminary data that supports this hypothesis. We found that the most prominent statistically significant change in a pilot study of a novel desensitization treatment, developed by Ann Polcari PhD for young adults exposed to high levels of parental verbal abuse, was reduced connectivity of the default mode network (DMN) with the left pars triangularis. This is consistent with the idea that the left pars triangularis may be modified by verbal abuse and that reducing connectivity of this region with the DMN may attenuate symptoms and foster compensation by diminishing the critical internal voice coming through when not engaged in specific tasks.

Our vision for the future is to develop an incisive methodology to identify which nodes need to be targeted in a given individual to enable them to compensate effectively. This information may derive from their history of exposure to maltreatment during specific sensitive periods, and/or from neuroimaging parameters. We would then need to couple this with an understanding of the effects of various treatments on Neff or top-down regulation of specific regions. Putting these components together would then enable us to effectively match patients to available treatments and to test the efficacy of novel treatments designed to target nodes that are inadequately addressed by current strategies.

Implications of reported neuroimaging findings and conclusion

These neuroimaging findings present strong evidence for the overarching perspective that brain changes in maltreated individuals represent adaptations instead of non-specific damage. Furthermore, the close correspondence between type of maltreatment experienced and associated sensory system abnormalities provides neuroimaging evidence for the veracity of retrospective self-reports regarding the type of abuse experienced. This is significant in bolstering the confidence of self-reports in a clinical setting and their utility in determining the appropriate treatment modality for patients.

Type and timing of maltreatment also provides a greater understanding of why individuals may exhibit certain psychiatric disorders or neurocognitive problems. Khan *et al.* (2015) provide evidence that exposure at age 14 to parental nonverbal emotional abuse in males, and to peer emotional abuse in females, was for each sex, the most important risk factor for depression. Schalinski *et al.* (2017) recently reported that abuse at 10–11 years of age was the most important predictor of the severity of positive psychotic symptoms in hospitalized individuals with psychotic disorders.

In *The Body Keeps the Score: Brain, Mind, and Body in the Healing of Trauma*, Bessel van der Kolk reflects on his experience and emphasizes the importance of finding the preferred treatment modality for the individual (van der Kolk, 2014). He reflects that although the common approach to addressing trauma involves guiding the individual to share their story, trauma is often not remembered as a story but as sensory imprints of images, sounds, and physical sensations that are joined with intense emotions of terror and helplessness. Multiple studies have underscored how childhood maltreatment may continue to contaminate new encounters and events based on alterations in brain structure, function, connectivity, circuitry, and network architecture. This embedded trauma leads many individuals to be too numb to absorb new experiences and diminishes their alertness to dangers. On the other hand, others become too hypervigilant to fully experience life.

These reflections highlight the necessity of critically considering neurobiology and brain network architecture. This perspective appreciates the power of our brain in ensuring survival even under grim conditions while acknowledging the importance of the imprint of the past. Furthermore, this approach underscores the importance of taking a thorough developmental and maltreatment history for greater understanding of how an individual's childhood can lead to specific alterations in brain structure. These alterations then may be associated with changes in cognition, behavior, and psychopathology. Additionally, the perspective assists individuals in connecting current challenges with past experience, especially as each person has a unique history with differing ages and durations of exposure to different arrays of abusive experiences. This may provide encouragement for self-compassion in maltreated individuals, as this narrative highlights that their neurobiological adaptations were developed for success in a different environment and there is an opportunity to work with their brain in the environment they currently inhabit.

Overall, we hope this chapter has elucidated the implications of neuroscientific research and revealed potential avenues for how our community can work together to ensure children are treated according to their specific experiences of trauma. As research continues to develop and further our understanding of the impacts of maltreatment, we are hopeful for continued advancement on how we can best prevent, pre-empt, and treat maltreatment.

Acknowledgement

Financial support was provided by US National Institute of Mental Health R01 Award MH-091391, National Institute on Drug Abuse

R01 Award DA-017846, and National Institute of Child Health and Human Development R01 Award HD-079484 to M.H.T.

References

Andersen, S.L. and Teicher, M.H. (2008). Stress, sensitive periods and maturational events in adolescent depression. *Trends in Neurosciences*, 31(4), 183–191.

Badura-Brack, A., McDermott, T.J., Heinrichs-Graham, E., Ryan, T.J. *et al.* (2018). Veterans with PTSD demonstrate amygdala hyperactivity while viewing threatening faces: A MEG study. *Biological Psychology*, 132, 228–232.

Baker, L.M., Williams, L.M., Korgaonkar, M.S., Cohen, R.A., Heaps, J.M. and Paul, R.H. (2013). Impact of early vs. late childhood early life stress on brain morphometrics. *Brain Imaging and Behavior*, 7(2), 196–203.

Baker, S.T., Lubman, D.I., Yucel, M., Allen, N.B. *et al.* (2015). Developmental changes in brain network hub connectivity in late adolescence. *Journal of Neuroscience*, 35(24), 9078–9087.

Baloch, H.A., Brambilla, P. and Soares, J.C. (2009). Corpus callosum abnormalities in pediatric bipolar disorder. *Expert Review of Neurotherapeutics*, 9(7), 949–955.

Carrion, V.G., Weems, C.F. and Reiss, A.L. (2007). Stress predicts brain changes in children: A pilot longitudinal study on youth stress, posttraumatic stress disorder, and the hippocampus. *Pediatrics*, 119(3), 509–516.

Champagne, D.L., Bagot, R.C., van Hasselt, F., Ramakers, G. *et al.* (2008). Maternal care and hippocampal plasticity: Evidence for experience-dependent structural plasticity, altered synaptic functioning, and differential responsiveness to glucocorticoids and stress. *Journal of Neuroscience*, 28(23), 6037–6045.

Choi, J., Jeong, B., Polcari, A., Rohan, M.L. and Teicher, M.H. (2012). Reduced fractional anisotropy in the visual limbic pathway of young adults witnessing domestic violence in childhood. *NeuroImage*, 59(2), 1071–1079.

Choi, J., Jeong, B., Rohan, M.L., Polcari, A.M. and Teicher, M.H. (2009). Preliminary evidence for white matter tract abnormalities in young adults exposed to parental verbal abuse. *Biological Psychiatry*, 65(3), 227–234.

Cowell, R.A., Cicchetti, D., Rogosch, F.A. and Toth, S.L. (2015). Childhood maltreatment and its effect on neurocognitive functioning: Timing and chronicity matter. *Development and Psychopathology*, 27(2), 521–533.

De Bellis, M.D., Keshavan, M.S., Clark, D.B., Casey, B.J. *et al.* (1999). A.E. Bennett Research Award. Developmental traumatology. Part II: Brain development. *Biological Psychiatry*, 45(10), 1271–1284.

De Bellis, M.D., Keshavan, M.S., Shifflett, H., Iyengar, S. *et al.* (2002). Brain structures in pediatric maltreatment-related posttraumatic stress disorder: A sociodemographically matched study. *Biological Psychiatry*, 52(11), 1066–1078.

Derntl, B., Habel, U., Windischberger, C., Robinson, S. *et al.* (2009). General and specific responsiveness of the amygdala during explicit emotion recognition in females and males. *BMC Neuroscience*, 10, 91.

Di Martino, A., Fair, D.A., Kelly, C., Satterthwaite, T.D. *et al.* (2014). Unraveling the miswired connectome: A developmental perspective. *Neuron*, 83(6), 1335–1353.

Edmiston, E.E., Wang, F., Mazure, C.M., Guiney, J. *et al.* (2011). Corticostriatal-limbic gray matter morphology in adolescents with self-reported exposure to childhood maltreatment. *Archives of Pediatrics and Adolescent Medicine*, 165(12), 1069–1077.

Gerritsen, L., Tendolkar, I., Franke, B., Vasquez, A.A. *et al.* (2012). BDNF Val66Met genotype modulates the effect of childhood adversity on subgenual anterior cingulate cortex volume in healthy subjects. *Molecular Psychiatry*, 17(6), 597–603.

Geuze, E., Vermetten, E. and Bremner, J.D. (2005). MR-based in vivo hippocampal volumetrics: 2. Findings in neuropsychiatric disorders. *Molecular Psychiatry*, 10(2), 160–184.

Glahn, D.C., Lovallo, W.R. and Fox, P.T. (2007). Reduced amygdala activation in young adults at high risk of alcoholism: Studies from the Oklahoma family health patterns project. *Biological Psychiatry*, 61(11), 1306–1309.

Goodman, M., Carpenter, D., Tang, C.Y., Goldstein, K.E. *et al.* (2014). Dialectical behavior therapy alters emotion regulation and amygdala activity in patients with borderline personality disorder. *Journal of Psychiatric Research*, 57, 108–116.

Green, J.G., McLaughlin, K.A., Berglund, P.A., Gruber, M.J. *et al.* (2010). Childhood adversities and adult psychiatric disorders in the national comorbidity survey replication I: Associations with first onset of DSM-IV disorders. *Archives of General Psychiatry*, 67(2), 113–123.

Grotegerd, D., Stuhrmann, A., Kugel, H., Schmidt, S. *et al.* (2014). Amygdala excitability to subliminally presented emotional faces distinguishes unipolar and bipolar depression: An fMRI and pattern classification study. *Human Brain Mapping*, 35(7), 2995–3007.

Heim, C.M., Mayberg, H.S., Mletzko, T., Nemeroff, C.B. and Pruessner, J.C. (2013). Decreased cortical representation of genital somatosensory field after childhood sexual abuse. *American Journal of Psychiatry*, 170(6), 616–623.

Herringa, R.J., Burghy, C.A., Stodola, D.E., Fox, M.E., Davidson, R.J. and Essex, M.J. (2016). Enhanced prefrontal-amygdala connectivity following childhood adversity as a protective mechanism against internalizing in adolescence. *Biological Psychiatry: Cognitive Neuroscience and Neuroimaging*, 1(4), 326–334.

Jensen, S.K., Dickie, E.W., Schwartz, D.H., Evans, C.J. *et al.* (2015). Effect of early adversity and childhood internalizing symptoms on brain structure in young men. *JAMA Pediatrics*, 169(10), 938–946.

Khan, A., McCormack, H.C., Bolger, E.A., McGreenery, C.E. *et al.* (2015). Childhood maltreatment, depression, and suicidal ideation: Critical importance of parental and peer emotional abuse during developmental sensitive periods in males and females. *Frontiers in Psychiatry*, 6, 42.

Kleinhans, N.M., Richards, T., Weaver, K., Johnson, L.C. *et al.* (2010). Association between amygdala response to emotional faces and social anxiety in autism spectrum disorders. *Neuropsychologia*, 48(12), 3665–3670.

Klumpp, H., Angstadt, M., Nathan, P.J. and Phan, K.L. (2010). Amygdala reactivity to faces at varying intensities of threat in generalized social phobia: An event-related functional MRI study. *Psychiatry Research*, 183(2), 167–169.

Koob, G.F. and Volkow, N.D. (2010). Neurocircuitry of addiction. *Neuropsychopharmacology*, 35(1), 217–238.

LeDoux, J.E. (1993). Emotional memory systems in the brain. *Behavioural Brain Research*, 58(1–2), 69–79.

Lozier, L.M., Cardinale, E.M., VanMeter, J.W. and Marsh, A.A. (2014). Mediation of the relationship between callous-unemotional traits and proactive aggression by amygdala response to fear among children with conduct problems. *JAMA Psychiatry*, 71(6), 627–636.

Luders, E., Narr, K.L., Bilder, R.M., Thompson, P.M. *et al.* (2007). Positive correlations between corpus callosum thickness and intelligence. *NeuroImage*, 37(4), 1457–1464.

Luders, E., Narr, K.L., Hamilton, L.S., Phillips, O.R. *et al.* (2009). Decreased callosal thickness in attention-deficit/hyperactivity disorder. *Biological Psychiatry*, 65(1), 84–88.

Moser, E.I., Kropff, E. and Moser, M.B. (2008). Place cells, grid cells, and the brain's spatial representation system. *Annual Review of Neuroscience*, 31, 69–89.

Nadel, L., Campbell, J. and Ryan, L. (2007). Autobiographical memory retrieval and hippocampal activation as a function of repetition and the passage of time. *Neural Plasticity*, 2007, 90472.

Navalta, C.P., Polcari, A., Webster, D.M., Boghossian, A. and Teicher, M.H. (2006). Effects of childhood sexual abuse on neuropsychological and cognitive function in college women. *Journal of Neuropsychiatry and Clinical Neurosciences*, 18(1), 45–53.

Ohashi, K., Anderson, C.M., Bolger, E.A., Khan, A., McGreenery, C.E. and Teicher, M.H. (2017). Childhood maltreatment is associated with alteration in global network fiber-tract architecture independent of history of depression and anxiety. *NeuroImage*, 150, 50–59.

Ohashi, K., Anderson, C.M., Bolger, E.A., Khan, A., McGreenery, C.E. and Teicher, M.H. (in press). Susceptibility or resilience to maltreatment can be explained by specific differences in brain network architecture. *Biological Psychiatry*.

Rao, H., Betancourt, L., Giannetta, J.M., Brodsky, N.L. *et al.* (2010). Early parental care is important for hippocampal maturation: Evidence from brain morphology in humans. *NeuroImage*, 49(1), 1144–1150.

Sapolsky, R.M., Krey, L.C. and McEwen, B.S. (1985). Prolonged glucocorticoid exposure reduces hippocampal neuron number: Implications for aging. *Journal of Neuroscience*, 5(5), 1222–1227.

Schalinski, I., Breinlinger, S., Hirt, V., Teicher, M.H., Odenwald, M. and Rockstroh, B. (2017). Environmental adversities and psychotic symptoms: The impact of timing of trauma, abuse, and neglect. *Schizophrenia Research*. doi:10.1016/j.schres.2017.10.034.

Schumann, C.M., Bauman, M.D. and Amaral, D.G. (2011). Abnormal structure or function of the amygdala is a common component of neurodevelopmental disorders. *Neuropsychologia*, 49(4), 745–759.

Schutter, D.J. and Harmon-Jones, E. (2013). The corpus callosum: A commissural road to anger and aggression. *Neuroscience and Biobehavioral Reviews*, 37(10 Pt 2), 2481–2488.

Sheridan, M.A., Fox, N.A., Zeanah, C.H., McLaughlin, K.A. and Nelson, C.A., 3rd (2012). Variation in neural development as a result of exposure to institutionalization early in childhood. *Proceedings of the National Academy of Sciences of the United States of America*, 109(32), 12927–12932.

Shin, L.M. and Liberzon, I. (2010). The neurocircuitry of fear, stress, and anxiety disorders. *Neuropsychopharmacology*, 35(1), 169–191.

Suslow, T., Lindner, C., Dannlowski, U., Walhofer, K. *et al.* (2013). Automatic amygdala response to facial expression in schizophrenia: Initial hyperresponsivity followed by hyporesponsivity. *BMC Neuroscience*, 14, 140.

Taylor, S.E., Eisenberger, N.I., Saxbe, D., Lehman, B.J. and Lieberman, M.D. (2006). Neural responses to emotional stimuli are associated with childhood family stress. *Biological Psychiatry*, 60(3), 296–301.

Teicher, M.H., Anderson, C.M., Ohashi, K., Khan, A. *et al.* (2018). Differential effects of childhood neglect and abuse during sensitive exposure periods on male and female hippocampus. *NeuroImage*, 169, 443–452.

Teicher, M.H., Anderson, C.M., Ohashi, K. and Polcari, A. (2014). Childhood maltreatment: Altered network centrality of cingulate, precuneus, temporal pole and insula. *Biological Psychiatry*, 76(4), 297–305.

Teicher, M.H., Dumont, N.L., Ito, Y., Vaituzis, C., Giedd, J.N. and Andersen, S.L. (2004). Childhood neglect is associated with reduced corpus callosum area. *Biological Psychiatry*, 56(2), 80–85.

Teicher, M.H. and Samson, J.A. (2016). Annual Research Review: Enduring neurobiological effects of childhood abuse and neglect. *Journal of Child Psychology and Psychiatry*, 57(3), 241–266.

Teicher, M.H., Samson, J.A., Anderson, C.M. and Ohashi, K. (2016). The effects of childhood maltreatment on brain structure, function and connectivity. *Nature Reviews: Neuroscience*, 17(10), 652–666.

Tomoda, A., Navalta, C.P., Polcari, A., Sadato, N. and Teicher, M.H. (2009). Childhood sexual abuse is associated with reduced gray matter volume in visual cortex of young women. *Biological Psychiatry*, 66(7), 642–648.

Tomoda, A., Polcari, A., Anderson, C.M. and Teicher, M.H. (2012). Reduced visual cortex gray matter volume and thickness in young adults who witnessed domestic violence during childhood. *PLoS One*, 7(12), e52528.

Tomoda, A., Sheu, Y.S., Rabi, K., Suzuki, H. *et al.* (2011). Exposure to parental verbal abuse is associated with increased gray matter volume in superior temporal gyrus. *NeuroImage*, 54 Suppl 1, S280–286.

van der Kolk, B.A. (2014). *The Body Keeps the Score: Brain, Mind, and Body in the Healing of Trauma*. New York, NY: Viking.

PRACTICE REFLECTION

Joe Tucci, Janise Mitchell and Ed Tronick

In their chapter, Teicher and Munkhbaatar present a densely packed summary of the research which suggests a number of important points for those working in Therapeutic Care with children whose experiences of abuse and neglect are recent and vivid.

First, not all trauma is the same. Different types of abuse and neglect lead to different alterations in brain structure and functioning. For example, experiences of verbal abuse appear to affect the parts of children's brains that are implicated in language development. Some children who are exposed to verbal abuse also show aggressive behaviour due to frustration with their experience of not being able to communicate effectively. Similarly, children who are witness to family violence have parts of their visual cortex affected, which leads to them experiencing difficulties with processing visuospatial information.

Even more importantly, Teicher and Munkhbaatar point to research which highlights that there appear to be gender differences in the way that different types of abuse and neglect affect boys and girls. Boys under the ages of seven who experience neglect seem to suffer from decreased size and functioning of the hippocampus and the corpus callosum, meaning they are less able to be supported to change the way that they respond to emotional/sensory memories and are left to repeat complex behaviour that results from these brain changes. Equally, girls have sensitive developmental periods for their hippocampus which is most likely to be affected at the ages of 10–11 and 15–16 when they experience sexual abuse.

Teicher and Munkhbaatar's explanation of hippocampal functioning provides an important and useful means of understanding why children with trauma-based behaviour are easily triggered in the present by experiences of the past, and in particular the sensory dimensions of these experiences – sight, sound, taste, touch and smell. It develops the foundational basis for understanding why these often complex behaviours are difficult to change without children gaining a felt sense of safety in their relational and physical environment found through consistent support from trusted others.

Teicher and Munkhbaatar also reflect on the need to emphasise that as much as traumatic experiences can lead to damage, experiences which promote adaptability can lead to restoration and renewal. This revitalised focus on neuroplasticity is critical, regardless of a child's age, providing both the opportunity to redirect our interpretive lens away from a deficit-based way of understanding the impact of trauma to a strengths-based approach which supports the view that adaptability is the basis upon which change can be achieved.

Finally, Teicher and Munkhbaatar comments on recent research showing that new models of neuronal networks suggest that children who experience abuse or neglect have had specific relay points in their network architecture compromised so that they are prevented from spreading maladaptive information throughout the network. This finding supports their proposition that the experience of the abuse and neglect itself helps to create adaptive neuronal connections and formations within the brain/body system to help children survive even the most dire traumatic exposure.

The implications for practice are that children's care and support needs are experienced in real time and must be sensitively configured in the environment in which they find themselves. Children's state and its expression in challenging or complex behaviour arises when there is a mismatch between the demands they experience in their environment in the present and the way that their internal systems have developed to protect them from the full impact of the threat and violation they have experienced in their past. It is in these moment-to-moment ruptures between past and present that carers and others in the child's network find themselves offering unique opportunities to children to re-experience their past through different reactions to them in the here-and-now. It is also the boundary at which Therapeutic Specialists actively intervene to shape and reshape the relational responses that children need at those times – stabilising them, making them become routine and gradually changing the environmental composition to reduce the demands on children so that their internal systems can be tempted into adapting away from the adaptations they were required to make as a result of the abuse and violation they suffered in the past.

Teicher and Munkhbaatar suggest more than once that it is critical to gather and analyse a detailed history of the type and timing of the experiences of trauma in children's lives. They believe that therapeutic input needs to become more and more attuned to the specific consequences of different types of abuse which occur at different times for children according to their gender and other background factors. This is a valuable lesson for Therapeutic Care because it establishes an important principle that partialised knowledge of children's lived experiences of trauma is not as helpful as a coherent story which incorporates comprehensive details of what has happened to them.

It is a truism for Therapeutic Care practice that time spent getting to know children and their experiences is time well spent.

4

The Fundamental Role of the Mother in the Interpersonal Neurobiological Origins of Mutual Love

ALLAN N. SCHORE

Introduction

Across the body of my work I have offered interpersonal neurobiological models of both abnormal and normal early emotional development. Towards that end my research and clinical contributions have focused on the psychopathogenesis and treatment of early attachment trauma. Over the last three decades I have offered interdisciplinary evidence which supports the basic developmental principle that during critical periods of brain development the developing brain is malleable, and that the early relationship with the mother shapes the baby's brain *for better or for worse*. In this expansion of regulation theory (Schore, 1994, 2003a, 2003b, 2012) I offer data from very recent advances in neuroscience in order to shed light upon perhaps the most essential characteristic of the human experience: the adaptive ability of humans to express, receive and share love with a valued other. I will argue that the prototypical expression of how the mother shapes the baby's brain *for the better* is expressed in an early bond of mutual love, and that this growth promoting early emotional experience acts as a relational matrix for the emergence of the capacity to share a loving relationship at later stages of life.

The Shorter Oxford English Dictionary defines love as 'a state or feeling', '*deep affection, strong emotional attachment*'. This raises the matter of the relationship of love to attachment, especially in light of the transformational impact of the shift of modern attachment theory from behavior and cognition to affect and an emotional bond between intimate individuals (Schore and Schore, 2008). Love is defined as (1) a noun: a feeling of tenderness, passion and warmth; and (2) a verb: to feel love for another person – actions including expressions of physical affection, tenderness and acts of kindness. The first usage implies love as an intense intrapersonal emotion, the second as a strong interpersonal emotional communication. The contrast in these two definitions mirror the ongoing shift from a 'one person' intrapsychic to a 'two person' interpersonal perspective in psychology, including the most prominent theory in developmental psychology, attachment theory. To understand the attachment origins of the capacity to share a strong intimate emotional relationship with a valued other, we need to utilize the perspective of *interpersonal* neurobiology in order to elucidate the functional and structural development of the early bonds of *mutual* love. The mutual love between a mother and her infant is embedded in an optimal co-created, reciprocal, synchronized, bodily based, emotion-transacting attachment relationship. In this manner the relational mechanism of mutual love, '*strong emotional attachment*', is mediated by the mother's right brain, which is dominant for strong emotions, interacting with the infant's right brain.

In the following sections of this chapter I will utilize the dynamic relational perspective of regulation theory in order to interpret a body of neuroimaging research on love in infancy in order to more deeply understand the right-brain attachment origins and underlying psychoneurobiological mechanisms of the capacity to form and maintain a strong emotional bond of mutual love. After an introduction and background, I will discuss recent developmental neuroimaging and conceptualizations of mother's love, a model of the initial emergence of mutual love at 2–3 months and then mutual love at later stages of infancy, toddlerhood, childhood and adult life. This work suggests that the capacity for mutual love is an essential marker of what it means to be human.

Understanding the nature of love

Although love is mostly thought to be the province of the arts, poets, writers, actors, dancers and musicians, from the very beginnings of modern biology and psychology, science has also explored its origins and emotional expressions. Indeed, in his seminal work *The Expression of the Emotions in Man and Animals* (1872), Charles Darwin proposed:

> The emotion of love, for instance that of a mother for her infant, *is one of the strongest of which the mind is capable*… No doubt, as affection is a *pleasurable sensation*, it generally causes a gentle smile and some brightening of the eyes. A *strong desire* to touch the beloved is commonly felt. (pp.224–225, my emphasis)

Specifically referring to the origins of perhaps this most essential expression of the human species, he speculated:

> The movements of expressions in the face and body…serve as the first means of communication between the mother and her infant; she smiles approval and thus encourages her child on the right path or frowns disapproval. (p.385)

At the end of the nineteenth century Sigmund Freud began his pioneering studies in psychoanalysis and initiated the field's long history of interest in the essential role of love in human function and dysfunction. Referring to his evolving position on the developmental origins of love that I have suggested:

> Although for much of his career [Freud] seemed ambivalent about the role of maternal influences in earliest development, in his very last work he stated, in a definitive fashion, that the mother–infant relationship 'is unique, without parallel, established unalterably for a whole lifetime as the first and *strongest love-object and the prototype of all later love relations*' (Freud, 1940). (cited in Schore, 2003b, p.256, my emphasis)

But perhaps more than any of Freud's followers, Donald Winnicott studied the deepest origins of the capacity to love. He observed that 'the early management of an infant is a matter beyond conscious thought and deliberate intention. It is something that becomes possible only through love' and that the mother 'by expressing love in terms of physical management and in giving physical satisfaction enables the infant psyche to begin in the infant body' (1975, p.183). Thus, the early origins of love are expressed in the mother–infant experience of mutuality, and in this primordial context of mutual love: 'The main thing is a communication between the baby and mother in terms of the anatomy and physiology of live bodies' (Winnicott, 1986, p.258). Furthermore, Winnicott (1963) described two forms of love in the developing infant. 'Quiet love' is seen in moments when the mother holds and handles (soothes, comforts, caresses) the infant (for a visual representation see Figure A-7 in Schore, 2003a). 'Quiet love' has been characterized as 'a mutual dwelling of baby and mother where one and one make not two but one' (Ulanov, 2001, pp.49–50). On the other hand, 'excited love' occurs in moments of thrilling excitement and intense interest in interaction with the mother and contains an energetic potential (see Figure 6.3 in Schore, 1994). In an update of this model, I suggest that quiet love represents a parasympathetic dominant state, whereas excited love reflects a sympathetic autonomic state.

In the middle of the last century, John Bowlby (1953), another of Freud's followers, began his seminal writings on what would become attachment theory in *Child Care and the Growth of Love*. In that volume he asserted that a mother's love in infancy and childhood is as important for mental health as are vitamins and proteins for physical health. In his later writings Bowlby (1969) concluded:

> Many of the most *intense emotions* arise during the formation, the maintenance, the disruption, and the renewal of attachment relationships. The formation of a bond is described as falling in love, maintaining a bond as loving someone, and losing a partner as grieving over someone. (p.130, my emphasis)

Also in the mid-twentieth century, another of Freud's disciples, Erich Fromm (1956), wrote the classic *The Art of Loving*, in which he described love as 'the experience of union with another being', and 'becoming one with another'. In that volume Fromm described what he deemed to be the central problem in individual development: 'What meaning – in both women as well as men – does our longing for a mother have? What constitutes the bond to the mother?' (pp.26–27). He stated that motherly love is an unconditional affirmation of the child's life and needs, and that it is expressed in two different aspects:

> [O]ne is the care and responsibility absolutely necessary for the preservation of the child's life and his growth. The other aspect goes further than mere preservation... Motherly love, in this second

> step, makes the child feel: it is good to have been born; it instills in the child the *love for life* and not merely the wish to remain alive… Mother's love for life is as infectious as her anxiety. (pp.46–47)

Note the overlap between maternal 'care' and Winnicott's 'quiet love'; and between Fromm's maternal support of the child's love for life and Winnicott's 'excited love' that contains an energetic potential.

Indeed, further advances in the scientific study of love, like emotions in general, were not available to science until the 1990s. In that decade, emotion finally was being investigated by both researchers and clinicians. This period also began to forge links between brain and emotion, and neuroscientists began to offer models of the association of love and specifically the right brain. In this same period I began to publish my own studies of the impact of early attachment on the early developing right brain. In my first book (Schore, 1994) I set forth the argument that the right orbitofrontal cortex acts as the control center of attachment, earlier described by Bowlby (1969). Expanding this model in my second book *Affect Dysregulation and Disorders of the Self* (2003a), I offered the heuristic proposal, 'The infant's right brain is tuned to dynamically self-organize upon perceiving certain patterns of facially expressed exteroceptive information, namely the visual and auditory stimuli emanating from the smiling and laughing joyful face of a *loving mother*' (p.147). I presented evidence showing that over the course of the first year mutual emotional exchanges of interactively regulated heightened affective moments are imprinted into limbic amygdala, insula, cingulate and orbitofrontal areas of the infant's developing right brain. I thus concluded that 'the visual image of the *loving mother's* positive emotional face as well as the imprint of the mother's regulatory capacities are inscribed into the circuits of this lateralized prefrontal system' (p.278).

Building upon the long-standing tradition of scientific interest in the development of love, in this chapter I will discuss recent neuroimaging research on the effects of this 'strong emotional attachment' on brain development in both infancy and adulthood. A large body of studies clearly demonstrates that at all stages of the lifespan an attachment relationship that supports a loving emotional bond between two individuals is optimized when it is reciprocal and mutual. Overviewing attachment dynamics in adulthood,

Baumeister and Leary (1995) emphasized 'how important it is that caring, concern, and affection be *mutual and reciprocal*' and concluded: 'Apparently, love is highly satisfying and desirable only if it is mutual' (p.514, my emphasis).

At present a number of psychological and biological disciplines are experiencing a paradigm shift into a relational psychology and a relational brain (Schore, 2012). In parallel, both researchers and clinicians are moving from investigations of love as an emotional state within an individual to mutual love between two individuals. This is manifest in the shift in the study of love within a single mind/brain in a solitary context to mutual love that is communicated to a valued other in a relational context. That said, in both the intrapersonal and interpersonal perspectives, love is conceptualized as an intense emotion, indeed 'one of the strongest of which the mind is capable', which when shared by another forms an 'intense emotional union'.

Throughout the lifespan these intense nonverbal embodied expressions of the human heart are generated by subcortical limbic–autonomic circuits of the right brain, which are imprinted in the attachment relationship. Love between the mother and infant in early critical periods thus shapes the trajectory of development of the right brain in the later stages of life. All forms of the 'extraordinary affect state' of mutual love share common activations of right lateralized cortical–subcortical circuits that generate extremes of arousal, including amygdala, insula, cingulate and orbitofrontal areas of the right brains of both members of a loving dyad. Mutual love can be understood as the interactive regulation of a shared strong positive affective state that results from right-brain-to-right-brain resonance and amplification of intense emotional arousal. These evidence-based developmental models of mutual love are grounded in clinical studies and neurobiological research of the last century, and yet they are heuristic and testable in the current century's emergent neuroimaging research, which I shall now describe.

Maternal neuroimaging and conceptualizations of mother's love

In 2004 Sue Gerhardt offered *Why Love Matters: How Affection Shapes a Baby's Brain*. Incorporating my work, she set forth the proposition that love is essential to brain development in the early years of life, particularly to the development of social and emotional brain systems. Beginning in this same year, a number of international neuroscience laboratories began to publish neuroimaging studies of love in mother–infant (as well as adult romantic) dyads. These functional magnetic resonance (fMRI) studies, carried out on four continents, now added to a large body of interdisciplinary research on the structural and functional development of the infant brain. Much of this infant imaging continues to focus on the infant brain's perceptual processing of maternal visual facial, auditory prosodic and tactile gestural communications. Many of these studies utilize not just static pictures but dynamic videos or auditory recordings of their own mother.

In the groundbreaking seminal study 'The neural correlates of maternal and romantic love', Bartels and Zeki (2004) announced:

> The tender intimacy and selflessness of a mother's love for her infant occupies a unique and exalted position in human conduct… it provides one of the most *powerful motivations for human action*, and has been celebrated throughout the ages – in literature, art and music – as one of the most beautiful and inspiring manifestations of human behavior. (p.1155, my emphasis)

In order to study the long-lasting and pervasive influence of maternal love on the development and future emotional constitution of a child, they offer an fMRI study of mothers viewing a picture of their own child's face (as early as nine months). They posited that this attachment cue would be associated with activity in cortical and subcortical sites in the mother's brain.

These authors report that the '*extraordinary affect state*' of maternal love triggers activation in the mother's lateral orbitofrontal cortex, medial insula, anterior cingulate and fusiform cortex. Underscoring the right lateralization, they note activation in 'right orbitofrontal cortex, periaqueductal gray, anterior insula, and dorsal and ventrolateral putamen, when the mother viewed her own infant's attachment behaviors compared with other infants' attachment behaviors' (p.419). Interpreting these data, they state the lateral orbitofrontal cortex is activated by pleasant visual, tactile and olfactory stimuli (such as their infant's face), whereas the anterior cingulate suggests 'a potential link to the mother's feelings of empathy and urge to care for her infant' (p.1163). Activation is also seen in the mother's insula while she's experiencing a subjective state of love for her infant. They note this area is involved in the 'gut feelings' of emotive states, and in 'limbic touch' that evokes pleasant feelings and regulates emotional, hormonal and affiliative responses to caress-like, skin-to-skin contact between individuals. Maternal love is also associated with heightened activity in cortical areas, the fusiform gyrus that reads facial expressions, as well as in subcortical ventral tegmental dopamine neurons associated with 'highly rewarding experiences'.

The same year, Nitschke *et al.* (2004) published 'Orbitofrontal cortex tracks positive mood in mothers viewing pictures of their newborn infants'. In their introduction they describe the subjective state of maternal love:

> Positive affect elicited in a mother toward her newborn infant may be one of the *most powerful and evolutionarily preserved forms of positive affect in the emotional landscape of human behavior*... One form of positive emotion...is the affect that arises in a mother's relationship with her infant. Whereas reward paradigms capitalize on approach tendencies and pursuit of an appetitive goal, the form of positive emotion in maternal attachment is better characterized by warmth, nurturance, joy, and fulfillment. (p.1155, my emphasis)

These authors document that while in the scanner viewing photos of the mother's own *3–5-month-old* infant, 'Most mothers report *extremely strong* pleasant emotions when interacting with or thinking about their infants' (p.584). Observing a picture of their smiling infant, mothers describe their subjectivity as 'loving' and 'motherly'. In this emotional state the mother shows changes within the orbitofrontal cortex that linearly tracks 'the intensity of positive emotions that may underlie maternal attachment... The present study extends this work by highlighting the role of the orbitofrontal cortex in the representation of attachment-related positive affect (Bowlby, 1982)' (p.590). (See Schore, 1994, 2000, on the orbitofrontal cortex as the control center of attachment.) They conclude that individual differences in maternal orbitofrontal responses to positive stimuli 'may have important relevance for happiness and well-being as well as clinical implications' (p.590).

In the same year, Ranote *et al.* (2004) scanned mothers looking at videos of their own (vs. an unknown) *4–8-month-old* infants. They report activation in the mother's brain in her right anterior inferior temporal cortex (involved in facial emotional recognition and expression) and right occipital gyrus (involved in visual familiarity). Activation is also seen in her amygdala.

Noting a significant recent change in neurobiological conceptions of the amygdala, they note: 'The amygdala is commonly associated with the processing of fearful and unpleasant emotional stimuli, but has also been shown to play a part in processing of happy expressions of facial emotion' (p.1828). Confirming a right lateralization effect, they conclude:

> In healthy new mothers, the viewing of own infants elicited activation in the ventral visual processing stream and cerebellum. This was more marked on the right and extended to polar temporal cortex. This is consistent with previous findings reporting right sided effects of visual object recognition and face processing. (p.1827)

Four years later, in 2008, Noriuchi and colleagues published 'The functional neuroanatomy of maternal love: Mother's response to infant's attachment behaviors'. They boldly assert:

> Maternal love is one of the most powerful motivations for the maternal behaviors of mothers to care for and protect their infants. (p.415)

In this study, mothers of *16-month-old* infants were shown two videos of infant attachment behavior. In the first situation, the infant was smiling while playing with his/her mother, and in the second video, the infant was asking for her while being separated from his/her mother. In the video of the play context the smiling mother blew bubbles toward her infant, while in the video of separation context, the mother leaves the room and the infant is left alone 'unduly distressed', crying and calling for mother. They note: 'While mothers may feel joyful by watching video clips of their own infant in the first situation, they may feel anxious and protective when shown video clips of their own infant in the second situation' (p.415). They posit that maternal love and 'strong emotional attachment would be invariant regardless of whether she was expressing affectionate behavior or vigilance and protectiveness' (p.415).

In line with the earlier cited studies, these researchers report that maternal love activates the mother's right orbitofrontal cortex, a cortical-limbic structure that regulates both positive and negative affect. They state that the orbitofrontal cortex plays an important role in the positive reward system and at the same time its activation reflects selection of appropriate strategies to reduce the negative distress of her infant. This finding fits nicely with my ideas about the right orbitofrontal system encoding strategies of positive and negative affect regulation in the mother's internal working model of her relationship with her infant. In summary, they conclude that 'the amount of love with which a mother interacts with her infant is highly influential on the stability of the mother–infant relationship and the quality of the mother–infant attachment' (p.415).

One year later in the journal *Cerebral Cortex*, Minagawa-Kawai *et al.* (2009) offered a near-infrared spectroscopy (NIRS) study of *12-month-old* infants responding to movies of their own mother's smiling expression, as well as their mothers watching movies of their infant playing and rating their emotional mood from 0 to 6 (6 = 'most loving'). Note the age is the same as the classical attachment measure, the strange situation. The infants show activation in the right orbitofrontal cortex that is stronger when viewing their own mother's smile. On the other hand, mothers looking at their own infant also show activation in the right orbitofrontal cortex. They speculate that if a mother shows higher right frontal activation in response to her infant, then her infant could also show larger activations as a result of his/her mother's stronger affection probably observed in their daily life. The authors conclude that the orbitofrontal cortex both encodes and regulates the attachment system and that at one year of age infants share similar neuronal functions with their mothers. With respect to the lateralization effect they state: 'Our results are in agreement with those of Schore (2000) who addressed the importance of the right hemisphere in the attachment system' (p.289). Thus, the attachment functions of the right orbitofrontal area develop within the social world between the caretaker and their infant. They conclude: 'This type of emotional regulation is also a fundamental social skill to extend infants' social involvement beyond kinship and friendship, including *love*' (p.291, my emphasis).

Most recently, Barrett *et al.* (2012) reported an fMRI study demonstrating the importance of the mother's subcortical amygdala response to the facial affective signals of her *3-month-old* infant, the youngest age of these neuroimaging studies. At three months postpartum, mothers viewed and affectively responded to photos of their own and unfamiliar infants' positive and negative facial expressions. Repeating the finding of other laboratories, they report that mothers were more responsive to their own infant compared with an unfamiliar infant, for both positive and negative infant faces. Based on their observation that maternal responses to negative faces consisted of a mixture of positive and negative affect, they suggest that 'an infant face does not have to be overtly "happy" in order to function as a positive stimulus for mother' (p.263).

Neuroimaging data showed that although a number of areas of the mother's brain are activated while viewing photos of her own 3-month-old infant, two stand out to be centrally involved in maternal responsiveness: the anterior cingulate cortex, and the basolateral amygdala and its connections to the temporal pole. Activation of the mother's right anterior cingulate to their infant's negative face (crying or fussing) reflects greater maternal distress. In line with the earlier-discussed studies on the role of the amygdala in positive emotions, they report an increased maternal amygdala response to their infant's smiling face associated with 'positive feelings and attachment' and 'more pro-social aspects of maternal responsiveness, feelings, and experience'. Interestingly, this greater amygdala response was associated with '(1) lower maternal anxiety, lower parental distress, and fewer symptoms of depressed mood, and (2) more positive attachment-related feelings about her infant' (p.263).

Initial emergence of mutual love at 2–3 months

A central thesis of this chapter dictates that all forms of mutual love arise from early affective experiences of mother–infant mutual love, and that these first appear at about 2–3 months. In classic research, Stern (1985) describes the transition from an early forming 'emergent self' at birth into a 'core self' at 2–3 months. He observes:

> At the age of two to three months, infants begin to give the impression of being quite different persons. When engaged in social interaction, they appear to be more wholly integrated. It is as if their actions, plans, affects, perceptions, and cognitions can now all

> be brought into play and focused, for a while, on an interpersonal situation. (p.69)

With the onset of this emergent developmental function, the subjective social world is altered, and interpersonal experience operates in a different domain, a domain of core-relatedness. He concludes that at this stage the infant participates in shared 'observable interactive events' involved in 'bridging the infant's subjective world and the mother's subjective world' (p.119). Recall that Trevarthen's (1979) primary intersubjectivity and protoconversation also emerge at 2–3 months, suggesting that mutual love onsets with primary intersubjectivity.

Confirming the 2–3-month transition, Miall and Dissanayake (2003) document:

> Over time, mothers subtly adjust their sounds and movements to what the baby seems to want (or not want), and to its changing needs and abilities. They gradually move from the gentle, cooing reassurance of the first weeks to trying to engage the baby in increasingly animated mutual play. At 8 weeks utterances and facial expressions have become more exaggerated, both in time and space. (p.342)

In another study of this critical period of change of infant facial expression, voice and gesture, Dissanayake (2001) asserts:

> It should also be emphasized here that although mothers 'talk' to their babies, the multimodal messages in early interactions are nonverbal. What mothers convey to infants are not their verbalized observations and opinions about the baby's looks, actions, and digestion – the ostensible content of talk to babies – but rather positive affiliative messages about their intentions and feelings: You interest me, I like you, I am like you, I like to be with you, You please me, I want to please you, You delight me, I want to communicate with you, I want you to be like me. (p.91)

In the context of intense affect, these are the first communications of maternal love. More recently, Ammaniti and Galesse (2014) report:

> From the second month after birth, parents and infant begin to show a temporal structure in their interactions… In this period, the sharing of social gaze between parent and baby is the expression of

> coordinated interactions, which can occur between 30% and 50% of the time. At the same time, mutual gaze can be integrated with parents' and infants' affectionate touch... At around 3 months, parents tend to touch their baby in an affectionate way and infants tend to respond with an intentional affectionate touch. (p.147)

Note the increases of the mother's loving touch that emerge at this time period.

Integrating the studies in this section, I propose that the primordial expression of mutual love first appears at 2–3 months. In heightened moments of affect synchrony, vitality affects are amplified by interpersonal resonance, generating shared moments of intense positive arousal. In dyadic episodes of interactive repair, the contingently responsive mother who has misattuned to the infant's negative state adaptively psychobiologically reattunes in a timely manner, thereby sharing states of down-regulated intense negative arousal. The loving mother now interactively regulates both states of sympathetic 'excited love' and parasympathetic 'quiet love', allowing the infant to begin to integrate these two differently embodied affective psychobiological states. These dual patterns of synchronized face-to-face, right-brain-to-right-brain state sharing occur in critical periods of the early developing right brain, and thus experiences of mutual love structuralize Stern's 'core self' that appears at 2–3 months (for more see Schore and Marks-Tarlow, 2017).

Further expressions of mutual love in the second year and beyond

The co-creation of mother–infant mutual love, a bond of '*deep affection, strong emotional attachment*', represents the expression of an instinctual evolutionary mechanism that is continually activated over the stages of human infancy and beyond. Although it emerges at 2–3 months, the loving mother's right-brain-to-right-brain up-regulation of positive and down-regulation of negative intense emotional arousal continues to shape the child's right subcortical–cortical circuits over the human growth spurt of the first two years of life. Across the stages of infancy, the infant's amygdala, anterior cingulate and orbitofrontal cortex enter into critical periods of growth which are sensitive to and imprinted by events in the social emotional environment (Schore, 2003a, 2003b, 2014). In *intensely charged* synchronous affective communications of mother–infant love, the infant's right lateralized limbic–autonomic system learns how to perceive and respond with heightened perceptual awareness to the mother's spontaneous facial, auditory, olfactory and somesthetic affective expression (to consciously 'take in' the look, sound, smell and feel of the mother's love). The ongoing mother–infant attachment relationship acts as a growth-facilitating intersubjective matrix of the adaptive capacity to enter into a shared state of mutual love with a valued other.

In subsequent periods of toddlerhood, the mother switches from an affect mirroring object to a socialization agent, setting limits and creating a context for the child's emerging autonomy (Schore, 1994). Fromm (1956) observes that 'the real achievement of motherly love lies not in the mother's love for the small infant, but in her love for the growing child' (p.47). At about the same time as Darwin, the philosopher Søren Kierkegaard described how the loving, attuned mother supports the toddler's exploration and emerging autonomy in the second year:

> The loving mother teaches her child to walk alone. She is far enough from him so that she cannot actually support him, but she holds out her arms to him. She imitates his movements, and if he totters, she swiftly bends as if to seize him, so that the child might believe that he is not walking alone...and yet, she does more. Her face beckons like a reward, an encouragement. Thus, the child walks alone with his eyes fixed on his mother's face, not on the difficulties in his way. He supports himself by the arms that do not hold him and constantly strives towards the refuge in his mother's embrace, little supposing that in the very same moment that he is emphasizing his need for her, he is proving that he can do without her, because he is walking alone. (1846/1938, p.85)

Again, sensitive, responsive mothering is considered to be the optimal condition for early human development. Indeed, in intensely emotional moments in the second year, the infant's early developing right hemisphere, which is dominant over the course of human infancy (Chiron *et al.*, 1997), continues to be imprinted by the output of the mother's right hemisphere, which is dominant for 'emotional processing, and thus mothering' (Lenzi *et al.*, 2009, p.1131).

Furthermore, secure attachment is defined not only by a sense of safety but also a positively charged curiosity that fuels the burgeoning self's exploration of novel socioemotional and physical environments. According to McGilchrist (2009), at all points of the lifespan what is new must first be present in the right hemisphere, before it can come into focus for the left. It begins in wonder, intuition, ambiguity, puzzlement and uncertainty on the right. In 1965 Rachel Carson, author of the groundbreaking and transformative *Silent Spring*, wrote *The Sense of Wonder*. Emphasizing the central role of the sharing of emotions in early childhood, she asserted:

> A child's world is fresh and new and beautiful, full of wonder and excitement... *If a child is to keep alive his inborn sense of wonder... he needs the companionship of at least one adult who can share it, rediscovering with him the joy, excitement and mystery of the world we live in.* I sincerely believe that for the child, and for the parent seeking to guide him, it is not half so important to know as to feel. If facts are the seeds that later produce knowledge and wisdom, then the emotions and the impressions of the senses are the fertile soil in which the seeds must grow. The years of early childhood are the time to prepare the soil. It is more important to pave the way for the child to want to know than to put him on a diet of facts he is not ready to assimilate. (1965, pp.42–45, my emphasis)

Note the similarity to Fromm's (1956) description of the loving mother's infectious 'love of life'. Indeed, the early origins of relational capacity to engage in creativity as well as mutual love are both generated in the early developing right brain (Schore and Marks-Tarlow, 2017).

The synchronized right-brain-to-right-brain interpersonal neurobiological mechanism of mother–infant love continues to activate limbic–autonomic emotional circuits in later right-brain growth spurts in childhood, adolescence and adulthood, thereby allowing 'the emotional brain' to develop to more complexity and 'higher forms' of mutual love. Ammaniti and Gallese (2014) offer an evocative portrayal of Stern's model of interpersonal expressions of mutual love in early and later development:

> As Daniel Stern has written, expressions of love begin early in an astonishing way. Mother and child behavior overlaps with the behavior of two lovers. For example, mother and child look at each other without speaking, hold a physical closeness with faces and bodies in constant contact, display alterations in vocal expressions or synchrony of movements, and perform particular gestures like kissing each other, hugging, touching, and taking the face or the hands of the other... When parents speak to their child, or lovers talk with one another...they emphasize the musicality of the words instead of the meaning, they use baby talk, and they express a wide range of nonverbal vocalizations... Facial expressions assume a special register also, altering and emphasizing the facial mimic. There is also a choreography in the movements of mother and baby, like those of two lovers; they move in synchrony, getting closer and more distant on the basis of a common rhythm. (pp.110–111)

Recall that Bartels and Zeki's (2004) neurobiological studies show that maternal and romantic love share a crucial evolutionary purpose and a similar biological function, namely the maintenance and perpetuation of the species, and thereby similar brain circuits. Indeed, there is now consensus that 'the biological basis of parental and romantic attachment share similar mechanisms' (Weisman, Feldman and Goldstein, 2012, p.533).

Early attachment experiences associated with strong emotions epigenetically shape the individual's capacity for functioning in close proximity to another; that is, the adaptive emotional capacity to share an intimate subjective state with a valued other. Porges and Carter (2010) conclude:

> Although the brain retains plasticity and adaptability throughout life, early experience may set the parameters for that plasticity. Attachment may be said to set up social and emotional homeostasis, *designing future patterns for intimacy*. Emotional homeostasis resides in the subcortical brain structures and their links to cortical structures, all of which are shaped in early life. (p.13, my emphasis)

That said, this optimal context for the development of the sharing of right-brain strong emotion and intimacy fails to emerge in all relationships, especially in insecure attachments. In her classic *The Leaven of Love*, Izette De Forest (1954) asserted:

> The offering of loving care cannot be given, either by parent or by psychotherapist, on demand or in answer to threat. It must be given freely and spontaneously as a genuinely felt emotional expression. And it must provide an environment of trust and confidence and hope... It must provide the environment...which is essential to growth, to the unfolding of individuality. In other words, the therapist must give to the patient a replica of the birthright of love which has denied him, as an infant or a growing child, but which, if granted, would have assured him full stature as an individual in his own right. (pp.16–17)

Early experiences of mutual love deeply imprint not only the individual but also the culture. In the last century Donald Winnicott, with keen foresight, put forth the developmental principle:

> If human babies are to develop eventually into healthy independent, and society-minded adult individuals, they absolutely depend on being given a good start, and this good start is assured by...the thing called love. (1975, p.17)

Thirty years later, Sue Gerhardt (2004) looked forward and asked:

> The babies who are born now and in the years to come will be the adults who nurse us in old age, who manage our industry, who entertain us, who live next door. What kind of adults will they be? Will they be emotionally balanced enough to contribute their talents, or will they be disabled by hidden sensitivities? Their early start, and the degree to which they felt loved and valued, will surely play an important part in determining that. (p.218)

Indeed, neuroscientists are currently asserting that the first expression of love, the one between a mother and her infant, represents 'one of the most powerful and evolutionarily preserved forms of positive affect in the emotional landscape of human behavior' (Nitschke *et al.* 2004, p.1155), that 'the phylogenetically ancient role of maternal care...appears to be underpinned by evolutionarily ancient structures' (Abraham *et al.*, 2014, p.9795), and that social epigenetic forces in the cultural environment can positively or negatively impact the evolutionary mechanism of attachment (Narvaez *et al.*, 2013). Explicitly alluding to Charles Darwin's magnum opus (1859), these scientists are now telling us that maternal love for the infant is 'a biologically essential mechanism for the *preservation of the human species*' (Noriuchi *et al.*, 2008, p.415, my emphasis). We must now pay very, very careful attention to these essential messages of current developmental science.

References

Abraham, E., Hendler, T., Shapira-Lichter, I., Kanat-Naymin, Y. and Zagoory-Sharon, O. (2014). Father's brain is sensitive to childcare experiences. *Proceedings of the National Academy of Sciences of the United States of America*, 111(27), 9792–9797.

Ammaniti, M. and Gallese, V. (2014). *The Birth of Intersubjectivity*. New York, NY: Norton.

Barrett, J., Wonch, K.E., Gonzalez, A., Ali, N. *et al.* (2012). Maternal affect and quality of parenting experiences are related to amygdala response to infant faces. *Social Neuroscience*, 7(3), 252–268.

Bartels, A. and Zeki, S. (2004). The neural correlates of maternal and romantic love. *NeuroImage*, 21(3), 1155–1166.

Baumeister, R.F. and Leary, M.R. (1995). The need to belong: Desire for interpersonal attachments as a fundamental human motivation. *Psychological Bulletin*, 117(3), 497–528.

Bowlby, J. (1953). *Child Care and the Growth of Love*. London: Pelican.

Bowlby, J. (1969). *Attachment and Loss, Volume 1: Attachment*. New York, NY: Basic Books.

Bowlby, J. (1982). *Loss: Sadness and Depression, Volume 3*. New York, NY: Basic Books.

Carson, R. (1965). *The Sense of Wonder*. New York, NY: Harper and Row.

Chiron, C., Jambaque, I., Nabbout, R., Lounes, R., Syrota, A. and Dulac, O. (1997). The right brain hemisphere is dominant in human infants. *Brain*, 120(6), 1057–1065.

Darwin, C. (1859/1958). *The Origin of Species*. New York, NY: Signet Classics.

Darwin, C. (1872/1965). *The Expression of the Emotions in Man and Animals*. Chicago, IL: University of Chicago Press.

De Forest, I. (1954). *The Leaven of Love: A Development of the Psychoanalytic Theory and Technique of Sándor Ferenczi*. New York, NY: Harper Brothers.

Dissanayake, E. (2001). Becoming Homo Aestheticus: Sources of aesthetic imagination in mother–infant interactions. *SubStance*, 30(1/2), 85–103.

Freud, S. (1940/1964). *An Outline of Psychoanalysis*, Standard Edition, 23. London: Hogarth Press.

Fromm, E. (1956). *The Art of Loving*. New York, NY: Harper and Row.

Gerhardt, S. (2004). *Why Love Matters: How Affection Shapes a Baby's Brain*. New York, NY: Brunner-Routledge.

Kierkegaard, S. (1846/1938). *Purity of Heart*. New York, NY: Harper and Row.

Lenzi, D., Trentini, C., Pantano, P., Macaluso, E. *et al.* (2009). Neural basis of maternal communication and emotional expression processing during infant preverbal stage. *Cerebral Cortex*, 19(5), 1124–1135.

McGilchrist, I. (2009). *The Master and His Emissary: The Divided Brain and the Making of the Western World*. New Haven, CT: Yale University Press.

Miall, D. and Dissanayake, E. (2003). The poetics of babytalk. *Human Nature*, 14(4), 337–354.

Minagawa-Kawai, U., Matsuoka, S., Dan, I., Naoi, N., Nakamura, K. and Kojima, S. (2009). Prefrontal activation associated with social attachment: Facial-emotion recognition in mothers and infants. *Cerebral Cortex*, 19(2), 284–292.

Narvaez, D., Panksepp, J., Schore, A.N. and Gleason, T.R. (2013). *Evolution, Early Experience and Human Development: From Research to Practice and Policy*. New York, NY: Oxford University Press.

Nitschke, J.B., Nelson, E.E., Rusch, B.D., Fox, A.S., Oakes, T.R. and Davidson, R.J. (2004). Orbitofrontal cortex tracks positive mood in mothers viewing pictures of their newborn infants. *NeuroImage*, 21(2), 583–592.

Noriuchi, M., Kikuchi, Y. and Senoo, A. (2008). The functional neuroanatomy of maternal love: Mothers' response to infant's attachment behaviors. *Biological Psychiatry*, 63(4), 415–423.

Porges, S.W. and Carter, C. (2010). Neurobiological Bases of Social Behavior across the Life Span. In M.E. Lamb, A.M. Freund and R.M. Lerner (eds), *The Handbook of Life-Span Development, Volume 2: Social and Emotional Development*. Hoboken, NJ: John Wiley and Sons.

Ranote, S., Elliott, R., Abel, K.M., Mitchell, R., Deakin, F.W. and Appleby, L. (2004). The neural basis of maternal responsiveness to infants: An fMRI function. *NeuroReport*, 15(11), 1825–1829.

Schore, A.N. (1994). *Affect Regulation and the Origin of the Self: The Neurobiology of Emotional Development*. Mahwah, NJ: Erlbaum.

Schore, A.N. (2000). Attachment and the regulation of the right brain. *Attachment and Human Development*, 2(1), 23–47.

Schore, A.N. (2003a). *Affect Dysregulation and Disorders of the Self*. New York, NY: Norton.

Schore, A.N. (2003b). *Affect Regulation and the Repair of the Self*. New York, NY: Norton.

Schore, A.N. (2012). *The Science of the Art of Psychotherapy*. New York, NY: Norton.

Schore, A.N. (2014). Early interpersonal neurobiological assessment of attachment and autistic spectrum disorders. *Frontiers in Psychology*, 5, Article 1049, doi:10.3389/fpsyg.2014.01049.

Schore, A.N. and Marks-Tarlow, T. (2017). How Love Opens Creativity, Play, and the Arts through the Early Right Brain Development. In T. Marks-Tarlow, M. Solomon and D.J. Siegel (eds), *Play and Creativity in Psychotherapy*. New York, NY: Norton.

Schore, J.R. and Schore, A.N. (2008). Modern attachment theory: The central role of affect regulation in development and treatment. *Clinical Social Work Journal*, 36(1), 9–20.

Stern, D.N. (1985). *The Interpersonal World of the Infant*. New York, NY: Basic Books.

Trevarthen, C. (1979). Communication and Cooperation in Early Infancy: A Description of Primary Intersubjectivity. In M. Bullowa (ed.), *Before Speech: The Beginning of Interpersonal Communication*. New York, NY: Cambridge University Press.

Ulanov, A.B. (2001). *Finding Space: Winnicott, God, and Psychic Reality*. Louisville, KY: Westminster John Knox Press.

Weisman, O., Feldman, R. and Goldstein, A. (2012). Parental and romantic attachment shape brain processing of infant cues. *Biological Psychiatry*, 89(3), 533–538.

Winnicott, D.W. (1963). The development of the capacity for concern. *Bulletin of the Menninger Clinic*, 27, 167–176.

Winnicott, D.W. (1975). *The Child, the Family, and the Outside World*. Harmondsworth: Penguin.

Winnicott, D.W. (1986). *Home Is Where We Start From*. New York, NY: W.W. Norton and Company.

PRACTICE REFLECTION

Joe Tucci, Janise Mitchell and Ed Tronick

As always, Schore has provided a wonderfully detailed account of the emergence of love in the dynamic of caring relationships that hold infants so tenderly and warmly. It is important to note that his focus draws on research paying attention to traditional forms of caring relationships – the mother–child dyad. However, the themes that he explores are relevant for children in out-of-home care, no matter whether they are being raised by foster parents, grandparents, uncles, aunts or as part of other kinship relationships. It is the dynamics of the relational experience for children that makes all the difference to their development and well-being.

To this end, Schore highlights the powerful intimacy that develops between child and caregiver as they move synchronously through interactions using voice, touch, gaze, facial expression; these interactions are based on right-brain-to-right-brain communication, implicating a number of neural regions and networks. In particular, it is worth noting his comment that love has an ongoing positive impact on the 'emotional landscape of human behavior' and is different to the effect of immediate rewards that accompany the attainment of a specific goal.

The presence of loving relationship is the accompaniment to children's development. It is one of the most powerful drivers of human behaviour. It awakens in the relational space between infant and caregiver. It is intensely felt in reciprocal and mutual synchronous experiences which are needed for it to continue to grow. Caregivers feel it in their minds and bodies as much as their children do. For caregivers, it is not only the sense of care, commitment and closeness; it is also manifested in vigilance and protectiveness of the infant.

Children receive clear embodied messages about their value and worth. They experience being held by adults who want them, are enlivened by the experience of having them, and who act to keep them safe. As they do, they internalise the reference points that are associated with being loved into their own implicit memory systems, holding the sensory input of their experience in ways that they can draw on as they evolve and relate to others. As Schore points out, the capacity to be loved and love in return emerges in those moments of quiet love that hold the infant's preciousness as an expression of the human heart. It is, as we have known from the attachment literature, the very mechanism through which the intrapersonal is shaped through the experiences of early interpersonal interactions.

The implications for Therapeutic Care practice rests in understanding how this experience of love can be disrupted and how vulnerable such compromise leaves children in a world where relationships are life. Tronick's reconceptualisation of the emphasis on synchronous attunement as the basis for normal attachment (Tronick, 2017; Tronick and DiCorcia, 2015; Tronick and Gianino, 1986) adds an important counterpoint in this discussion. Tronick's findings over many years have led him to conclude:

> [T]he infant and mother were in synchronous or matching states, states in which they were doing the same thing together – looking and smiling at each other – only a small proportion of the time: the rest and predominant proportion of time they were in mismatching states – the infant looking toward the mother with an interested facial expression and the mother looking away with a sad facial expression… [T]hus, mismatching and dyssynchrony – not synchrony – characterise the interaction. (Tronick, 2017, pp.563–564)

The movement between matching and mismatching states and back again underpins the dyadic regulatory process and is part and parcel of the dynamics that produce the attachment bond – the felt experience of a loving relationship between infant and caregiver. As Tronick has postulated from his body of work:

> [R]eparation, the experience of it, and the extent of its occurrence, is the social-interactive mechanism that drives and modifies infants' development. In normal dyads reparation is ubiquitous. Interactive mismatches have a high rate of occurrence, but they are quickly repaired. In studies of face-to-face interaction, repairs occur at a rate of once every 3–5 seconds, and more than one-third of all repairs occur by the next step in the interaction. In other Western

> and non-Western cultures, reparation is seen but with different rates and patterns that are perhaps analogous to dance partners: one culture doing a messy waltz and another doing a messy tango. (Tronick, 2017, pp.564–565)

These reparatory experiences are pivotal to infants' development, especially in the evolution of what Tronick describes as the establishment of a 'positive affective core'.

> Reparatory experience leads to the elaboration of communicative and coping skills, and the development of an understanding of culturated interactive rules and conventions. Reparations are associated with positive affect and with the experiential accumulation of successful reparations and the attendant transformation of negative affect into positive affect… This internal positive core is a resource that allows the infant to come to new situations feeling positive about him or herself and the unknown situations… [T]he infant develops a representation of himself or herself as effective, of his or her interactions as positive and reparable, and the caregiver as reliable and trustworthy. (Tronick, 2017, p.565)

Therapeutic Care is concerned with the ways in which micro-opportunities exist in between the interactions between children and carers to build moments of repair that are deposited into children's bank of implicit memories that accumulate over time and provide a reservoir of deepening compensatory experiences for the failure of such repair to have been offered to them in their relationships in which the abuse and neglect occurred.

It is in the microlevel interactions that such repair occurs and love emerges, activating, as Schore has suggested, a cascade of neural connections which deliver ongoing formulations of acceptance and belonging. In these moments, children are being given embodied messages from their carers that invite them to see themselves and relationships differently:

- 'You may have not been interesting to others before me, but you interest me now and into the future.'
- 'You may not have always been liked by those before me, but I like you. I will always find you likeable and lovable.'

- 'You may not have felt that others before me were like you, but I am. We belong to a family now. This is our family. It may not feel like your family, but I am hoping it will one day. I am going to do everything I can to help you feel that and believe that.'
- 'You may not have pleased others before me, but you are delightful. I am interested in you and what you do. I like spending time learning about you. I hope you like spending time with me too.'
- 'You may not have felt that others have been on your side, but I will always be on your side. We are in this together.'

Therapeutic Care keeps as its focus ways to amplify small actions of repair that occur in one relationship in the network around a child in out-of-home care so that its impact spreads out to others. It uses one outcome in one context to tailor and transport the opportunity to find synchrony after a rupture in another context. In this way, children's relationships harness their own vitality – their own internal resources – to shift previously mismatched attenuations to matched states of love and engagement. The therapeutic impact of multiple relationships working in unison is multiplied in Therapeutic Care.

References

Tronick, E. (2017). The caregiver–infant dyad as a buffer or transducer of resource enhancing or depleting factors that shape psychobiological development. *Australian and New Zealand Journal of Family Therapy*, 38(4), 561–572.

Tronick, E. and DiCorcia, J.A. (2015). The Everyday Stress Resilience Hypothesis: A reparatory sensitivity and the development of coping and resilience. *Children Australia*, 40(2), 124–138.

Tronick, E. and Gianino, A. (1986). Interactive mismatch and repair: Challenges to the coping infant. *Zero to Three*, 6(3), 1–6.

5

'Support and Love and All That Stuff'

Evidence of Impact in the Treatment and Care for Kids Program

JANISE MITCHELL, LYNNE MCPHERSON AND KATHOMI GATWIRI

Introduction

The title of this chapter is drawn from the words of a young man who has lived with his foster carers in the Treatment and Care for Kids (TrACK) Program for more than a decade. He is now a young adult who has aged out of the care system and continues to be a member of his foster family, who according to him were able to give him 'support and love and all that stuff'.

He is one of 48 children, aged 16 years or less at the time of the referral, who have been cared for in the TrACK Program since its commencement in 2003. He, along with the other children referred to the program, had been defined by the child protection system as having a constellation of complex needs and challenging behaviours that had led to multiple placement breakdowns, and was deemed unable to live in a family-based placement. Many of the children admitted into the TrACK Program had multiple failed foster and kinship placements and were residing in residential care.

The TrACK Program was the first therapeutic foster care program to be implemented in Australia and one of the first in the world. The program was designed to provide long-term care for children and young people for whom reunification with family was not possible and for whom other placement models were unsuccessful. It was driven by a belief that no one should give up on children and young people in out-of-home care because their behaviours and needs were confronting and at times overwhelming in their intensity and frequency. There is an inherent responsibility in a child protection system to develop a context of care and support for these children that would enable them to recover, or at least significantly improve, from their early adversity and trauma caused by abuse and neglect.

The TrACK Program was developed at a time when the major trends and issues faced by the Australian out-of-home care system paralleled those in other Western countries, including increasing numbers of children entering out-of-home care, children in care presenting with more complex and challenging needs, a lack of coordination and access to specialist services, insufficient available and appropriate placement options, high levels of placement instability, a reduction in placement resources, and difficulty in recruiting and retaining carers (Mitchell, 2008). Although foster care sought to provide a safe and nurturing environment for abused and neglected children, it was less commonly conceptualised as a form of therapeutic resource through which children are helped to recover from their emotional difficulties and supported to modify any challenging behavioural patterns (Sinclair, 2005; Wilson, 2006). Many had long argued that foster care should be viewed as 'active intervention' (Ruff, Blank and Barnett, 1990), with foster parents conceptualised as appropriate and capable therapeutic agents of change and recovery for children (Christiansen and Fine, 1979).

This chapter describes the approach of the TrACK Program and the context within which it operates. It then explores the difference it has made in the lives of the 48 children and young people who have lived in the program through the findings of two independent evaluations in 2005 and 2017.

The key to stability is a resourced network of relationships of care and support around children

Placement stability is most often cited as a principal indicator and predictor of positive outcomes for children in care. Research has repeatedly shown the significant adverse effects on children of placement instability, including poor educational, employment, social and psychological outcomes (Johnson *et al.*, 2011) as well as behavioural and emotional problems (Australian Institute of Family Studies, Chapin Hall Center for Children at the University of Chicago, and NSW Department of Family and Community

Services, 2015). Less well conceptualised is the critical need for a stable network of relationships around children through which children can receive support and which grow with children over time and throughout their life.

The TrACK Program is informed by the neuroscience of child development, attachment and trauma. It gives central prominence to the complex and pervasive impact that complex trauma has on a child's development, worldview and interpersonal relationships. The theoretical frame establishes the context through which the therapeutic experiences offered to children during their placement are interpreted and ultimately given meaning (Durrant, 1993). It also serves to orient the practice of staff, shapes the activities of the program and defines how children relate to their families and other critical adults in their network. The theoretical frame unifies expectations about the placement and how it works. It enables the placement to provide the basis for growth and transformation to occur.

The program is premised on the notion that if relationships have been the site of hurt and harm for children, then relationships are the necessary site of healing. In doing so, the TrACK Program challenged traditional doctrine about the nature of relationships between children and carers in out-of-home care. For example, it was, and still is, commonplace to exclude carers from decision-making processes about the children in their care on the basis that they lack the 'professional knowledge' to contribute to conversations about a child's best interests. Carers are often cautioned about not becoming 'too attached' to children in their care. Carers and children are often actively prevented from having ongoing contact with each other in the event of a placement change, for fear that it will undermine the ability of the child to settle into their next placement. As a result, children are exposed to repeated experiences of relationships stopping and starting, often for reasons that are never explained to them, triggering feelings of mistrust, abandonment, rejection, anger and grief.

The TrACK Program holds the view that traumatised children need and deserve a resourced network of relationships that they know and who know them, within which they experience safety and trust, who are attuned to their needs, accept them unconditionally and will be there for them now and into their future. Children themselves tell us this is also what they want. Mitchell's (2008) review of research privileging the voices of children in care highlights the primary importance of relationships, connection and belonging for these children. The research clearly demonstrates that children in care desire normality, want to feel that they belong in or are connected to their foster family and that they are treated in the same way as other children, to experience a genuine relationship within which they feel loved, cared about and cared for, feel accepted by carers who show patience as they struggle to understand and accept rules, especially following a change from one home to another. The same review also indicated that children, with support, want and can manage multiple significant relationships with both their foster and biological families, with their siblings and friends, with an appreciation that their feelings about their relationships with family can fluctuate over time. Confirming earlier research, a more recent survey of more than 1000 children, aged 8–17 years, in care across Australia, found that children were happiest in placements when they felt loved and cared for, had a positive relationship with the other people in the household and had some privacy and space to themselves (McDowall, 2013).

Reinforcing the desired lifelong nature of relationships, a longitudinal study of outcomes for young people who age out of care identified that 'felt security' while in care and continuity and social support beyond care were the key determinants of positive outcomes for young people 4–5 years after leaving care (Cashmore and Paxman, 2006). They concluded that stability was important as it supported the development of a sense of belonging and security and an enduring network of social support for children in out-of-home care.

To be loved, cared for and cared about

Although love holds multiple interrelated meanings in the literature such that its meaning is often lost or misinterpreted, the critical components of loving relationships or interactions are encapsulated in experiences of care, acceptance, empathy, sympathy, compassion, presence, recognition, respect, honesty, commitment, trust and a sense of community (Vincent, 2016). These are the relationships that the TrACK Program seeks to support and resource around children.

While craving them, many traumatised children shy away from relationships of care and love, driven by feelings of worthlessness or repeated experiences of loss, rejection or abandonment. Others simply may not have experienced feeling cared for and cared about, having lived a life of self-reliance, taught to them by repeated relationships that have let them down, been unreliable or even dangerous. Children need repeated opportunities to tolerate loving relationships, to trust them, slowly let them in and believe in them, and through them learn to see themselves as lovable and valuable.

The TrACK Program resources carers and other significant relationships in the child's life to develop loving relationships with children in their care. The program actively fosters attachment, celebrating instances of connection and belonging, creating opportunities for attuned relationships within which trust, safety and acceptance are felt experiences for children. It is through these repeated experiences that children are able to challenge their worldviews about relationships, themselves and what is possible in their own lives.

The TrACK Program, while providing long-term placements, shares the view of Thich Nhat Hanh (2007) that every relationship, whether brief or long-lasting, creates a space that holds the potential for loving interaction. This orientation informs the work of the Therapeutic Care Team approach used by the program and assists those both in caring and non-caring roles (such as teachers) to conceptualise the importance of what they are communicating to the child in every interaction they have with them in the lifespace (Smith, 2005; Taylor, 2005; Torrenon, 2006). Central to the program is a commitment to meaning-making, viewing behaviour as a form of communication and seeking to understand the meaning behind behaviours. The program supports the carer and care team to bring into conscious awareness the meaning behind both what is said and what is done on the part of both the child and themselves. In this way, carers are resourced to actively communicate love and care to children in a way that is both 'embodied and performative...brought into existence by doing' (Lanas and Zembylas, 2014, p.36, as cited in Vincent, 2016).

The relational space as the focus for intervention

The TrACK Program is predicated on the belief that relationships are the primary vehicle for change and recovery and are thus therapeutic in nature. Children who have experienced complex trauma bring particular challenges to those who would seek to be in relationship with them. It is these challenges that so often see carers unable to sustain the care of the children and relinquish their care.

Garfat and Fulcher (2012) draw the distinction between having a relationship and being in a relationship, the latter involving meaningful, attentive engagement that has an impact on both individuals involved. Such positioning enables the TrACK Program to conceptualise the relational space between individuals as the site for the intervention (Garfat and Fulcher, 2012; Gharabaghi, 2008). In doing so, the program considers the needs of the child, the needs of the carer and others in a relationship with the child and the space between them, each influenced by the other individual, their unique life experiences and knowledge, as well as the shared interactions between them (Gharabaghi, 2008).

The TrACK Program uses reflective practice to support carers and care team members to review the relational space between themselves and the child, to seek to understand what the child is experiencing and needs in the context of each interaction and what the adults themselves are experiencing and need. The program orients carers and care team members to the impact on themselves of being in a relationship with a traumatised child, and provides support to be able to stay present in the relationship to the child's needs while holding awareness of one's own needs that must also be addressed at a later time. The carers are assisted to reframe the trauma-based behaviour of children in terms of its function in helping survival and/or as a response to situational or relational triggers. This reframing supports different perspective taking and enables compassionate and attuned ways of making meaning of the behaviour, replacing traditional behavioural approaches to responding to challenging behaviour. Reframing behaviour as an adaptation allows carers to consider and address the underlying needs the behaviour is communicating, utilising the relationship to co-regulate and resource the child to manage at times when feeling overwhelmed by the situation. Crucially, this entails a shift from thinking 'what is wrong with you?' to 'what happened to you?' and 'what do you need?'.

The quality, stability, predictability and consistency of relationships between children, their carers and others in the care team are critical to the achievement of placement stability and successful outcomes for children in the program. As such, foster carers and members of the care team require adequate recognition, support and training in order that they are sufficiently resourced to engage in these therapeutic relationships with traumatised children. Strategies to address these needs must be integrated and supported by theoretical frameworks, principles and processes that ensure all carers and key stakeholders are respected and arrive at a shared ethos and approach to understanding and responding to the needs of traumatised children in care.

Position relationships and environments as therapeutic

The TrACK Program pays attention to the nature of the therapeutic environment through:

- the planning and management of routine experience
- the handling of the unplanned or unexpected
- carer responses to the everyday challenges/experiences of children to help them to feel safe, valued and understood
- the sensory dimensions of the physical environments.

The program's approach to the creation of therapeutic environments or milieu is developmentally appropriate (Taylor, 2005) and draws from Maier's (1979) seminal paper 'The core of care: Essential ingredients for the development of children at home and away from home'. As outlined below, Maier identified seven vital components in the core of care that still remain relevant today.

Bodily comfort

As a child's bodily comforts are met, they feel treated with care. Throughout life a sense of well-being and care is experienced when one's body is free of stress. The experience of discomfort makes people feel unwelcome, worthless and isolated. Children need to have private spaces that are unconditional.

Differentiations

Individual children all have different temperaments. This requires that caregivers differentiate in the way they respond to them. Temperamental differences impinge on development. Some young people require bodily contact as part of close personal interactions, while others need some distance and rely on eye and marginal body contacts.

Rhythmic interactions

Rhythmic experiences promote feelings of belonging and continuity. These can be simple things like walking, laughing or clapping together. Playing ball games can also create these rhythms. Rituals are the social counterpart to psychological rhythmicity. Formal rituals might be the kind of things that happen on birthdays.

The element of predictability

To know what is likely to happen in the future lends a sense of order and power to people's lives. Although predictability is important, Maier cautions that a healthy sense of order does not come from a book of house rules but needs to grow out of the lived experience of those who live in the household.

Dependability

When repetition, rhythmicity and predictability are combined, the child will feel good and cared for because these experiences establish a sense of certainty. The feeling of dependence creates attachments and intimacy which are pleasurable and safe.

Personalised behavioural training

It is only when a trusting relationship has been established with caregivers that effective behaviour training starts. This is because behaviour is moulded largely by the caring person whom the child perceives as being on his or her side.

Care for the carer

It is essential that the carers are nurtured and given caring support to enable them to transmit this quality of care to others. Carers are enriched or limited as agents of care according to the care they receive.

Carers, teachers and others are also supported to establish environments in the care and school settings that create a 'holding environment' (Ward, 2003) for children such that the environment fosters:

- a culture of belonging, providing an element of 'giving' and tolerance in relationships, so that children felt genuinely cared for and looked after
- a culture of safety, providing suitable boundaries for behaviour and the expression of emotion, so that strong feelings can be expressed but do not get 'out of hand'
- a culture of openness that works towards clarity in communication, thus avoiding or dealing promptly with misunderstandings or confusion
- a culture of participation and citizenship
- a culture of empowerment.

Drawing on the work of Smith (2005), Taylor (2005), Torrenon (2006), who argued in favour of the central place of 'life space', or Ward's (2006) 'opportunity-led' approach, all interactions between children and carers and others are conceptualised by the program as potentially therapeutic in nature. Ward differentiates between reacting (in a kneejerk way) and responding in a considered planned way to children. He suggests:

> [D]aily life can be viewed as potentially offering a series of everyday challenges and opportunities for children in which they will need more or less support, encouragement or even correction, according to the nature and degree of their trouble. (Ward, 2006, p.123)

Such an approach helps children make connections between the past, present and future, is goal-oriented and uses everyday opportunities to reinforce these (Smith, 2005). Working in the lifespace requires ongoing assessment, planning and review of children's needs and progress (Feilberg, 2007) and is the focus of the Therapeutic Specialist and the Therapeutic Care Team.

The TrACK Program has adapted Torrenon's (2006) notion of 'community' in residential settings wherein she noted that adults and children produce their everyday life in their collective interactions, with children being active negotiators of the everyday experience and able to regulate the quality of their interaction with different carers and adults. Within the TrACK Program, the concept of 'community' is considered more broadly as the experience of belonging, be it in the foster family, the school community or with their family of origin, with the focus of the program being that of resourcing and supporting the network of relationships around the child.

Carers and others in the Therapeutic Care Team are supported to hold a 'therapeutic attitude' in their interactions with children. Hughes (1998) conceptualises this attitude as Playful, Accepting, Curious and Empathic. Cairns (2002) suggests an attitude which is Secure, Attentive, Friendly and Empathic. The 'therapeutic attitude' underpins the lifespace approach of the program. It is in the everyday moments that carers and others can assist children to increase their flexibility and adaptability in the face of their trauma triggers, feelings, thoughts and behaviours, and build new relationships which serve to support the child in their growing understanding of themselves and how to relate to others. Thus, throughout the daily experience of living, the child is offered compensatory experiences to counteract the negative effects of earlier traumatic experiences as well as complementary experiences that build adaptability and resilience.

The program also considers the impact of sensory stimulation on stress regulation and the relationship between these issues and the physical environment. Each of the senses is involved in processes of stimulation and relaxation. The physical environment has a powerful effect on traumatised children.

Sensory experience that arouses a reaction in the sympathetic nervous system produces stimulation. Sensory experience that reduces arousal in the sympathetic nervous system and arouses a reaction in the parasympathetic system produces soothing. In general, traumatised children are reactive through the sympathetic nervous system, even to stimuli that in others would elicit parasympathetic responses. It is this hypersensitivity that we aim to soothe through environmental changes (Akamas, 2007). As such, the Therapeutic Specialist supports carers and the Therapeutic Care Team to consider the sensory needs of the child within the care, school and other environments in order that they support regulation, engagement and belonging.

Elements of the TrACK Program

The broad aim of the TrACK Program is the creation of therapeutic relational and physical environments for children who have experienced abuse and trauma in their lives within which they can recover from the negative developmental consequences of their experiences. The program aims to provide children with holistic, dependable, predictable environments of care and support which can be used to challenge the negative, direct and secondary aspects of their abusive experiences.

The program is predicated on the belief that all forms of intervention with children who have suffered abuse have the potential to ameliorate the degree of trauma they experience. The outcomes of such intervention depend significantly on the confidence and competence of carers, networks and professionals to:

- communicate effectively with children about their experiences and the meaning they draw from them about their identity and relationships
- provide therapeutic contexts for children that promote recovery from the effects of complex trauma
- consider the cultural background and/or special needs of children in planning and executing programs aimed at supporting recovery
- embed their practice in an appreciation of the current research findings about the psychobiological effects of trauma for children
- use ethical decision-making frameworks that promote the restructuring of abusive family relationships in order to focus on meeting the emerging needs of children.

The program supports the multiple environments within which children live, learn and play. A primary objective of the program is to resource carers and other significant relationships in the life of the child to provide nurturing, therapeutic, reparative care and support to the child using a trauma framework. Interventions are viewed as most successful when carers, families, support networks and professionals enact collaborative and intersecting functions that can achieve protective, reparative and restorative goals for children.

The program has a clearly articulated theoretical and evidence-informed model of practice which is used as the basis for training, support, assessment, planning and review. All foster carers undergo a comprehensive assessment before being accredited to provide care for children in the TrACK Program. All foster carers are provided with foundational and advanced modules of training based in the theoretical foundations of the program, with the aim of equipping them with the necessary knowledge and frameworks for understanding the needs of traumatised children and using their relationships as therapeutic agents of change for children.

The model of practice is integrated and embedded across the program with the support of a Therapeutic Specialist who provides assessment, clinical leadership and reflective practice with the carer and the network of people in relationship with the child. The key aim of the therapeutic support offered by the Therapeutic Specialist is to develop and resource relationships of care and support around the child over the short, medium and long term to create environments of care and support that are safe, congruent, stable and predictable. The relational space is a key focus of activity.

In order to resource the network of relationships around the child, the program uses a Therapeutic Care Team approach that includes the carer, foster care worker, teacher, family members (as appropriate) and mechanisms for including the views and wishes of the child. The Therapeutic Specialist runs and coordinates this collective process. Other people with relationships of significance to the child are also invited to participate in the Therapeutic Care Team. Tailored training is provided to support the development of a shared way of understanding and meeting the needs of the children in the program.

A Therapeutic Care Team is formed around every child in the TrACK Program to support and resource key relationships and promote the development of a shared approach to the child, regardless of what setting the child is in. Therapeutic Care Teams are an important aspect of the program, helping to provide a 'therapeutic web' in the system of relationships around the child. The Therapeutic Care Team is seen as a powerful antidote to the fragmentation of service delivery that is often the experience of many children with complex needs. The Therapeutic Care Team meeting provides a tool for key people in the child's life to come together to share information, expertise and to problem solve. The Therapeutic Specialist provides opportunities for critical reflection in the meetings and to carers and other team members outside of meetings with the aim of enhancing understanding, and the development of shared and consistent strategies for responding to the critical needs of children within and across settings. Effective and timely support from the Therapeutic Specialist is a significant component of the TrACK Program and is considered highly effective in informing and shaping decision-making processes.

The TrACK Program utilises the phases of therapeutic care approach as developed by the Australian Childhood Foundation (2004) and drawn from the work of Brown, Scheflin and Hammond (1998) Cairns (2002) Hughes (1997). Within the program model, a child's process of healing moves through several, clearly identifiable stages or phases. This framework suggests what children's needs are at each phase of recovery and change, and what the carer and Therapeutic Care Team need to provide to promote the child's recovery.

The key phases of therapeutic care as expressed in the TrACK Program are the following.

1. Placement orientation

During this phase the child is oriented into the foster family. The carers are also oriented to understanding the child's specific abuse and trauma issues and how the impact is manifested by the child. Carers and the Therapeutic Care Team are supported to assist the child through this transition stage and begin familiarising the child to their new foster family, living environment and any other changes that have occurred as a result of the move, such as a change of school.

The primary goal for this phase is to assist the child and the carers to orient themselves to each other and begin to experience opportunities for matched physiological and narrative states.

2. Placement integration

During this phase the child's healing is the primary focus. Stabilisation of the placement promotes the child's capacity to address the more specific details of his/her trauma experiences.

The child will gradually become less hypervigilant to his/her surroundings, develop improved capacity to co-regulate his/her states with the carer and others, and start to experience deep visceral safety in relation to the carer and others who are close to him/her.

There will be evidence of the child's ability to reintegrate shame that arises from limit setting and consequences for negative behaviours. He/she will also begin to demonstrate a capacity to enjoy life and a tolerance for light, fun interactions.

3. Placement consolidation

During this phase, the core changes will be reflected in the child's development of a sense of self and personal agency. Self-esteem and self-confidence are critical growth factors which now allow the child to discover the delights of social connectedness and the natural ability of human beings to enjoy social relationships. The child understands and accepts their place in the family and the place of their birth family in their life.

As the child moves into and through this final stage of recovery, his/her pride and confidence in him/herself will be clearly evident. Self-care, hygiene and personal appearance become significant. The child will also demonstrate an ability to have healthy relationships, clear attachments and an extended support and social network. The child will show an understanding of emotional literacy and a capacity for emotional regulation. He/she will be able to accept adult authority, and take risks in relationships, tasks, activities and family interactions.

Movement through the phases is often not unidirectional. As such, the child and care context must be frequently reassessed. As the child progresses, each new stage of recovery may destabilise and produce new terrors. Then, there needs to be a new period of grounding and stabilising for the child to re-establish her or his sense of safety and assurance that she or he will not be overwhelmed. Sometimes a child may regress to an earlier stage if a major event occurs (e.g. death of birth parent, changes to court orders or changes to a birth mother's circumstances such as marriage, pregnancy). The length of these changes in direction may be difficult to predict. It is necessary for carers and the Therapeutic Care Team to understand, however, that these changes are temporary and will last until the child feels emotionally safe to return to her or his prior place in the recovery process. It is the Therapeutic Care Team's responsibility to be cognisant of these possibilities and be prepared for them.

Evaluating outcomes achieved by the TrACK Program

Since its development in 2003, TrACK has achieved long-term positive outcomes for children in care. This was reflected in an early independent qualitative evaluation undertaken in 2005 (SuccessWorks, 2005). The aim of the evaluation was to benchmark the program against best practice elements in the literature, evaluate the effectiveness of the TrACK Program and provide recommendations regarding strengthening future service developments. The evaluation reviewed seven children and their carers, six of whom had been in the TrACK Program for approximately 18 months and the other at least six months.

The evaluation noted that the TrACK Program is underpinned by

> theoretical frameworks including the neurobiology of abuse related trauma and attachment in understanding disrupted developmental pathways for chronically traumatised children and its impact on emotional, psychological and behavioural functioning. Children's experiences of trauma are privileged as a means of understanding their complex matrix of needs and responding to their behaviour. (p.3)

The evaluation identified that for all children there were significant changes in critical areas of emotional, psychological and social function including self-esteem, ability to verbalise fears and worries, acceptance of limits, routines and carer roles, participation in family tasks and ability to establish and maintain relationships with carers and demonstrate affection. There was substantial improvement across a range of behaviours commonly referred to as 'challenging' in the care environment, including the minimisation of violent behaviours, property damage, problematic sexual behaviours and absconding. Of note the evaluation commented:

> [F]or all children there have been significant changes in critical areas of emotional, psychological and social functioning… Indeed, 3 children have ceased long term medication for issues such as ADHD and anxiety since placement within the TrACK Program. The reasons for this appear directly related to the quality and effectiveness of the care they are currently receiving. (p.3)

The program was seen to act as a catalyst for reducing placement breakdowns and unplanned changes – a characteristic of this group of children prior to their entry into the program. The evaluators concluded:

> [T]he TrACK Program effectively demonstrates the essential components of 'therapeutic foster care', marrying the contribution of trauma and attachment theories to practices within a home based care setting. The centrality of the carer's role in care planning and treatment further confirms the program's adherence to current best practice standards in therapeutic fostering. The training and secondary consultation provided by the program coupled with the intensive casework and support are clearly essential in maintaining placement stability and are highly valued by foster carers. (p.4)

A second independent evaluation was commissioned in 2017 to examine the longer-term effectiveness of the program. With some 15 years of client data, the program was well positioned to evaluate its impact with a cohort of children who had been in the program for a significant period of time. Undertaken by Southern Cross University, the study aimed to determine whether the TrACK Program had been successful in creating safety, stability and connections for children and young people. The evaluation used a mixed-methods approach, drawing upon multiple sources of information and varied perspectives. Data collection included examining client files and interviewing TrACK carers and other Therapeutic Care Team members, including foster care workers and Therapeutic Specialists. In addition, some young people who had experienced the Therapeutic Care program since its inception 15 years ago were individually interviewed. Informed by narrative inquiry methodology, data were analysed. A detailed description of the methodology and findings is reported on elsewhere (McPherson *et al.*, 2018). Ethics approval to conduct the evaluation was granted by both Southern Cross University and Anglicare Victoria. What follows is a summary of the key findings of the evaluation illustrated by the narrative of young people, carers and other members of the Therapeutic Care Team.

Key outcomes of the TrACK Program

The TrACK Program was found to have demonstrated 'during care' outcomes for children in the following areas: placement stability, emotional recovery and caregiver relationship stability. Caregiver relationship stability was strongly supported by a Therapeutic Care Team offering a consistent relationship with the carer. In relation to 'post care' outcomes, there is some evidence of longer-term stability in relationships and connectedness to community. These findings are summarised and discussed below in the context of the voices of carers and young people.

Placement stability

The file analysis revealed that children placed in the TrACK Program had frequently experienced multiple placement moves. Twenty-nine of the 48 children who had experienced TrACK had experienced more than three placements. Fifteen children had lived in more than six placements before program entry. Seven of these children had experienced more than ten placements, with one child having experienced 18, and another child, 30 placements, prior to entering the program. In addition, file analysis and interviews with carers and professionals revealed that children typically entered the TrACK Program with a high level of adverse childhood experience. Each of the 48 children accepted into TrACK were profiled as having either been in residential care (n=19) or at risk of being placed in residential care in light of their challenging, trauma-based behaviours. The number and severity of adverse childhood experiences indicated in file records and confirmed at interview was reported to be extreme. In the context of this client profile, TrACK has achieved stabilisation for children who had witnessed violence or attempted parental suicide, endured torture – including severe sexual exploitation at the hand of paedophile rings – and experienced extreme and inhumane deprivation. Put simply, children who have been highly unstable prior to entry into the TrACK Program almost always stabilise once in the program. For former clients, the period of stay ranged from five months to nine years and two months.

Of 32 former clients, only six identified an unplanned exit from TrACK. The remaining 26 children exited the program having achieved stability and in a planned manner. The following stories illustrate the journey toward stability.

One of the current children in TrACK, a six-year-old girl, was described by her carer in the following way:

> She's got a lot of baggage; her parents are in jail for what they've done to her mentally, physically, sexually and she depends on [the carer] like 24/7. If [the carer] leaves the house, our house overlooks the main road, she stands at the window like this waiting – until she's coming down the street – [asking] "Where's mum? Where's mum?" So she's got attachment issues... – she can't communicate properly because they used to lock her in a room out of the house and they were on drugs so they didn't teach her how to talk... So her speech is absolutely terrible. You wouldn't understand half of the words she's saying. (Sally, carer)

In spite of what could be seen as extreme presentations on entry to the program, a consistent picture of stability emerged, based on the persistent and proactive relational responses from carers. For some this was a slow and at times painstaking process:

> The first couple of years she used to scream if I went anywhere near her, like scream and scream and scream and scream, couldn't go into her room to say goodnight, so it was sort of like that blocked care, like quite severe blocked care because I...like I couldn't do anything, I couldn't have any sort of relationship with her at all. And then gradually when we got the older one on side and that was with a lot of support from the Care Team about ways to make that happen, like the practicalities of it, we eventually got her to move into her own room so that they were in separate rooms, so after the couple of years of screaming with the younger one... – it progressed... (Jenny, carer)

The 'progression' described was the slow consolidation of relational and placement stability. Now three years on, with no established end date, this carer talks about the future for the sisters in a hopeful manner, while acknowledging the ongoing challenges. There are no plans for the sisters to leave her care.

Another story highlights stability at home and in school:

> [H]e was 7 [when he came into the TrACK Program] and he was very animal-like and he could not read and write. He never went to school – well, he went to school but they sat him in the middle of a room, you know how they have the middle room between two rooms in primary school? With a martial arts man. And that was his school experience until I met him. (Holly, carer)

Four years later this boy delights in the ordinary moments of family life and is described as having a sense of humour and a close relationship with his foster 'brother', a 24-year-old young man who has aged out of the TrACK Program and continues to live in the family home.

Emotional recovery

Each child who has experienced the TrACK Program (n=48), including those who did not complete the TrACK Program in a planned manner, was reported to have made gains in their capacity to self-regulate and ability to use relationships to support effective decision-making, especially in relation to future planning and addressing areas of risk in their behaviour.

> He's eight now. He was five when he came to us. And just the distance between the violence now… – it's not daily, like he's not screaming in my face how much he hates me and wants to kill me and kill himself. Now it will happen but we'll have days when it doesn't happen. And he's also very affectionate. Like I think of him as my son, like I sometimes forget, like we'll go to do something and then the other side of him sort of comes back, the deep down stuff comes back. There's no way we would have lasted and there's no way he would have got to a point now of being vulnerable around us without all that extra support and he will continue to need it… yeah, so that's probably our biggest measure of success is when we forget that he's actually our foster son, like he's just… (Josie, carer)

The program typically offers children opportunities to understand their need to self-regulate:

> The other really powerful thing that I've seen around regulation is for kids learning about what is happening in their body and that they're flipping their lid and they can't access the thinking part of their brain. So, that kind of very basic for young children, and then with older adolescents, talking about that sort of window of tolerance type idea. And I had one adolescent do to me…he really got that and he was like, yes, mine's this wide. And then talking about how the work we need to do is about widening that for you and how to help you. I recently heard a young boy say to his carer: 'I need to regulate.' 'Mum, I need to regulate, I've got that feeling, I need to regulate', so he'll go on his rocker or he'll go and punch the bag: 'I think I'm nearly there mum.' (Wendy, Therapeutic Specialist)

Caregiver-child relationship as the critical ingredient for healing

The child–caregiver relationship was consistently identified as the critical ingredient for healing and change. Almost all of the children were able to develop warm and trusting relationships with their carers, which contributed to their recovery and capacity for growth and development. For some the relational progress was painfully slow, with carers noticing small signs of progress:

> So this year, she has just like really blossomed, you know, from last year wanting to kill herself and really isolating herself at school. (Daphne, carer)

This carer talked about her own advocacy and persistence to have the child's complex needs addressed and for the importance of the child to experience success and connectedness within the wider community.

Carers typically described a long-standing commitment to the program, enabling young people to develop lasting and long-standing relationships. Some had an experience of generalist foster care prior to becoming TrACK Program carers. A critical difference for TrACK Program carers was the experience of their own relational support by a Therapeutic Care Team who were identified as trustworthy and available.

> Having done both [generalist foster care and care within the TrACK Program], there's no comparison really with the level of support

> you get. So way more support, way more help in advocating for their needs to get met, you know, whether it's educational, assessments or...do you know what I mean? Without the assistance of the Track [Care] Team... (Josie, carer)

In the words of another carer, who had been supporting a young woman who was chronically suicidal:

> [W]e all weren't sure of where it was all going you know, because it was so intense and I remember one of my workers saying to me that we're standing over an abyss and we're looking into the black and I'm going 'are you sure?' and she's going 'nope, but I'm coming with you'. So the trust, when you need like trust that no one else can give you and no one else wants to know about what's going on because it's just too much. (Sally, carer)

Another carer revealed that when she felt the pain and distress associated with caring for children who had trauma histories, the Therapeutic Care Team validated this by telling her:

> '[Y]ou're a good carer because you're feeling all that, because you're feeling that pain that the children are feeling all the time and you're –' because if you're not – if you're sort of 'oh well, whatever' and it's water off a duck's back, you're not that connected with them, that's what she was saying. If you're really feeling it, if they're really stabbing you in the heart, that means it's hurting because you've got a connection with them, otherwise it wouldn't hurt, you wouldn't care what they said. (Maxine, carer)

Finally, another carer summed up her experience of Therapeutic Care Team relationships:

> I just hope that you guys do know, is just the amount of time they give us...like I know I can pick up my phone, any hour, any day and get support, and I've had days where I've had three, four hours and the next day the same – like the hours and hours when you're in crisis, the availability is absolutely phenomenal... And the creativity of what they offer, you know, they're there, they're at the school, they'll appear, they'll deliver food if you need, they'll be getting people to repair the [wall] – you know, just the flexibility of whatever different people need. (Simone, carer)

Predicted trajectory versus outcomes

A reasonable prediction for the future of those children referred to the TrACK Program would have been that they were at substantially elevated risk of a range of mental health difficulties, including posttraumatic stress disorders, conduct problems and attachment difficulties, as well as associated indices of poor functioning, including poor school attainment and, later, higher rates of unemployment, homelessness, substance abuse and contact with the criminal justice system (Fuemmeler *et al.*, 2009).

This evaluation found that this risk has almost always been averted by the TrACK Program. After more than 18 years of operation, the dominant theme in care is one of being stable, connected and settled as young people approach adulthood. In addition, there is some emerging evidence indicating that TrACK Program graduates are healthy, stable young adults. 'Stability' is defined by carers and young people as secure relationships within a family environment and stability in knowing the long-term connection to an extended family. It includes stability of 'place' and connections to their local community based on the hobbies and interests of the child and family. It involves stability of informed professionals who form a team around the child. It involves knowing and being known by the school and being a stable and active participant in learning and friendships. It involves having hopes, dreams and aspirations for the future without concern or fears about basic survival.

In the words of one young man who had aged out of care, the TrACK Program offered

> guidance really, and support. Support and love and all that stuff. That was the big thing, because me and my brother were in it as well... They [the carers] love a laugh, a chat, no matter what time of day or night... (David, young person)

This young man described having a sense of connection to the regional town that he lived in and stability of relationships and in employment. He was proud to also reveal that he had been in a stable relationship for five years with a young woman and planned to be married: 'I've got a fiancée now and everything.'

A second young person, also aged out of care yet continuing to live with his carers, described his hopes and plans for the future in a way that mirrored the values and interests of his carer family.

This family were very interested in outdoor recreation and had involved their TrACK children in family adventures, including travelling overseas. This, combined with a commitment to charitable work in developing countries, had helped to shape the attitudes and values of the young person who was now, as a young adult, engaged in fundraising activities of his own. He too expressed a sense that he did not know what his life might have been like had he not had the stability and care that the TrACK Program had offered him, summarising his current post-TrACK life in the following way:

> I think the main thing [about why TrACK works for me] would be just knowing that you've got that support behind you, I would say...I feel 100% that this is the right place, I have settled down. (Simon, young person)

At least three former TrACK clients continue to live with 'their' families as young adults. They know they have a home: a place to belong and a family to love them and support them until they are ready to be on their own – or not. 'Claiming the child' is a phrase used by the Therapeutic Care Team in the TrACK Program to illustrate the process of the carer 'internalising' the child. The process through which the child has also developed enough trust to internalise the carer is the ultimate indication of integration. This appears to create the foundations for developing the essential sense of worthiness and belonging that children need for internal stability.

Conclusion

The TrACK Program pioneered therapeutic foster care in Australia, providing effective care and positive outcomes for a cohort of children with a range of complex needs and challenging behaviours that the system to date had failed. A history of multiple placement breakdowns within a context of behaviours and needs that overwhelmed the care system was characteristic of the children in the program over the last 15 years. In many ways the system had given up on these children, conceiving that somehow they were to blame for their poor placement history and outcomes.

The TrACK Program has shown a strong capacity to change the trajectory for these children. Independent evaluation findings are very promising, finding that the program produces tangible and lasting results for children. The most compelling finding is that children who had experienced many placements and years of threat and deprivation (McLean, 2016) before they entered the TrACK Program were almost always able to achieve stability as a result of the program. Clearly, the program is creating viable alternatives for young people entering residential care, or as a pathway supporting young people to leave residential care and to be looked after in family-based care.

A number of carers have developed a sense of permanence with their children, from childhood through to young adulthood, and continued to show explicit commitment to them beyond 18 years when foster care in Australia officially ends. Engaging with children and young people in this way future-orientates the relationships.

One of the foster care managers summed up her experience of TrACK in the following way:

> I've been a foster care case manager in the TrACK Program for about seven years. I worked in child protection before and I think I saw a lot of children with complex needs being moved around and having a lot of broken relationships and that sort of thing. And I feel very passionate about this program in terms of, you know, we provide an intensive level of support to children and carers. And I think that the outcomes that we see, we see, you know, more placement stability, you know, better quality relationships and that sort of thing. (Sarah, foster care manager)

The TrACK Program has demonstrated significant outcomes for the children it has cared for. Since its establishment, the key elements of the TrACK model have been used to replicate similar therapeutic foster care and kinship care models across a number of states and territories in Australia, catering for children in statutory care requiring short-, medium- and long-term care.

Note: The TrACK Program has been delivered in partnership between the Australian Childhood Foundation, Anglicare Victoria and the Department of Human Services in the Eastern Metropolitan Region of Melbourne, Victoria, Australia.

References

Akamas (2007). About healing environments. Extracted from 'Working with Traumatised Children' Level 4 BTEC Qualification, available online from Akamas.

Australian Childhood Foundation (2004). *TrACK Program Manual*. Melbourne: Australian Childhood Foundation.

Australian Institute of Family Studies, Chapin Hall Center for Children at the University of Chicago, and NSW Department of Family and Community Services (2015). *Pathways of Care Longitudinal Study: Outcomes of Children and Young People in Out-of-Home Care in NSW. Wave 1 Baseline Statistical Report*. Sydney: Department of Family and Community Services.

Brown, D., Scheflin, A. and Hammond, D. (1998). *Memory, Trauma Treatment and the Law*. New York, NY: W.W. Norton and Company.

Cairns, K. (2002). *Attachment, Trauma and Resilience: Therapeutic Caring for Children*. London: British Association of Adoption and Fostering.

Cashmore, J. and Paxman, M. (2006). Predicting after-care outcomes: The importance of felt security. *Child and Family Social Work*, 11(3), 232–241.

Christiansen, G. and Fine, P. (1979). Corrective socialisation in foster care of children. *Child Psychiatry and Human Behaviour*, 10(1), 15–34.

Durrant, M. (1993). *Residential Treatment: A Cooperative, Competency-Based Approach to Therapy and Program Design*. New York, NY: W.W. Norton and Company.

Feilberg, F. (2007). Teaching lifespace working by using the lifespace in teaching. *Scottish Journal of Residential Child Care*, 6(1), 32–36.

Fuemmeler, B., Dedert, E., McClernon, F. and Beckham, J. (2009). Adverse childhood events are associated with obesity and disordered eating: Results from a U.S. population-based survey of young adults. *Journal of Trauma and Stress*, 22(4), 329–333.

Garfat, T. and Fulcher, L. (2012). Characteristics of a Relational Child and Youth Care Approach. In T. Garfat and L. Fulcher (eds), *Child and Youth Care in Practice*. Cape Town, South Africa: The CYC-Net Press.

Gharabaghi, K. (2008). Values in child and youth care. *Child and Youth Services*, 30(3/4), 185–209.

Hughes, D. (1997). *Facilitating Developmental Attachment: The Road to Emotional Recovery and Behavioral Change in Foster and Adopted Children*. Lanham, MD: Rowman and Littlefield Publishers.

Hughes, D. (1998). *Building the Bonds of Attachment: Awakening Love in Deeply Troubled Children*. Lanham, MD: Rowman and Littlefield Publishers.

Johnson, G., Natalier, K., Liddiard, M. and Thoresen, S.H. (2011). Out in the World with No-One: A Qualitative Study of the Housing Pathways of Young People who have Recently Left State Out-of-Home Care. In P. Mendes, G. Johnson and B. Moslehuddin (eds), *Young People Leaving State Out-of-Home Care*. North Melbourne: Australian Scholarly Publishing.

Maier, H. (1979). The core of care: Essential ingredients for the development of children at home and away from home. *Child Care Quarterly*, 8(3), 161–173.

McDowall, J.J. (2013). *Experiencing Out-of-Home Care in Australia: The Views of Children and Young People (CREATE Report Card 2013)*. Sydney: CREATE Foundation.

McLean, S. (2016). *The Effect of Trauma on the Brain Development of Children: Evidence-based Principles for Supporting the Recovery of Children in Care (CFCA Practitioner Resource)*. Melbourne: Child Family Community Australia Information Exchange, Australian Institute of Family Studies.

McPherson, L., Gatwiri, K., Tucci, J., Mitchell, J. and Macnamara, N. (2018). A paradigm shift in responding to children and young people who have experienced trauma: The Australian Treatment and Care for Kids Program. *Children and Young People and Youth Services Review*, doi:10.1016/j.childyouth.2018.08.031.

Mitchell, J. (2008). A Case Study in Attempted Reform in Out of Home Care: A Preliminary Examination of the Introduction of the Circle Therapeutic Foster Care Program in Victoria. Unpublished Masters Thesis, Monash University.

Ruff, H., Blank, S. and Barnett, H. (1990). Early intervention in the context of foster care. *Developmental and Behavioural Paediatrics*, 11(5), 265–268.

Sinclair, I. (2005). *Fostering Now: Messages from Research*. London: Jessica Kingsley Publishers.

Smith, M. (2005). Working in the 'Lifespace'. *In Residence*, 2. Glasgow: Scottish Institute for Residential Child Care.

SuccessWorks (2005). *Evaluation of the Treatment and Care for Kids (TrACK) Program*. Melbourne: SuccessWorks.

Taylor, L. (2005). Theoretical Perspectives. In M. Smith, B. Forrest, P. Garland and L. Hunter (eds), *Secure in the Knowledge: Perspectives on Practice in Secure Accommodation*. Glasgow: CELCIS.

Thich Nhat Hanh (2007). *Teachings on Love*. Rocklin, CA: Parallax Press.

Torrenon, M. (2006). Community in a children's home. *Child and Family Social Work*, 11(2), 129–137.

Vincent, J. (2016). Perspectives on love as a component of professional practice. [Joint Special Issue, Love in Professional Practice] *Scottish Journal of Residential Child Care*, 15(3) and *International Journal of Social Pedagogy*, 5(1), 6–21. doi: https://doi.org/10.14324/111.444.ijsp.2017.02.

Ward, A. (2003). The Core Framework. In A. Ward, K. Kasinski, J. Pooley and A. Worthington (eds), *Therapeutic Communities for Children and Young People*. London: Jessica Kingsley Publishers.

Ward, A. (2006). Models of 'ordinary' and 'special' daily living: Matching residential care to the mental health needs of looked after children. *Child and Family Social Work*, 11(4), 336–346.

Wilson, K. (2006). Can foster carers help children resolve their emotional and behavioural difficulties? *Clinical Child Psychology and Psychiatry*, 11(4), 495–511.

PRACTICE REFLECTION

Joe Tucci, Janise Mitchell and Ed Tronick

In this chapter, Mitchell, McPherson and Gatwiri describe the elements of a pioneering Therapeutic Foster Care Program that has been running for almost two decades. They also then outline the results of a retrospective longitudinal study of the children, young people and carers who have benefited from it.

The most critical finding is the impact of the TrACK Program on achieving stability of care for children whose history of placement disruptions leading up to their entry into the program was extreme. The most heart-warming outcomes are found in the voices of the children, young people and their carers themselves. They all described how love, which was so difficult to find at the beginning, emerged as carers were patient, predictable and attuned. Many of these children have stayed on to live with their foster families well beyond the legal age that they were required to do so. The foster families became their families. It was whom they could trust, who they could believe in and who they could belong to. The trauma-based behaviours subsided, enabling behaviours that were based in reciprocity, compassion and understanding to take their place.

TrACK has enacted the principles of Therapeutic Care that were articulated in Chapter 2. Its elements indeed inspired this form of practice. It is critical that child protection systems value the paradigm shift that Therapeutic Care symbolises. It offers these systems the opportunity to act from a different starting point – the relational needs of children. These are the needs that give expression to what care means. As they are met in the here-and-now, they radiate backwards and forwards through time, kickstarting children's development where trauma has held it hostage in the past and bracing the future vulnerabilities of children with care, attention and relationally crafted responses. Therapeutic Care creates the change in stuck systems that can only be possible when intimate relationships around children are organised, resourced and supported to know how, why and when to respond to these children along their journey through care and beyond.

6

The Neurosequential Model

A Developmentally Sensitive, Neuroscience-Informed Approach to Clinical Problem-Solving

BRUCE D. PERRY

Introduction: Origins of the Neurosequential Model

The Neurosequential Model© (NM) is the umbrella for three interrelated programs: the Neurosequential Model of Therapeutics© (NMT), the Neurosequential Model in Education© (NME) and the Neurosequential Model in Caregiving© (NMC). The NM originated as the clinically focused NMT, but has evolved over the last ten years to provide a set of parallel and complementary program elements for various target populations and settings.

The most fully developed element of the NM is the NMT. The NMT is both an evidence-based and 'evidence-generating' approach that has shown effectiveness with a wide range of clinical populations in multiple settings, including early childhood (Barfield *et al.*, 2012; Ryan, Lane and Powers, 2017), outpatient mental health (Zarnegar *et al.*, 2016), foster care (Grove, 2012; Wang *et al.*, 2015), special education (Australian Council for Education Research, 2015), education (Anich and King, 2013; Whyde and Boldman-Buzard, 2017), juvenile justice and residential treatment (Hambrick *et al.*, 2018) and inpatient psychiatric settings (De Nooyer and Lindgard, 2016). The NMT was designated a 'promising practice' by the National Quality Improvement Center for Adoption and Guardian Support and Preservation (QIC-AG.org) in 2015. The NM has been incorporated into the practice framework for many organizations, including Casey Family Programs, and government systems, including Alberta Human Services.

The origins of the NM trace back to the work of an interdisciplinary clinical research group studying the effects of stress and trauma on neurodevelopment based at the University of Chicago (Center for the Study of Child Trauma and Laboratory of Developmental Neurosciences). When Dr. Perry moved to Baylor College Medicine in 1992, the Center became the CIVITAS ChildTrauma Programs, and in 1995 was renamed the ChildTrauma Academy (CTA). In 2001, the CTA became a free-standing non-profit organization functioning as a Community of Practice (Wenger, 1988). The CTA's Neurosequential Model Network is currently comprised of more than 2000 affiliated organizations and individual clinicians engaged in research, program development, direct service and training in child trauma, maltreatment, education, child welfare, juvenile justice and a host of related areas.

The NMT draws on research from multiple disciplines (e.g. the neurosciences, anthropology, sociology, developmental psychology, public health) to create a semi-structured, practical way for an interdisciplinary clinical team to quantify elements of the client's developmental history and current functioning. The NMT includes a set of 'metrics', the NMT Clinical Practice Tools, developed to help the clinician practice in an evidence-based, developmentally sensitive and trauma-informed manner (Brandt *et al.*, 2012). The goal of this semi-structured process is to ensure that the clinician/clinical team systematically considers key developmental factors that may contribute to the client's current functioning (see Figure 6.1). The NMT assessment elements are meant to complement and not replace other metrics or assessment elements; each organization and clinical team has developed some assessment process, and the NMT is designed to provide a neurodevelopmental framework for the data obtained in these various assessments. The functional data for a client, gathered in either quantitative (e.g. Wechsler Intelligence Scale for Children, Wide Range Achievement Test, Child and Adolescent Functional Assessment Scale, Child and Adolescent Needs and Strengths, Child Behavior Checklist, Trauma Symptom Checklist for Children, Parent Stress Index) or qualitative ways, is organized into a neuroscience-focused 'map'. This heuristic 'brain map' provides the clinical team with an approximation of current functional organization of the client's brain (see Figure 6.2).

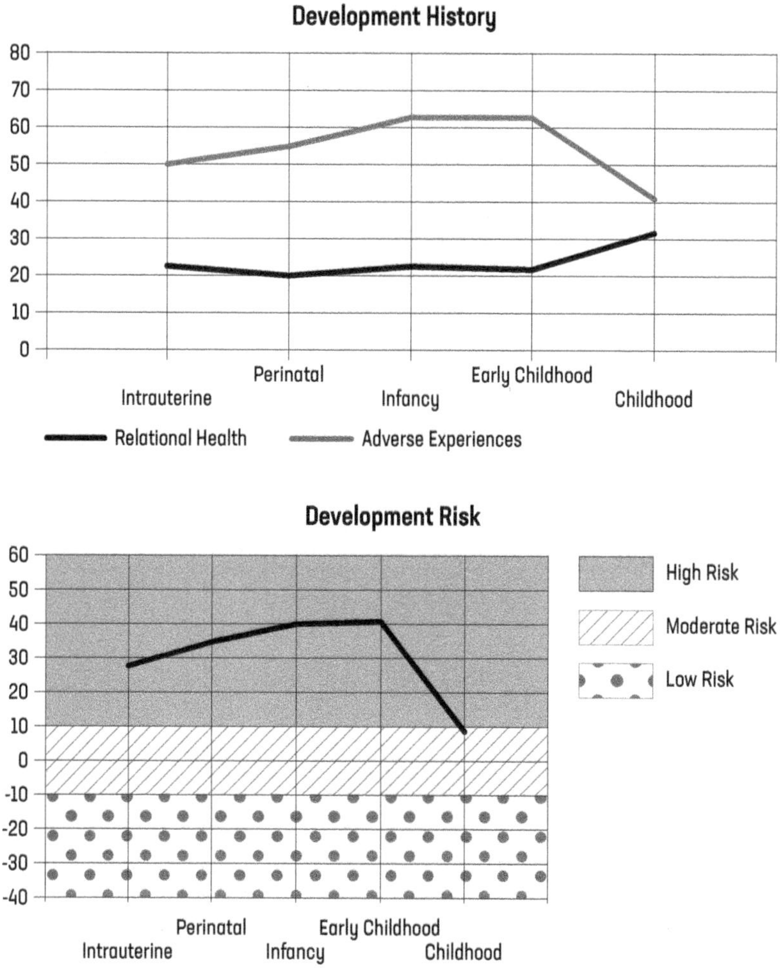

Figure 6.1 Graphic representation of NMT Clinical Practice Tools (Parts A and B)

The NMT assessment process examines both past and current experience and functioning. A review of the history of adverse experiences and relational health factors helps create an estimate of the timing and severity of developmental risk that may have influenced brain development (see graphs). In the sample graphs, both the timing and severity of risk and resilience factors are plotted (top graph) to generate an overall developmental risk estimate (bottom graph). In this case the individual was at high risk for developmental disruptions – with potential significant functional consequences – during the entire first five years of life.

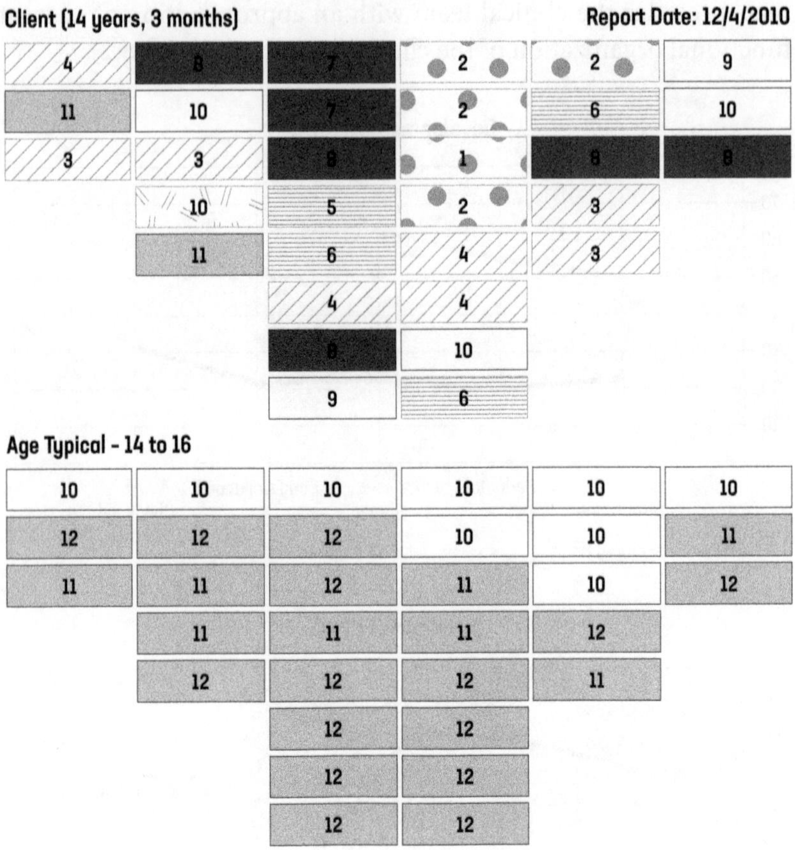

Figure 6.2 Central Nervous System Functional Status Measure ('brain map')

This is an example of a functional 'brain map' produced by the web-based NMT Clinical Practice Tools application. The top image (with the red squares) corresponds to a client. (Each box corresponds to brain functions mediated by a region/system in the brain. The map is coded, with dots indicating significant problems, dark grey indicating moderate compromise and mid-grey indicating fully organized and functionally capable.) The bottom map is a comparative map for a 'typical' same-age child. The graphic representation allows a clinician, teacher or parent to quickly visualize important aspects of a child's history and current status. The information is key in designing developmentally appropriate educational, enrichment and therapeutic experiences to help the child.

Development of the NMT

A primary focus of the NM from the outset was integrating fundamental principles of neuroscience into an understanding of the child, youth and adult. This neurodevelopmental 'bias' is not intended to replace other theoretical perspectives on human behavior; rather, it seeks to complement and enrich other perspectives. The recognition that the NM is an evolving 'model' – and that all models are wrong or incomplete in some way (see George E.P. Box as quoted in Draper, 1987) – drives the 'growth mindset' of the community of NM practitioners and developers. The creation of the NMT was in response to the frustrating awareness that a more traditional clinic-based, medical model was ineffective in working with children and youth impacted by severe neglect and trauma who presented with a host of developmental challenges including profound attachment problems (see Perry, 2017). By 2000, the CTA was beginning to use an alternative method for assessment and intervention, the NMT, which evolved from the research and clinical experiences of the CTA team (Perry, 2006; Perry, 2009). Detailed theoretical background and rationale for the NMT have been reported previously (Perry, 2006; Kleim and Jones, 2008; Perry, 2009; Ludy-Dobson and Perry, 2010).

A multi-year process of beta-testing various versions of the NMT took place within the clinical settings of the ChildTrauma Academy in Houston, Texas. The NMT was used in multiple clinical populations across the full developmental spectrum (infants to adults), including maltreated children and youth (e.g. Barfield *et al.*, 2012; Hambrick *et al.*, 2018). Approximately 1000 clients were evaluated in the CTA Clinics using the NMT Clinical Practice Tools (i.e. the NMT Metrics). Based upon these experiences, modifications were made to the assessment to make it more practical, affordable and exportable. The intention was to provide a useful set of capacity-building, assessment and implementation capabilities for other clinicians and clinical sites.

By 2008, inter-rater reliability and face validity of the Clinical Practice Tools (the web-based 'NMT Metrics': see below) had been established to a sufficient degree that the CTA felt comfortable sharing this approach using a certification process, and the NMT approach was 'manualized' for export (see Perry and Szalavitz, 2017). In 2010 the NMT Metrics were converted to a web-based program with certified individuals used a web-based interface to enter, score and create reports. This stimulated significant growth of the NMT-certified community (see Figure 6.3).

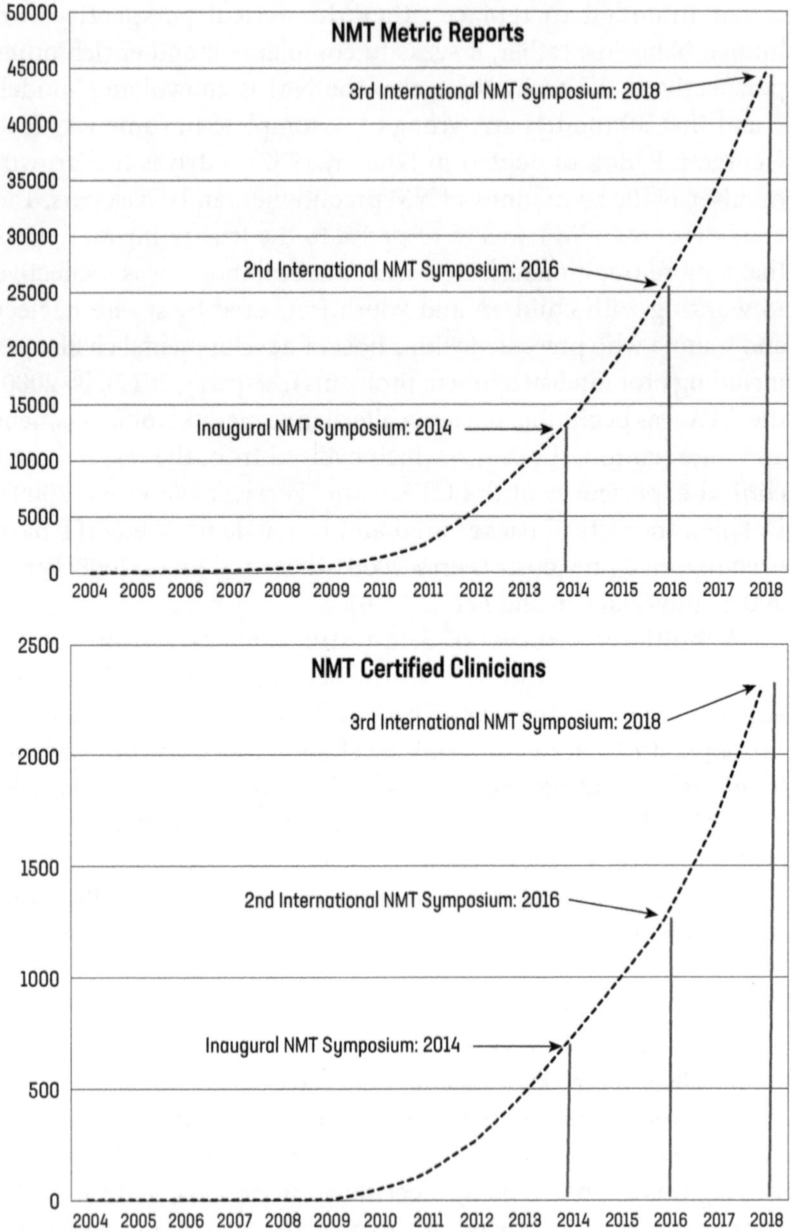

Figure 6.3 Growth of the NMT

The bottom graph illustrates the growth of NMT-certified clinicians. Since the NMT Certification process was introduced, the number of NMT-certified clinicians has grown from 0 in 2008 to more than 2000 in 2018. The top graph illustrates the growth of NMT metric reports in the web-based dataset, projected to be over 60,000 by 2020.

Considering the typically 'slow' nature of the dissemination of new clinical innovations, the growth of the NMT is relatively rapid. Few translational medicine efforts see the light of day; only 14% of the practices developed in clinical research actually reach clinical 'practice' (Balas and Boren, 2000). Further, it takes, on average, 17 years for these innovations to go from clinical investigation to standard of practice (see Morris, Wooding and Grant, 2011). The growth of the NMT is ahead of the typical rate of dissemination as it has evolved over the last ten years from science-based practice to promising practice to an evidence-based practice (see Figure 6.3). Much of this growth is due to the general enthusiastic (sometimes over-enthusiastic) word of mouth from program to program, clinician to clinician. Since 2008, more than 2500 clinicians and 200 organizations or programs in 24 countries have become certified. The manualized and web-based training elements developed for the NMT Certification process continue to be updated and revised as the field grows. To ensure the systematic, high-fidelity dissemination of the core concepts and mastery of the NMT Clinical Practice Tools (see below) and NMT-guided treatment planning process, ongoing access to the web-based NMT Metrics requires participation in an ongoing biannual NMT Fidelity exercise for all NMT Metrics users. Over 85% of certified users routinely obtain high or acceptable inter-rater reliability. In one recent study, Cronbach's was .95 for Part C (CNS Functioning) and .84 for Part D (Current Relational Health) (Hambrick, Brawner and Perry, 2018).

The NMT Clinical Practice Tools

The NMT Clinical Practice Tools (aka NMT Metrics) help to provide a structured assessment of the developmental history of adverse experiences and relational health, as well as current brain-mediated functioning and relational health (connectedness). These NMT Metrics are designed to complement, not replace, existing assessment tools (e.g. CANS, CAFAS) and psychometrics (e.g. CBCL, IES, WISC, WRAT). They are designed to allow use across multiple systems using multiple assessment packages. The primary goal of the NMT Metrics and assessment is to ensure that the clinical team is organizing the client and family's data (and planning) in a developmentally sensitive and neurobiology-informed manner.

The NMT 'mapping' process helps identify systems (areas) in the brain that appear to have functional or developmental problems; in turn, this helps to guide the selection and sequencing of developmentally appropriate (and age-acceptable) interventions. These interventions are designed to replicate the normal sequence of development, beginning with the lowest, most abnormally functioning systems of the brain (e.g. those originating in the brainstem) and moving sequentially up the brain as improvement is seen. The NMT is grounded in an awareness of the sequential development of the brain and sequential, bottom-up processing of all incoming experience (i.e. sensory input). Cortical organization and functioning depend upon previous healthy organization and functioning of lower neural networks originating in the brainstem and diencephalon. Therefore, a dysregulated individual (child, youth or adult) will have a difficult time benefiting from educational, caregiving and therapeutic efforts targeted at, or requiring, 'higher' cortical networks. This sequential approach is respectful of the normal developmental sequence of both brain development and functional development. Healthy development depends upon a sequential mastery of functions; a dysregulated individual will be inefficient in mastering any task that requires relational abilities (cortico-limbic) and will have a difficult time engaging in more verbal/insight-oriented (cortical) therapeutic and educational efforts.

This clinical approach helps professionals determine the strengths and vulnerabilities of the child and create an individualized intervention, enrichment and educational plan matched to his/her unique needs. The goal is to find a set of therapeutic activities that meet the child's current needs in various domains of functioning (i.e. social, emotional, cognitive and physical). An individual demonstrating significant problems in brainstem and diencephalic functions may end up with recommended activities that are primarily rhythmic, repetitive and somatosensory in nature, such as music, dance, yoga, drumming, various sports or therapeutic massage, or more traditional play therapy, sand tray therapy or other art therapies. Later in the treatment process, with improved somatosensory processing and self-regulation, the 'therapeutic front' shifts to more complex, higher networks in the brain. The treatment recommendations would shift to more relational and cognitive-behavioral-focused interventions including a range of evidence-based treatments (EBTs) such as parent–child interaction therapy (PCIT) or trauma-focused cognitive-behavioral therapy (TF-CBT). Over the course of any client's NMT-guided treatment, then, a set of EBTs may be used depending upon the nature and timing of the client's needs.

A. The NMT Clinical Practice Tools (NMT Metrics)

The NMT Metrics (see Box 6.1) are divided into four main parts and some supplemental tools. The four main components of the NMT Metrics are Part A (Developmental Adversity), Part B (Relational Health), Part C (Central Nervous System (CNS) Functioning: Current) and Part D (Current Relational Health).

Box 6.1 NMT Clinical Practice Tools

1. **Demographics**
2. **History - Developmental**
    a. Genetic
    b. Epigenetic
    c. Part A. Adverse Events measure
    d. Part B. Relational Health measure
3. **Current Status**
    a. Part C. Central Nervous System (CNS) Functional Status measure
        i. Brainstem
        ii. Diencephalon/CBL
        iii. Limbic
        iv. Cortex/Frontal Cortex
    b. Part D. Relational Health measure
4. **Recommendations**
    a. Therapeutic Web
    b. Family
    c. Client
        i. Sensory Integration
        ii. Self-Regulation
        iii. Relational
        iv. Cognitive
5. **Caregiving Challenge Estimator**
    a. Caregiving resources
        i. Internal resources/demands
        ii. External resources/demands
    b. Caregiving demand
        i. Children (number)

In Part A (Adversity), clinicians score a range of potentially traumatic and/or adverse experiences during the following periods of life: Perinatal (birth to two months), Infancy (two months to 12 months), Early Childhood (13 months to four years) and Childhood (four years to 11 years). The six experiences assessed per developmental period are quality of primary caregiving, caregiver drug/alcohol use, neglect, domestic violence, transitions/chaos and 'other trauma'. Clinicians rate the severity of each experience from 1 to 12, ranging from None/Minimal (1–3) to Mild (4–6), Moderate (7–9) and Severe (10–12). Although the metrics are only completed by clinicians, clinicians use information from any available source including clinical interviews, child welfare case files, observations of child/family, medical records, psychosocial assessments, etc. When clinicians are uncertain about a child's specific adverse experiences (or relational health: see below), the scoring rules instruct the clinician to provide a neutral score and, when partial information is available, score in a manner that will, if anything, underestimate developmental risk.

B. The NMT Metric Report and Treatment Planning

The resulting report provides a three-page, graphic representation of the child's developmental history (see Figure 6.1) and a heuristic of their brain's current functional status relative to same-age peers (Figure 6.2). This report also uses the data from Part C to create an estimate of the client's executive functioning, the 'cortical modulation ratio', as well as the relative functional status in four major domains: sensory integration, self-regulation, and relational and cognitive functioning. These results are used to select and sequence enrichment, educational and therapeutic activities that can plausibly influence the targeted neural networks (e.g. motor, relational) with adequate nature, pattern and frequency of experience to effect positive change. The core principles of neuroplasticity help guide this treatment planning process (see Kleim and Jones, 2008), and multiple examples of a detailed therapeutic process using the NMT Metrics to guide treatment selection and sequencing have been described elsewhere (Perry and Dobson, 2013; Perry, 2014; Gaskill and Perry, 2017; Perry and Szalavitz, 2017; Steinkopf, Bræin and Nordanger, 2017).

Central to NMT recommendations is the recognition of the importance of the therapeutic, educational and enrichment opportunities provided in the broader community, especially the home and school. The power of relationships and the mediation of therapeutic experiences in culturally respectful relational interactions are core elements of the NMT recommendations (Ludy-Dobson and Perry, 2010). Although not a formal wraparound, the NMT recommendation process starts with a focus on the therapeutic web – the collective of healthy invested adults and peers who provide the relational milieu of the child; the quality and permanence of this relational milieu is one of the most essential elements of successful outcomes (see Mears, Yaffe and Harris, 2009; Bruns *et al.*, 2010). Ideally, this is where the Neurosequential Model in Education (NME) can be a component of the intervention (see below). The school personnel often need support and psychoeducation to better understand the child and create realistic expectations and services to 'meet' a client where he or she is developmentally. In clinical situations where the school is 'trauma-informed' and the client's teachers understand the effects of trauma, attachment disruptions, neglect and related adversities (e.g. food and housing insecurity), a more seamless treatment process can create therapeutic opportunities throughout the school day.

The next set of recommendations focuses on the family, often the key to the therapeutic approach. In many cases, the parents' history will mirror the child's developmental history of chaos, threat, trauma or neglect. When this is the case, the NMT will include the parents and provide recommendations to help address their multiple needs in addition to those of their child. Transgenerational aspects of vulnerability and strength in a family play important roles in the child's educational, enrichment and therapeutic experiences. When the caregivers and parents are healthy and strong, their capacity to be present, patient, positive and nurturing is enhanced. When the parents' needs are unmet and their own mental health is compromised as a result, it is unrealistic to expect that they will have the energy or capacity to meet all of the therapeutic needs of challenging maltreated children. In other cases, caregivers (e.g. biological parents, foster parents or adoptive parents) may be experienced and nurturing but not very 'trauma-informed'; maltreated children can present with complex and confusing problems that even a team of professionals do not understand. This is where a capacity-building and ongoing psychoeducational approach is essential to help them help their child: the Neurosequential Model in Caregiving (NMC) helps address this. As described later, the NMC can help build capacity, encourage self-care and increase connectedness for the family.

The final stage of treatment planning involves the client. Individual recommendations are based upon the client's neurodevelopmental organization. The selection and timing of various enrichment, educational and therapeutic experiences are guided by the developmental capabilities and vulnerabilities of the child, as determined from the results of the NMT Metric assessment. The NMT Metric report suggests some, but not all, activities that can provide patterned, repetitive and rewarding experiences. The goal is to help create therapeutic experiences that are sensitive to developmental status in various domains and that are aware of the individual's regulatory state: 'Know the Stage (of development) and Watch the State (of regulation)'.

C. Certification in the NMT

The NMT Certification process is 150 hours of didactic and case-based training designed to introduce the NMT assessment process, the NMT Clinical Practice Tools/Metrics, and the core concepts of neurodevelopment, neuroplasticity, attachment theory, traumatology and child development that inform work with traumatized and maltreated children, youth and adults. The Certification process consists of three phases.

Phase I is the introduction to the NMT and the key principles that underlie the clinical applications used with the model. The primary goals of Phase I are for clinicians to build comfort with, and experience in, organizing clinical information in a neurodevelopmentally informed way and develop mastery in using the NMT Metrics package. Phase II provides training in advanced clinical concepts, and is intended for a Train-the-Trainer component of the model. Internal fidelity and sustainability is provided by a cohort of Trainers completing Phase II phase. Post completion of NMT Phases I and II, the Maintenance Phase begins. The intention of this phase is to ensure that clinicians are provided ongoing access to any enhancements to the NMT Practice Tools and related improvements in the NMT process. This phase also provides the CTA opportunity to help assure fidelity to the NMT.

NMT database, outcomes and research

As the NMT Metrics are web-based, all of the data (deidentified) is gathered on a central database. Therefore, the developmental experiences and current functioning of all of the clients (and a set of 'typical' individuals) are on a central database, which can be used to better understand the impact of experience on development. There are approximately 1700 providers throughout the world who have achieved acceptable reliability in using the NMT Metrics. The Metrics, as described above, provide a way of organizing information regarding a child's developmental experience and current functioning. This dataset is unique and growing, with roughly 20,000 cases provided by NMT users who have acceptable or high fidelity. To date, several important observations regarding the timing of developmental trauma (i.e. adversity in the first two months of life is the major contributor to functional outcomes in youth) and the power of relational connectedness (the best predictor of current functioning in youth is current relational health, not history of adversity) have been reported (Hambrick, Brawner and Perry, 2018; Hambrick *et al.*, in press). This large NM dataset will allow a much more nuanced and granulated examination of the relationships between developmental experiences, good and bad, and various functional outcomes in multiple domains.

Development of the Neurosequential Model in Education (NME) and NM for Caregivers (NMC)

The first use of the NMT outside of the CTA's clinic was in an early childhood setting in 2006. Dr. Rick Gaskill and colleagues brought the NMT to a preschool setting serving at-risk children with high rates of dysregulation and various social and emotional delays. In this version of the NMT, the senior clinical consultant (RG) and staff with advanced clinical training (Master of Social Work or higher) carried out the assessments, implemented treatment plans and provided psychoeducational support to frontline staff and parents.

The results were promising, with the children having parents who participated in the NMT-guided activities at the school experiencing the best outcomes (Barfield *et al.*, 2012). It became clear, however, that if these children matriculated to a public school setting where the staff and teachers were not 'developmentally sensitive' or 'trauma-informed' (like the staff at the NMT-trained preschool), the positive effects faded. These children were misunderstood, and punitive, marginalizing interventions were used to address behavioral problems. The positive impact of the NMT in that setting faded without ongoing 'developmentally sensitive' educational practices. Two things were clear from this and related clinical experiences: (1) schools needed support to better understand maltreated and traumatized children and youth; and (2) parents and families needed to be engaged and supported to optimize any benefits provided in the school or clinic.

This was a major impetus to create the Neurosequential Model in Education (NME) and the Neurosequential Model in Caregiving (NMC). A major component of the NMT is the 'capacity-building' component which focuses on teaching the core concepts and heuristics intended to introduce basic neuroscience, neurodevelopment, attachment, trauma, neglect, resilience, epigenetics and a host of other topics key to understanding and working with maltreated or traumatized children and their families. In 2010, elements of this 'psychoeducational' content were modified to create materials and a process with a focus on the educational setting (NME). Beta versions of the NME were provided to selected schools with good success. An NME Trainers model (a modification of the NMT Train-the-Trainer program) was developed in 2012. By 2018, 1000 individuals with access to more than 6000 schools in 34 states and ten countries have become NME Trainers – and this NME community continues to grow. Preliminary outcome data from these schools has been very promising; many report fewer critical incidents, increased attendance, fewer teacher sick days and improved standardized test scores (Australian Council for Education Research, 2015; McNally and Ewing, 2018; Whyde and Boldman-Buzard, 2017).

For many years, a major focus of feedback from our NMT Community was the need for further translation of these NM concepts for non-professionals, including parents, kinship carers and foster and adoptive parents. Several of the CTA's partners (e.g. Cal Farley's Boys and Girls Ranch in Texas and Mount St. Vincent Home in Denver) have created modifications of the core content of the NM to use with caregivers. In 2016 the CTA started a pilot of the NMC with a state-wide collaborative of child- and family-serving organizations in Arizona led by the Arizona Council of Human Service Providers. A modification of the core concepts and teaching heuristics of the NMT provide the curricular framework, and ongoing web-based case discussions of challenges facing foster, kinship and adoptive parents provide the context for capacity-building. The feedback has been positive. Independent evaluation data (LT Partners for Change, 2018) demonstrate that the majority (92%) of participants agreed or strongly agreed when asked if their participation in the webinars helped them be a better caregiver to the children in their care. Almost 90% of respondents stated that their participation in the webinars positively changed their approach with their child and/or situations with their child, and 96% of respondents said the information will improve their caregiving skills. An exportable version of the NMC will be available in 2019.

Summary and future directions

The Neurosequential Model offers multiple cost-effective ways to integrate core concepts of developmental psychology and neurobiology into clinical practice, education and the home. This approach has been used in public systems, thereby allowing the systematic assessment of large numbers of complex children with relatively high fidelity. This is allowing better studies of the complex clinical phenomenology and neurobiology associated with maltreatment (e.g. Hambrick, Brawner and Perry, 2018). As with any approach, there are shortcomings – primarily the time required to become trained to use the NMT Metrics with fidelity and the challenge of having the resources and capacity to act on the NMT-derived recommendations. We believe these are outweighed by the capacity to track outcomes, ensure acceptable fidelity and help create a developmentally sensitive, trauma-informed lens through which to understand complex children and their families.

Ongoing studies of outcomes at several large clinical settings using the NMT will allow a more comprehensive evaluation of this approach in comparison with treatment as usual. Several key questions need to be addressed. Which aspect of this multidimensional approach resulted in the positive outcome? Was it the 'in-room' aide? The therapeutic massage or OT-directed activities? The psychoeducation for the foster family? Stopping the medications? The challenge of tracking outcomes and developing an 'evidence base' and outcome studies for the clinical settings using the NMT will have to be dissected, to some degree, from the application of specific treatments (many of them evidence-based treatments), that end up being recommended by the NMT process.

NMT is still a 'young' approach – only ten years have passed since the first systematic exporting of the model using a certification process. Despite this, the web-based nature of the NMT Metrics allows collection of data at a very rapid pace. This dataset is now large enough to allow more detailed examination of important relationships between developmental experience (including the timing and nature of adversity, as well as resilience-related factors) and functional outcomes (e.g. Hambrick, Brawner and Perry, 2018). At present, we have more than 40,000 children, youth and adults in the current data set. The projected number of NMT-assessed individuals will approach 60,000 in 2020.

Current NM-related activities of the CTA include: (1) ongoing evaluation and modification of NMT Metrics (including modification of gender-related items and development of culturally sensitive certification and training elements); (2) development of data analysis packages and statistical models for research and site-related QI/QA evaluation; (3) development of university-based NMT/NME certification packages (an effort pioneered by Dr. Christie Mason of Loyola University, Chicago School of Social Work); (4) additional targeted versions of the Neurosequential Model including the NMT Early Childhood Version and the Neurosequential Model in Sport (NM-S); (5) modification and revision of all NM-related multimedia content in collaboration with two federally funded projects, CORE Teen (https://spaulding.org/professionals/spaulding-institute/core-critical-on-going-resource-family-education) and the NTDC (National Training and Development Curriculum for Foster/Adoptive Parents: https://ntdcportal.org); and (6) development of advanced and proactive NM training opportunities (both advanced clinical workshops and NMT/NME boot camps) in collaboration with our new NM College. Collectively, we are hopeful that we will continue to learn from our colleagues and clients and remain hopeful that a developmental and neuroscience-informed approach can help individuals and advance our field.

References

Anich, Z. and King, E. (2013). Trauma, neuroscience and SEBN: An evaluation of training. Presentation at Annual Conference for Educational Psychologists in Scotland.

Australian Council for Education Research (2015). ACER Social-Emotional Wellbeing Survey. Summary School Report RADAR (Tasmania).

Balas, E.A. and Boren, S.A. (2000). Managing clinical knowledge for health care improvement. *Yearbook of Medical Informatics*, 2000(1), 65–70.

Barfield, S., Dobson, C., Gaskill, R. and Perry, B.D. (2012). Neurosequential Model of Therapeutics in a therapeutic preschool: Implications for work with children with complex neuropsychiatric problems. *International Journal of Play Therapy*, 21(1), 30–44.

Brandt, K., Diel, J., Feder, J. and Lillas, C. (2012). A problem in our field. *Zero to Three*, 32(4), 42–45.

Bruns, E.J., Walker, J.S., Zabel, M., Matarese, M. *et al.* (2010). Intervening in the lives of youth with complex behavioural health challenges and their families: The role of the wraparound process. *American Journal of Community Psychology*, 46(3–4), 314–331.

De Nooyer, K.M. and Lingard, M. (2016). Applying principles of the Neurosequential Model of Therapeutics across an adolescent day program and inpatient unit. *Australasian Psychiatry*, 25(2), 150–153.

Draper, N.R. (1987). *Empirical Model-Building and Response Surfaces*. New York, NY: Wiley.

Gaskill, R.L. and Perry, B.D. (2017). A Neurosequential Therapeutics Approach to Guided Play, Play Therapy, and Activities for Children Who Won't Talk. In C.A. Malchiodi and D.A. Crenshaw (eds), *What to Do When Children Clam Up in Psychotherapy: Interventions to Facilitate Communication*. New York, NY: Guilford Press.

Grove, T. (2012). Outcomes from a pilot project examining the NMT in a residential treatment center. Report to Shaw Foundation (NMT Grant to St. Aemelian-Lakeside), Milwaukee, WI.

Hambrick, E., Brawner, T. and Perry, B.D. (2018). Examining developmental adversity and connectedness in child welfare-involved children. *Children Australia*, 43(2), 105–115. doi:10.1017/cha.2018.21.

Hambrick, E., Brawner, T., Perry, B.D., Brandt, K., Hofeister, C. and Collins, J. (in press). Beyond the ACE Score: Examining relationships between timing of developmental adversity, relational health and developmental outcomes in children. *Archives of Psychiatric Nursing*.

Hambrick, E., Brawner, T., Perry, B.D., Wang, E. *et al.* (2018). Restraint and critical incident reduction following introduction of the Neurosequential Model of Therapeutics (NMT). *Residential Treatment for Children and Youth*, 35(1), 2–23.

Kleim, J.A. and Jones, T.A. (2008). Principles of experience-dependent neural plasticity: Implications for rehabilitation after brain damage. *Journal of Speech, Language and Hearing Research*, 51(1), 225–239.

LT Partners for Change (2018). *Arizona's Neurosequential Model in Caregiving Project: Webinar Survey Results*. Phoenix, AZ: Arizona Council of Human Service Providers.

Ludy-Dobson, C. and Perry, B.D. (2010). The Role of Healthy Relational Interactions in Buffering the Impact of Childhood Trauma. In E. Gil (ed.), *Working with Children to Heal Interpersonal Trauma*. New York, NY: Guilford Press.

McNally, E. and Ewing, B. (2018). A journey to calm: Utilizing the Neurosequential Model to effect school turn around. Presented at 3rd International Neurosequential Model Symposium, Banff, Canada.

Mears, S.L., Yaffe, J. and Harris, N.J. (2009). Evaluation of wraparound services for severely emotionally disturbed youths. *Research on Social Work Practice*, 19(6), 678–685.

Morris, Z.S., Wooding, S. and Grant, J. (2011). The answer is 17 years, what is the question: Understanding time lags in translational research. *Journal of the Royal Society of Medicine*, 104(12), 510–520.

Perry, B.D. (2006). The Neurosequential Model of Therapeutics: Applying Principles of Neuroscience to Clinical Work with Traumatized and Maltreated Children. In N. Boyd Webb (ed.), *Working with Traumatized Youth in Child Welfare*. New York, NY: Guilford Press.

Perry, B.D. (2009). Examining child maltreatment through a neurodevelopmental lens: Clinical application of the Neurosequential Model of Therapeutics. *Journal of Loss and Trauma*, 14(4), 240–255.

Perry, B.D. (2014). The Neurosequential Model of Therapeutics in Young Children. In K. Brandt, B.D. Perry, S. Seligman and E. Tronick (eds), *Infant and Early Childhood Mental Health: Core Concepts and Clinical Practice*. Washington, DC: American Psychiatric Press.

Perry, B.D. (2017). Trauma- and Stress-Related Disorders. In T.P. Beauchaine and S.P. Hinshaw (eds), *Textbook of Child and Adolescent Psychopathology*, 3rd Edition. New York, NY: Wiley.

Perry, B.D. and Dobson, C. (2013). Application of the Neurosequential Model (NMT) in Maltreated Children. In J. Ford and C. Courtois (eds), *Treating Complex Traumatic Stress Disorders in Children and Adolescents*. New York, NY: Guilford Press.

Perry, B.D. and Szalavitz, M. (2017). *The Boy Who Was Raised as a Dog: And Other Stories from a Child Psychiatrist's Notebook. What Traumatized Children Can Teach Us About Life, Loss and Healing*, Revised and Updated Edition. New York, NY: Basic Books.

Ryan, K., Lane, S.J. and Powers, D. (2017). A multidisciplinary model for treating complex trauma in early childhood. *International Journal of Play Therapy*, 26(2), 111–123.

Steinkopf, H., Bræin, M.K. and Nordanger, D.Ø. (2017). Kartlegging av barn med 'The Neurosequential Model of Therapeutics'. *Journal of the Norwegian Psychological Association* (Tidsskrift for Norsk Psykologforening), 10, 958–969.

Wang, E., Wilkes, T.C., Perry, B.D. and McMaster, F. (2015). Open trial of the Neurosequential Model of Therapeutics (NMT) approach in a clinical setting. 28th Annual Sebastian Littman Research Day, University of Calgary.

Wenger, E. (1998). *Communities of Practice: Learning, Meaning, and Identity*. Cambridge: Cambridge University Press.

Whyde, J. and Boldman-Buzard, J. (2017). *Building Better Lives: Promoting Healthy Children, Strong Families and Thriving Communities.* Columbus, OH: Franklin County Family and Children First Council.

Zarnegar, Z., Hambrick, E., Perry, B.D., Azen, S. and Peterson, A. (2016). Clinical improvements in adopted children with fetal alcohol spectrum disorders through neurodevelopmentally informed clinical interventions: A pilot study. *Clinical Child Psychology and Psychiatry*, 21(4), 551–567.

PRACTICE REFLECTION

Joe Tucci, Janise Mitchell and Ed Tronick

In his chapter, Perry has elegantly described the culmination of his pioneering work in developing the Neurosequential Model in its application in therapeutic, educational and care contexts. He raises a number of important principles that apply to the practice of Therapeutic Care.

The primary objective of this work is to help create therapeutic experiences that are sensitive to, and ultimately support, the developmental states across various domains of children's lived experiences. As such, it is critical to develop a detailed picture of the extent to which children are functioning at or below the expected developmental stage for their age. This enables the resources offered to children to match their developmental stage and rebuild the architecture of their internal systems in the sequence that should have occurred and which has been altered as a result of their experiences of abuse and neglect. Perry has been a major proponent of the view that many traumatised children, regardless of their age, require access to sensory-rich, repetitive, rhythmical opportunities as the starting point for intervention. This facilitates the stabilisation of lower-order brain regions such as the brainstem before moving on to more emotional and cognitive therapeutic forms.

As Badenoch (2018) has highlighted, rhythms are important to regulation individually and socially and it is not coincidental that there is a connection between the two.

> Our current culture has moved far away from the rhythms of communal life. At that time, the group came together throughout the day around the sound of corn being ground, the slap of clothes on rocks as they were washed, the rhythm of butter being churned. Babies were rocked in time with the tribe's life, and children often organised their games in harmony with these daily activities as well. (Badenoch, 2018, p.111)

Children's progression through their developmental stages cannot be fudged. If they miss out on those experiences at the time their internal systems were being recruited, they will benefit from going back and engaging with similar experiences, giving them the chance to make up for missing out. The neurobiological sequence of needs that underlies the development for children, in particular those who have suffered trauma in their young lives, cannot be left without it being respected, understood and resourced.

It is important to map the relational network around children and acknowledge how vital relational connections are to the transformation of children's trauma. Perry describes starting with a therapeutic web, those people with a vested and real interest in the well-being of the child. This is similar to the concept of the Care Team we introduced as a core element of Therapeutic Care practice. This web or team offers multiple points for children to experience their internal states in the present in different ways to what they have experienced in the past. This is why it is critical for Perry to ensure that each participant in the web understands the basic knowledge about child development, the impact of trauma and the strategies that can be used to support children's neurobiological functioning, independent of the context they share with children at school, home and/or while they are engaged in recreational activities or hobbies.

Highlighting relationships as key vehicles for recovery and change, Perry emphasises the critical need of Therapeutic Care to assess not only the needs and capacities of children but also those of the caregiver and other key relationships in the life of children and the interface between the two. Such an understanding both informs the resources available to children through these relationships and provides essential insights into the support needs of caregivers and children to build, strengthen and sustain these relationships.

Finally, Perry offers confirmation about the need to develop a comprehensive understanding of the child's lived experiences so that a unique plan can be pieced together that is matched specifically to her or his individually configured developmental and relational needs. It is a fundamental principle of Therapeutic Care that all children need to be treated uniquely, that plans should be tailored to their needs and that systems should be resourced to resist the temptation to describe and work with children in out-of-home care as if they were a homogenous population that share histories and features. They are not. Each is unique.

Reference

Badenoch, B. (2018). *The Heart of Trauma: Healing the Embodied Brain in the Context of Relationships*. New York, NY: W.W. Norton and Company.

7

Dabakan Kooyliny - Go Slowly, Walk Slowly, Walk Together

Culturally Strong Therapeutic Care for Aboriginal and Torres Strait Islander Children, Families and Communities

GLENDA KICKETT, SHAUN CHANDRAN AND JANISE MITCHELL

We would like to acknowledge the Elders – Doolann Leisha and Walter Eatts – for assisting with the Nyungah language and wording used in this chapter.

Introduction

Nyungah people have lived in the South West of Western Australia for more than 45,000 years. *Dabakan kooyliny* comes from Nyungah language meaning 'go slowly, walk slowly, walk together'. It is with this orientation that we come together to write this chapter. As authors we all come from different cultural backgrounds. Glenda is a Whadjuk and Ballardong Nyungah woman with many family and cultural connections throughout Nyungah country. Shaun is of Indian, Chinese, Thai and Portuguese ancestry, moving from Singapore to Australia as a young person. Janise is the daughter of British migrants who came to Australia after the Second World War. Together, we have a deep commitment to working alongside Aboriginal and Torres Strait Islander families, communities and organisations to respond to the needs of their children and young people in care.

Many Aboriginal and Torres Strait Islander children and young people live with experiences of trauma and disadvantage resulting from both the present day and as a consequence of the reverberating impacts of trauma experienced in families and communities over many generations as a result of colonisation and the continuing dispossession of their traditional communities, lands and cultures. They face considerable vulnerability across all socio-economic indicators, including entrenched poverty, housing and homelessness, education, law and justice, health and well-being, and are over-represented in the child protection and juvenile justice systems (Family Matters, 2017). Although they only make up 5.5% of all children aged 0–17 years in Australia (Australian Institute of Health and Welfare (AIHW), 2018b), Aboriginal and Torres Strait Islander children are almost ten times more likely than non-Indigenous children to be placed in out-of-home care, making up 36.9% of all children in care (AIHW, 2018a, 2018b).

It is vital that Aboriginal and Torres Strait Islander children and young people who have experienced trauma have access to culturally strong, protective and therapeutic programs of support and care (Atkinson, 2013). In this chapter we will explore the impact of trauma on Aboriginal and Torres Strait Islander children, families and communities over many generations and the healing to be found in culture. Using these understandings, we will explore what children, families and their communities have taught us are important in the provision of culturally strong therapeutic care and its application in one approach to the provision of therapeutic kinship care for Aboriginal and Torres Strait Islander children and families.

Adopting a position of cultural humility

The chapter is written with cultural humility (Australian Childhood Foundation, 2019; Hook, 2013). Cultural competency has been a long-held ideal for organisations and practitioners in the social welfare services. However, definitions and approaches to cultural competency vary widely depending on worldview, discipline and practice context. Within social welfare and beyond, cultural competency has been challenged for its failure to account for the structural forces that shape individuals' and communities' experiences and opportunities.

In contrast, cultural humility does not focus on competence or confidence and recognises that the more you are exposed to cultures different from your own, the more you will realise how much you don't know about others. That is where humility comes in. Cultural humility involves humbly acknowledging oneself as a learner when it comes to understanding another's experience. It is defined not as a discrete end-point but as a commitment to lifelong learning, continuous self-reflection on one's own assumptions and practices (privilege is invisible to those who have it), comfort with 'not knowing', and recognition of the power/privilege imbalance that exists between service users and professionals. Cultural humility takes into account the fluidity of culture and challenges structural racism. This is the attitude we wish to encourage in all who work with children and families from cultures other than their own. Cultural humility builds mutual trust and respect and enables cultural safety.

Kaditj - Reflecting on the impact of colonisation and intergenerational trauma as a context for developing therapeutic approaches to care

Kaditj comes from Nyungah language meaning 'to reflect'. An understanding of the past is critical to understanding the present and creating the future.

Prior to colonisation, Aboriginal and Torres Strait Islander peoples, Australia's First Nations peoples, lived on mainland Australia and the islands of the Torres Strait long before time began, when the land and waters were being formed by the spirit beings who also gave specific instructions to the people to look after and care for the land and waters, and everything in it.

Aboriginal and Torres Strait Islander peoples were many and diverse across Australia, living in their language and clan groups within their own traditional lands, practising complex kinship and social systems which ensured the passing down of information in regard to language, dance and songs, country and places, family relationships, lore and law for behaviour and responsibilities, as well as stories about connection to and relationship with Mother Earth. Elders, who were the knowledge holders, watched over their family groups to ensure that everyone cared for each other through the interconnecting elements of family relationships, looked after places in country, told Creation and Dreaming stories, and participated in ceremonial songs and dances (Kickett, 2019).

From the settlement of traditional lands and waters by European colonisers, Aboriginal and Torres Strait Islander peoples felt the loss of their traditions, languages, family kinship and social systems, cultural knowledges and worldviews about relationships to and stories about country, family and cultural connections.

Since settlement, successive government policies have subjected Australia's First Nations peoples to practices that have sought to make decisions on behalf of and for them, to care for and protect them, to segregate and assimilate them to mainstream society. In doing so, these practices saw the removal of whole groups of families away from their traditional country to missions and reserves, forcibly removing children and young people from their families and country. The ongoing practices of removal of children from family and country are acknowledged as the Stolen Generations. These practices have impacted, and continue to impact, generations of families through the intergenerational transmission of trauma, with the inadequacy of state interventions creating dependencies and dysfunctions that have retraumatised our First Nations peoples (Atkinson, 2013).

Potently summarising the pervasive felt impacts today of these past practices on Aboriginal and Torres Strait Islander families and communities, McKendrick *et al.* (2013) noted:

> Today Aboriginal people are the most socioeconomically disadvantaged group in Australia and their health status is well below that of the general community, with an average life expectancy 10–20 years less than that of other Australians. Assimilationist policies such as the forced removal of Aboriginal children from their families have disrupted the fabric of Aboriginal family and community life. Aboriginal people are incarcerated up to 20 times more than the general Australian community, high school retention rates are many times lower and unemployment rates many times higher than for the general population. Chronic psychological distress has been shown to be associated with both longstanding environmental difficulties and intermittent acute stressors, such as physical illness in self and significant others, frequent bereavement, poverty and lack of educational opportunity. (p.12)

These impacts are widely understood as intergenerational trauma. Mu'id (2004) provides a conceptualisation of intergenerational trauma as being:

> the subjective experiencing and remembering of events in the mind of an individual or the life of a community, passed from adults to children in cyclic processes as 'cumulative emotional and psychological wounding'. (p.9)

Reflecting on the impacts of intergenerational trauma, Brokenleg (2012) suggested that it sculpts thinking and feelings, shapes social dynamics and impacts spirituality. Highlighting the perpetuating nature of trauma across families, communities and generations, Atkinson (2013) observed that the multiple layers of problems experienced in the present day, such as the prevalence of family violence, substance abuse, grief and loss, are now as much symptoms of past trauma as they are causes of traumatic stress in the present. The Aboriginal and Torres Strait Islander Healing Foundation Development Team (2009) took this notion further, suggesting:

> Where trauma is left unresolved, people can begin to internalise shame and guilt; and, in more severe and sustained cases, whole communities can begin to think that pain and chaos is normal. (p.4)

Giving consideration to the impact of intergenerational trauma on Aboriginal and Torres Strait Islander children and young people growing up today, Milroy (2005) summarises it well:

> The trans-generational effects of trauma occur via a variety of mechanisms including the impact on the attachment relationship with caregivers; the impact on parenting and family functioning; the association with parental physical and mental illness; disconnection and alienation from extended family, culture and society. These effects are exacerbated by exposure to continuing high levels of stress and trauma including multiple bereavements and other losses, the process of vicarious traumatisation where children witness the on-going effect of the original trauma which a parent or other family member has experienced. Even where children are protected from the traumatic stories of their ancestors, the effects of past traumas still impact on children in the form of ill health, family dysfunction, community violence, psychological morbidity and early mortality. (p.xxi)

Kaaditjn – The centrality of culture to Aboriginal and Torres Strait Islander peoples' well-being

Kaaditjn comes from Nyungah language meaning 'knowledge'. In a world increasingly driven by 'evidence', it is easy to lose sight of the powerful knowledge that sits within Aboriginal and Torres Strait Islander cultural practices which across many thousands of years have produced abiding evidence of 'what works' in bringing up safe, happy and strong children.

The application of cultural practices and reclaiming a sense of cultural identity is the key to alleviating the impacts of trauma, grief and loss. In this sense, Aboriginal culture is strength and acts as a protective force for children and families (Anderson *et al.*, 2017; Lohoar, Butera and Kennedy, 2014; Victorian Aboriginal Child Care Agency, 2013).

Culture is at the very core of the experience of living for Aboriginal people. Understanding the dynamics of culture is not just about seeing the 'tip' of the cultural identity 'iceberg' of food, dress, music, language and art, but is concerned with the more subtle ways in which culture impacts on how individuals and communities see and engage with the world (St. Onge, Cole and Petty 2003, as cited in Bamblett, Harrison and Lewis, 2010). It defines identify, beliefs and values, forms of communication and the ways in which relationships are formed and maintained. It is passed down the generations in the complexity of relationships, protocols, languages, social organisation and life experiences that bind diverse individuals, families and communities together. Culture is a living process. It changes over time to reflect the changed environments and social interactions of people living together (Atkinson, 2002). Aboriginal and Torres Strait Islander cultures have many elements which connect and interconnect children and young people to their family, extended family and country through language, stories, songs and dance. Aboriginal and Torres Strait Islander children and young people who can grow up strong in culture develop a sense of strength, confidence, pride, belonging, peace and security that has the potential to guide and protect them through adolescence and adulthood (Bamblett *et al.*, 2010).

Family is the cornerstone of Aboriginal culture. It is the set of relationships which transcend through the lifespan of Aboriginal people, giving birth to identity, knowledge, role and, ultimately, social meaning. With this in mind, Bamblett reminds us all of our collective responsibilities:

> Organisations must rise to the challenge of protecting their cultural identities. If we neglect this aspect of our children's best interests, we deny them the cultural and spiritual life that is their birth right. We also risk fundamentally damaging their wellbeing, growth, education and life prospects. Our children need to know their culture and for Aboriginal and Torres Strait Islander children, culture and family are inextricably linked. Culture and spirituality are part of the meaningful ways in which Aboriginal and Torres Strait Islander people interact with their families and communities and their land. There are no short cuts to keeping our children culturally and spiritually strong: maintaining connections to family and community is the only way. (cited in Commission for Children and Young People, 2013, p.21)

It is hard to conclude anything from this other than that for any therapeutic care program that accommodates Aboriginal and Torres Strait Islander children to be effective, it must be grounded in the resources that emanate from cultural ways of living and relating. As holders of cultural knowledge, it is essential that Aboriginal families and communities participate fully in the development and implementation of these programs – the ways it is to be interpreted, the ways it is to be accessed and how it might be brought to bear on problems that are experienced by children, families and communities.

'I keep my tears in my heart' - Culturally strong approaches to therapeutic care

'I keep my tears in my heart' are the words of a young boy living with his sibling in the care of their grandmother. Over time he slowly told us the story of himself, his brother and his family. We learned about the meanings his experiences had generated for him. We talked about meaning-making for the parts of his story that he had not yet been able to make sense of, and slowly he found shared meanings with his brother, grandmother and family. Our work with this family and many others like them taught us much about what is helpful through stories, deep listening and the power of connection.

The Aboriginal and Torres Strait Islander Healing Foundation Development Team (2009) argued for the need for services to not focus on symptoms, as has happened in the past, but on the causes of trauma. It also suggested the need for a wider shift in perceptions around trauma and healing, noting the critical need for the integration of cultural and trauma-informed healing approaches. There is wide agreement that the best approach is a combined approach – a Western approach and a traditional cultural approach with a significant focus on understanding the intersection between Western and traditional understandings of trauma and well-being (Aboriginal and Torres Strait Islander Social Justice Commissioner, 2008; McCoy, 2008). This is often referred to as the third cultural space (Davis, 2008, as cited in Department of Education and Training, 2010). In the third cultural space the Western and Aboriginal systems are acknowledged and valued equally, and the overlapping and merging of views represents a new way of doing things.

Healing through trauma-informed, cultural approaches addresses the whole health and well-being of Aboriginal and Torres Strait Islander children and young people, not only their social and emotional well-being, but in building the capacity of their families and communities to respond to their needs and to raise them healthy and strong in culture. Leading Aboriginal mental health practitioner Helen Milroy (as cited by the Aboriginal and Torres Strait Islander Healing Foundation Development Team, 2009) conceptualised healing in this way:

> Healing gives us back to ourselves. Not to hide or fight anymore. But to sit still, calm our minds, listen to the universe and allow our spirits to dance on the wind. It lets us enjoy the sunshine and be bathed by the golden glow of the moon as we drift into our dreamtime. Healing ultimately gives us back to our country. To stand once again in our rightful place, eternal and generational. (p.16)

She goes on to say:

> Healing is not just about recovering what has been lost or repairing what has been broken. It is about embracing our life force to create a new and vibrant fabric that keeps us grounded and connected,

wraps us in warmth and love and gives us the joy of seeing what we have created. Healing keeps us strong and gentle at the same time. It gives us balance and harmony, a place of triumph and sanctuary forevermore. (p.22)

Conceptual Framework

Using these ideas, we propose a conceptual framework for a culturally strong approach to practice in therapeutic care (see Figure 7.1 and the sections below). The framework comprises the overlapping themes of 'Connection', 'Deep Listening' and 'Stories'. It is underpinned by an understanding of the impact of trauma in the present and across generations, and privileges Aboriginal and Torres Strait Islander ways of knowing and being.

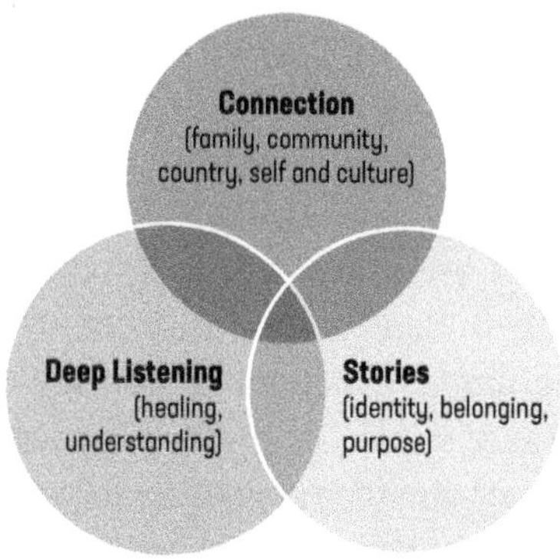

Figure 7.1 Conceptual framework for a culturally strong approach to practice in therapeutic care

Connection

The theme of connection is a central premise underpinning both cultural ways of knowing and being and the ways in which the impact of trauma in the lives of children, young people and their carers and families is understood and responded to. Linking concepts of connection and safety, Aboriginal young people themselves identify relationships across their families and communities, including the important role of Elders, and connection to culture as central to their experience of safety (Aboriginal Child, Family and Community Care State Secretariat, 2017).

Aboriginal and Torres Strait Islander cultures view the individual as living and being in relationship with the family, the community, the land and the spiritual beings of the Dreaming. It is inherently interrelational and interdependent. The intergenerational trauma arising from the practices of colonisation had the profound impact of dislocating, fragmenting and disintegrating these important connections.

Complex trauma is viewed as having a disintegrative and isolating impact on the developmental trajectories of children and young people. Critically, prolonged exposure to toxic stress and trauma, as described in detail by numerous authors (Atkinson, 2002, 2013; Badenoch, 2018; Hughes, 2015; Porges, 2014; van der Kolk, 2014), separates children from relationships of care and support that foster connection and belonging, support healthy physical, emotional and psychological development, and enable the emergence of a strong sense of identity.

Responding to the needs of Aboriginal and Torres Strait Islander children in care must integrate an understanding of what may be happening in the family and community context. Importantly, in recognising the ongoing consequences of intergenerational trauma, effective therapeutic care for children and young people can only occur with concurrent engagement of and support for their carers and families to heal from their own experiences of dislocation and trauma (SNAICC, 2005). Adopting such a stance generates ways of understanding and working that are non-judgemental, less stigmatising and more compassionate. Metaphors of integration and connection are viewed within the conceptual framework as key outcomes for children, young people and their carers and families, with relationships being the key site of intervention. Children and families need to be connected to each other and their communities, culture and lands in order first to survive and then to thrive.

The experience of appropriate, supportive adult–child relational exchanges is instrumental to the well-being of all children and often more challenging to achieve for traumatised children. The trauma-based behaviours and needs of the children can be overwhelming for carers, often triggering their own trauma. These relationships require sensitive, attuned support from a trusted other who can hold the safety of each person and build a sense of confidence and hope in the relationship. However, trust is undermined by trauma. Relationships can become in themselves the sites of tension and distress. The building of trust takes time. As practitioners providing support to carers and children, it is important to remain cognisant of both the power imbalance that exists between ourselves and families and the meaning this holds for the children, carers and the family. We must enact an approach that aims to build connection through *dabakan kooyliny* – to go slowly, walk slowly – and walk together with respect, building trust, shared understandings and shared ambitions for the children at the centre of our collective concern. Developing an effective partnership takes time. For most Aboriginal and Torres Strait Islander people, who you are is more important than the role you play (Kickett, 2019).

Aboriginal and Torres Strait Islander cultures are collective cultures with all family members holding important cultural obligations and responsibilities. It is critical to understand the places held in the kinship system by both the carer and the child and their sets of obligations and responsibilities to other family members. Children may hold concurrent roles and responsibilities of sibling, cousin and aunt/uncle depending on their place in the kinship system, each coming with unique roles to play in the enactment of cultural practices and the passing on of stories. It is important that children are provided with opportunities to enact their place in the kinship system. Equally, it is important to understand the obligations and responsibilities of the carer within the broader family group. The carer will likely hold a range of responsibilities across two generations that can have significant impacts on their capacity to care for a child in formal care. They will also hold obligations and responsibilities to care for other family members that may, at times, place additional strain or burden on the carer, or create significant levels of tension and stress. Understanding the family connections, obligations and responsibilities within the kinship group is critical to effective practice with children, carers and families.

Within the kinship system also come a range of potential resources for children and carers as a result of the shared responsibilities for raising and educating children that sit within the kinship group. It is important to understand the broader family system that sits around the child and family to develop ways of building an inclusive network of care and support around the child and the carer, to understand what each person is able to bring to promote a positive outcome, address areas of tension, and to draw on the collective wisdom and capacity of these networks to address the challenges which may threaten the stability of the placement and the safety and well-being of the child and the carer. Family meetings are a useful mechanism for creating shared understanding and a network of support around the child and carer. This is based on the view that:

- extended families know their members best and are usually the best sources of expertise on what should be done for their children
- children are usually best cared for within their extended kin network
- extended families can create the sort of therapeutic conditions necessary for supporting connection, belonging and the building of identity
- generating greater family ownership of the plan and building their capacity to develop lasting solutions are more likely to be effective and sustainable.

Kaadininy – *Deep listening and learning*

Kaadininy comes from Nyungah language meaning 'listening and learning'. Connected to listening and learning are other words that have meaning – hearing, thinking and understanding – which provide instructions for how we listen to stories and learn the meanings in them to work appropriately with Aboriginal and Torres Strait Islander peoples (Kickett, 2019). Brearley (2010) described deep listening as tuning in to the stories, the silences and the spaces in between, drawing on many senses beyond what is heard. She suggests deep listening can be applied as a way of being together, in connection with each other.

The words and meanings tell us how to listen and learn, to hear the stories and to find in the stories the ways we are to communicate with each other and relate to one another which are intertwined and connected. The listening involves hearing, thinking and understanding to follow cultural protocol, respect people and relationships, and know how to look after country. The thinking and doing is about how to relate to each other and the world around us, and is a process to build relationships, be respectful and work in cultural ways (Kickett, 2019).

To listen with an open heart and ears and closed mouth is also to listen when no one is talking and hearing the silence. It communicates to the person, 'I have heard you and your story,' and is saying, 'In listening and talking to you, I am learning from you. I learned about your culture, who you are, who your people are and where you come. I have learned your story is important because you have shared stories of sad times and happy times and challenges you have overcome and you have told me about your culture' (Kickett, 2019).

Through deep listening we are able to learn about:

- the ways in which the past experiences of parents/carers continue to reverberate into the present
- the strengths within the family that acted as resources for parents/carers in the past which may be helpful to their current challenges
- the ways in which parents/carers, children and other family members frame the needs of the children
- the intentions that the parents/carers, children and other family members continue to hold for themselves and their children.

We must sensitively hear and validate the experiences that children, carers and families want to share about their experiences. We also attend to the steps that carers engage in to protect themselves and their loved ones from the challenges they face and meet the range of needs that family members have. Through this process of deep listening, we are able to offer attuned interpersonal resources to the carer, child and family with whom we are speaking to support their arousal regulation. It acknowledges their pain and provides the carer, child and family with the experience that they are not alone in facing their challenges. This joining is the first step in building coalitions of commitment to work together towards a common goal.

Deep listening orients us to trying to understand the deeper meaning of the trauma or difficulties that the family is experiencing. This is the key to effective engagement. Deep listening seeks to engage carers and families in processes of reflection and thoughtful interactions that help to develop joint understanding of their children's needs and support them to meet those needs meaningfully and sustainably over time.

The healing power of stories

Storytelling is an oral tradition which many cultures and peoples around the world have used to tell their own mythological stories and legends and to communicate information from one person to another, from one generation to another (Kickett, 2019). Reflecting its importance, Atkinson (2007) suggested:

> Storytelling is in our life force. We think in story form, speak in story form to bring meaning to our lives through story. (p.224)

Storytelling links the past to the present and future, which is a continuum of all things from Dreaming stories and our lived experiences and knowledges of country, family and community (Kickett, 2019). Lawrence Bamblett, a Wiradjuri Koori man, in his study of the oral history of his family at Erambie mission in New South Wales, states that stories often focus on fulfilling the important task of establishing and maintaining connections to the past, connections to people and places – what Elder Norma calls 'the anchor of the strength of your identity, or who you are' (Bamblett, 2013, p.50).

Building relationships and finding commonalities is done through the telling of stories. Through the telling of stories, Aboriginal and Torres Strait Islander people from different traditional lands find common connection, setting protocols and processes for working together, building mutual respect for each other and their cultures and histories while recognising their shared story of colonisation.

Stories are based in cultural ways of connecting through family and kinship relationships and to country. The telling of story is about placing oneself in a place and time in country and about family and country, Dreaming and Creation. The cultural information is shared to talk and reflect on our common cultural elements about family, country, our belonging, who we are and where we belong, our past and our present. In Indigenous storytelling, stories are not straight-line stories because Indigenous people tell stories which move from one situation and one place to another, for 'we go all the way around' (Bamblett, 2013).

It is important to allow people collectively to tell and to make sense of their own stories, thereby allowing them to become experts of their stories and lives (Atkinson, 2013). Kirmayer *et al.* (2011) have researched the contribution to resilience of 'stories of identity and transformation at personal and collective levels'. They continue:

> The idea that resilience might reside in the ways we have of narrating our lives…making sense of their own predicaments and mapping possibilities for adaptation and a positive vision of the identity and future prospects by drawing on collective history, myths and sacred teachings. At the same time, these collective forms of narratives serve not only to help people make sense of their experience and construct a valued identity but also ensure the continuity and vitality of a community or a people. (pp.85–86)

In other words, strategies which aim to strengthen resilience focus on finding shared meaning across different members of a family or community about what has helped that family or community to survive and attempt to hold on to its values, beliefs, rituals and relationships, often in the face of overwhelming forces that have sought to destroy them. The modality used is collective dialogue, or yarning. Its purpose is to unearth symbolic and historical practices that have maintained people's connection to their cultural heritage. It is this common quality that is viewed as being the most significant factor in moving a community along a continuum from oppression to resistance to resilience (Tucci *et al.*, 2017).

Bacon (2013) paralleled the narrative approach to practice with the intrinsic storytelling traditions of Aboriginal and Torres Strait Islander people. She highlighted how facilitating conversations with Aboriginal and Torres Strait Islander people about the stories of themselves, their family and their community re-engaged them with their cultural heritage. It opened up the topic of how their culture had acted as a strength to resist the oppressions of colonisation. It also invited reflection on the relationships which have resourced them to survive in the face of such loss, trauma and grief.

Highlighting the significance of narratives and stories and the impact of trauma in the telling of these stories, White (2006, cited in Tucci *et al.*, 2017) reflected:

> No-one is a passive recipient of trauma. People always take steps in endeavouring to prevent the trauma they are subject to, and, when preventing this trauma is clearly impossible, they take steps to try and modify it in some way or modify its effects on their lives. These steps contribute to the preservation of, and are founded upon, what people hold precious. Even in the face of overwhelming trauma, people take steps to try to protect and preserve what they give value to. (p.28)

Drawing on White's approach, it is important to listen both to the stories of trauma and the stories of struggle and resistance in the face of trauma that hold on to conviction, belief, hope and value. As people reconnect with the story that preserved them, their family and their community, they come to see themselves with intent and power, rather than at the mercy of further harm and trauma in their lives (Tucci *et al.*, 2017).

Finding a shared language to negotiate how meaning is ascribed to experience is an important element of working effectively with Aboriginal and Torres Strait Islander people. It is critical to find the language of the child, carer and family that helps to shape the meaning of interactions which connect and disconnect people from each other. The aim is to find and engage with moments of affinity or interpersonal experiences of connection that generate understanding, mutuality, belonging, strength and hope (Tucci *et al.*, 2017).

Aboriginal and Torres Strait Islander people have strengths and resources for their own empowerment. Through storytelling comes the ability to focus on identifying, mobilising and honouring the resources, assets, wisdom and knowledge that every child, family or community has. The strengths approach demands practitioners to adopt a different way of looking at individuals, families and communities. Everyone must be seen in the light of their capacities, talents, competencies, possibilities, visions, values and hopes, however dashed and distorted these may have become through circumstance, oppression and trauma. The strengths approach requires an accounting of what people know and what they can do, however underdeveloped that may sometimes seem. Individuals' strengths are recognised, built on and validated, and new skills are developed as needed (strengths include personal qualities, traits, talents, virtues, interests and the person's knowledge of the world around them), which will build a strong platform for recovery from adverse experiences and trauma. Through deep listening and storytelling, practitioners take the time to identify these qualities and build on them, rather than focusing on the correction of skills, deficits or weaknesses. Strength-based principles do not deny shortcomings in family dynamics or individual motivation, knowledge and skills. Instead, they acknowledge that relational practice which rediscovers and amplifies strengths in families that have become less accessible over time because of the family's experiences of problems is the most effective way to engage and lead sustained change aiming to improve care outcomes for children.

Lessons from practice: The Woon-yah Ngullah Goorlanggass Program

Woon-yah Ngullah Goorlanggass comes from Nyungah language meaning 'caring for our children'. Developed using the framework described above, the Woon-yah Ngullah Goorlanggass Program is a therapeutic kinship care program developed by the Australian Childhood Foundation in partnership with Aboriginal and Torres Strait Islander children, young people and their families who are under the care of child protection services.

In their research with Aboriginal kinship carers, Kiraly and Humphreys (2011) found that the overwhelming theme from survey respondents was the lack of support available to them. Among other issues, they felt that they lacked information about entitlements, financial assistance, assistance with housing, counselling and help for distressed children, and information about responding to children's trauma. They described significant stress put on families and relationships. They concluded:

> The acute unmet support needs of kinship carers are nowhere seen as vividly as in the Aboriginal community, where larger numbers of children are being cared for by carers living in strained circumstances. As carers age and young children turn into teenagers,

> providing adequate support will become critical if the wellbeing of both children and their families is to be assured, and further family breakdown avoided. (p.34)

The lack of access to basic supports – financial, adequate housing, transport – was not uncommon for the families with whom we worked. It was not uncommon for a grandmother to be caring for up to six of her 'grannies' at once in housing that had only two bedrooms, to be walking an hour both morning and afternoon to take young children to school as a result of having no car big enough to transport them all around, or to worry about how she was going to make the money last.

The aim of the program was to deliver a culturally responsive, trauma-informed model of therapeutic care for the children and young people who were in the child protection and/or juvenile justice systems living with their kinship carers. The kinship carers referred to the program were mainly grandparents and great-grandparents to the children and young people in their care. They also regularly cared for other family members as part of their role in the kinship system. Referrals to the program came from the statutory child protection service and involved kinship placements that were facing high levels of stress and need, facing multiple challenges both in relation to basic physical needs and within their sets of relationships. Their relationship with formal systems of support (health and welfare services) was also commonly identified as a major source of stress. Despite previous attempts to support the carers using formal systems of support, many placements were still at risk of breaking down, with both carers and previous services referring to the limited helpfulness of the services offered.

Using the conceptual framework for a culturally strong approach to practice in therapeutic care outlined above, the program moved away from the traditional foster care approach that dominates kinship care support in Australia. In what we view as a paradigm shift within the formal system of child welfare and child protection in Western Australia where the program operated, we took a broader view of the relationships of care and support in the lives of the children and families with whom we worked. Consistent with a culturally strong approach, we included all the relationships of influence in the lives of the family and sought to understand their stories and collective shared meanings and collaborative ways of meeting the needs of the children, carers and family members. As such, we conceptualised the work of the program in understanding the stories of the child, the kinship carer, the child's parents and the broader family and community story, as depicted in Figure 7.2.

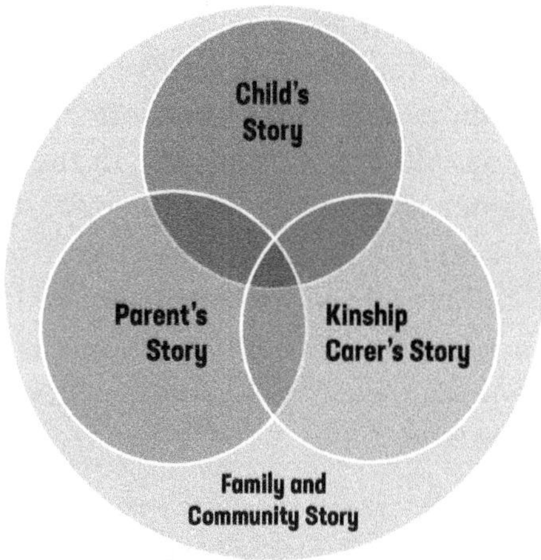

Figure 7.2 The sites of intervention for the Woon-yah Ngullah Goorlanggass Program

The program brought together these stories, listening for meanings, words and shared points of connection that could build into a shared story with a new meaning and opportunity for healing and recovery. The community story was inclusive of the formal and informal relationships and systems of support around the child, carer and family. Most often the stories held by formal systems of support (health and welfare services) were incomplete and often problem-focused to the exclusion of the strengths in the collective stories.

> Thank you for listening to me, hearing my story and walking with me to understand what is happening for my boys. (Kinship Carer in the Woon-yah Ngullah Goorlanggass Program)

Over time, through engaging and listening to their stories, we built relationships and trust in each other within which the carers, children and families felt safe. Through deep listening to the stories of the carers, we supported self-reflection on their own histories of trauma, resilience and strengths. They were enabled to use their own stories as a way of understanding their current relationships with family members and the needs of the children and young people in their care. Through the telling and re-telling of the stories, the carers and families were supported to get to know their children 'from the inside out'. They became more aware of the meanings behind the behaviours that challenged them and the needs they represented. They drew on their own knowledge of culture to shape their responses to children. They became more aware of their own triggers and were more able to be compassionate and responsive to changes in mood and levels of distress in their children. They developed confidence in knowing how to support the children to find calm and to find calmness in themselves. They learned how to motivate the children, to build opportunities for fun and play that is shared. They helped the children navigate novel and difficult situations with others in their life about which they expressed uncertainty and anxiety.

> You listened to my story, and there are many sad times in my life… But I love caring for these kids, they make me laugh. (Kinship Carer in the Woon-yah Ngullah Goorlanggass Program)

The families identified other family members that were important to the child and carers, those that were an actual or potential resource and support, and others that were a cause for concern in the family, often causing additional layers of stress and anxiety. The program found family members deemed safe and providing or able to provide support together in shared conversations about the needs of the child and carer, cooperatively planning to better resource and support the placement. Coalitions were built with family members to address issues of safety and protection. Relationships with family members were strengthened in the development of collective approaches to the care and support of the child.

> They built a good relationship with us. They really understood where our family was coming from…they really understood how things worked within our family. They didn't judge on us but worked with us. They found out our needs and wants. They asked 'How can we help you?' instead of saying 'I am coming here to help you.' They didn't presume what we wanted. (Kinship Carer in the Woon-yah Ngullah Goorlanggass Program)

Critical to the work of the program was its multi-systemic approach which also became its advocacy role within the formal systems of support and protection that surrounded the family, seeking to empower and give voice to the carers and families, often rendered silent by decision-making processes that had excluded them with outcomes that were not viewed by the families as culturally strong and safe. This, sadly, was at times the most challenging part of the work. Through active advocacy and the support of carers to express their views, we sought to shape case planning and other decision-making processes by ensuring that the cultural and familial context was well understood within these processes.

Through the trust in the program staff and empowered by the experience of feeling listened to, understood and validated, the carers and family felt more empowered and confident to advocate on their own behalf with the statutory child protection system with regard to the needs of the children and young people.

> If you've got no trust, you've got no relationship. They were easy to talk to. I can sit back and have a yarn like they are my family. They acknowledged us. They were there for us. They supported us all the way through. (Kinship Carer in the Woon-yah Ngullah Goorlanggass Program)

The capacity of the formal systems to adapt their approach to be more inclusive of the carers' voices, knowledge and wisdom was varied and largely dependent on the individual child protection case workers. This experience taught us much about the need to lay the foundations for programs that sit outside of the dominant paradigm.

> They spent a lot of time with the grandmother helping her make sense of her life. I have learnt a lot from them about the value of being able to slow down a bit and make time for how important it is to not just listen to our kinship carers but to really hear them. (Child Protection Worker for children in the Woon-yah Ngullah Goorlanggass Program)

Although highly regarded by the child protection system, on reflection we might have experienced greater success in collaborative and inclusive practice had we engaged in more preparatory steps with the child protection system to better understand the barriers and opportunities that were faced collectively and how at a systemic level these might have been overcome.

The multi-systemic approach of the program also included engagement with the schools of the children, as educational placements were often also at risk. The program worked with carers to support the school to develop a consistent approach to addressing the needs of the children across the home and school environments. This support was greatly welcomed by the schools involved.

Conclusion

The impact of colonisation has undermined Aboriginal and Torres Strait Islander cultures, family structures and systems of relationships to land and people, but it has not been destroyed. Traditions that were passed down from one generation to another are deep sources of strength and healing. We have proposed a model of culturally strong practice and its application which we believe holds great promise in improving the lives of Aboriginal and Torres Strait Islander children in care and their carers, families and communities. Through deep listening to children, carers and families, we have found the healing and power in stories which have given voice to the experiences of carers and their own trauma, and enabled them to make meaning of those experiences so they can build connection to self, family, community, land and culture, and support the child or young person to commence their healing.

Although this chapter has explored an approach to therapeutic care with Aboriginal and Torres Strait Islander children, carers and families, we believe that the underpinning principles and concepts in the approach are translatable to people from many cultural backgrounds. They are the elements that are universally valued by people from many cultures and traditions. As such, we encourage you to think about the application of these ideas and the resources that emerge in the often overlooked meanings that can be drawn from shared histories, traditions and practices of knowing and belonging.

References

Aboriginal Child, Family and Community Care State Secretariat (2017). *Youth Report: AbSec Youth Ambassador Program*. Sydney: AbSec.

Aboriginal and Torres Strait Islander Healing Foundation Development Team (2009). *Voices from the Campfires: Establishing the Aboriginal and Torres Strait Islander Healing Foundation*. Canberra: ATSIHF.

Aboriginal and Torres Strait Islander Social Justice Commissioner (2008). *Social Justice Report*. Canberra: Australian Human Rights Commission.

Anderson, P., Bamblett, M., Bessarab, D., Bromfield, L. *et al.* (2017). *Aboriginal and Torres Strait Islander Children and Child Sexual Abuse in Institutional Settings*. Report for the Royal Commission into Institutional Responses to Child Sexual Abuse, Sydney.

Atkinson, J. (2002). *Trauma Trails: The Transgenerational Effects of Trauma in Indigenous Australia*. North Melbourne: Spinifex Press.

Atkinson, J. (2013). Trauma-informed services and trauma-specific care for Indigenous Australian children. Resource sheet no. 21. Closing the Gap Clearinghouse, Canberra.

Atkinson, R. (2007). The Life Story Interview as a Bridge in Narrative Inquiry. In D. Jean Clandinin (ed.), *Handbook of Narrative Inquiry, Mapping Methodology*. Thousand Oaks, CA: SAGE Publications.

Australian Childhood Foundation (2019). *Reconciliation Action Plan*. Melbourne: Australian Childhood Foundation.

Australian Institute of Health and Welfare (2018a). *Child Protection Australia 2016–2017* (Child Welfare Series No. 68). Canberra: AIHW.

Australian Institute of Health and Welfare (2018b). *Child Protection Australia 2016–17*. Supplementary data tables. Canberra: AIHW.

Bacon, V. (2013). Yarning and Listening: Yarning and Learning through Stories. In B. Bennett, S. Green, S. Gilbert and D. Bessarab (eds), *Our Voices: Aboriginal and Torres Strait Islander Social Work*. South Yarra: Palgrave Macmillan.

Badenoch, B. (2018). *The Heart of Trauma: Healing the Embodied Brain in the Context of Relationships*. New York, NY: W.W. Norton and Company.

Bamblett, L. (2013). *Our Stories are Our Survival*. Canberra: Aboriginal Studies Press.

Bamblett, M., Harrison, J. and Lewis, P. (2010). Proving culture and voice works: Towards creating the evidence base for resilient Aboriginal and Torres Strait Islander children in Australia. *International Journal of Child and Family Welfare*, 13(1–2), 98–113.

Brearley, L. (2010). *Gulpa Ngawal Indigenous Deep Listening*. Melbourne: Royal Melbourne Institute of Technology.

Brokenleg, M. (2012). Transforming culture into resilience. *Reclaiming Children and Youth*, 21(3), 9–13.

Commission for Children and Young People (2013). *Residential Care Matters: A Resource for Residential Care Workers, Supervisors and Managers Caring for Young People*. Melbourne: Commission for Children and Young People.

Department of Education and Training (2010). *Embedding Aboriginal and Torres Strait Islander Perspectives in Schools: A Guide for School Learning Communities*. Brisbane: Department of Education and Training.

Family Matters (2017). *The Family Matters Report 2017: Measuring Trends to Turn the Tide on the Over-Representation of Aboriginal and Torres Strait Islander Children in Out-of-Home Care in Australia*. Melbourne: SNAICC.

Hook, J. (2013). Cultural humility: Measuring openness to culturally diverse clients. *Journal of Counseling Psychology*, 60(3), 353–366.

Hughes, D.A. (2015). The complex journey of traumatised children: Discovering safety in order to experience comfort, joy and self-discovery. *Children Australia*, 40(2), 147–151.

Kickett, G. (2019). Picking everlastings: A story to listen and learn. PhD Thesis (submitted), School of Social Work, University of Western Australia, Perth.

Kiraly, M. and Humphreys, C. (2011). *'It is the Story of All of Us': Learning from Aboriginal Communities about Supporting Family Connection* (Family Links: Kinship Care and Family Contact Research Series Report 2). Melbourne: Office of the Child Safety Commissioner and University of Melbourne.

Kirmayer, L.J., Dandeneau, S., Marshall, E., Kahentonni Phillips, M. and Jessen Williamson, K. (2011). Rethinking resilience from indigenous perspectives. *Canadian Journal of Psychiatry*, 56(2), 84–91.

Lohoar, S., Butera, N. and Kennedy, E. (2014). Strengths of Australian Aboriginal cultural practices in family life and child rearing. CFCA Paper No. 25, Australian Institute of Family Studies.

McCoy, B. (2008). *Holding Men: Kanyirninpa and the Health of Aboriginal Men*. Canberra: Aboriginal Studies Press, AIATSIS.

McKendrick, J., Brooks, R., Hudson, J., Thorpe, M. and Bennett, P. (2013). *Aboriginal and Torres Strait Islander Healing Programs: A Literature Review*. Canberra: Healing Foundation.

Milroy, H. (2005). Preface. Restoring Life and Spirit: Recovery from Trauma. In J.A. De Maio, S.R. Zubrick, S.R. Silburn, D.M. Lawrence, F.G. Mitrou and R.B. Dalby (eds), *Western Australian Aboriginal Child Health Survey: The Social and Emotional Wellbeing of Aboriginal Children and Young People*. Perth: Curtin University of Technology and Telethon Institute of Child Health Research.

Mu'id, O. (2004) '...Then I lost my spirit': An analytic essay on transgenerational trauma theory as applied to oppressed people of color nations. Masters Thesis, State University of New York, Stony Brook, NY. Accessed on 3/1/2019 at http://independent.academia.edu/OnajeMuid.

Porges, S.W. (2014). *The Pocket Guide to the Polyvagal Theory – The Transformative Power of Feeling Safe*. New York, NY: W.W. Norton and Company.

SNAICC (2005). *Achieving Stable and Culturally Strong Out of Home Care for Aboriginal and Torres Strait Islander Children*. Melbourne: Secretariat of National Aboriginal and Islander Child Care.

Tucci, J., Mitchell, J., Lindeman, M., Shilton, L. and Green, J. (2017). *Strengthening Community Capacity to End Violence: A Project for NPY Women's Council*. Alice Springs: NPY Women's Council and Australian Childhood Foundation.

van der Kolk, B.A. (2014). *The Body Keeps the Score: Brain, Mind, and Body in the Healing of Trauma*. New York, NY: Viking.

Victorian Aboriginal Child Care Agency (2013). Cultural Strengthening Programs. Accessed on 3/1/2019 at www.vacca.org/services/strengthening-culture.

White, M. (2006). Working with People Who Are Suffering the Consequences of Multiple Trauma: A Narrative Perspective. In D. Denborough (ed.), *Trauma: Narrative Responses to Traumatic Experience*. Adelaide: Dulwich Centre Publications.

PRACTICE REFLECTION

Joe Tucci, Janise Mitchell and Ed Tronick

> The word *safe*, both in the sense of being within the lore and in the sense of being cared for, is vital in well-being for Aboriginal individuals and groups. The experience of safety determines all the other factors of well-being. We know ourselves as strong, happy, knowledgeable, social responsible people when we are in a safe environment, cared for and caring for others. Lore is clear rules and boundaries. Lore provides a structure for proper behaviour, and creates a sense of safety. When we know lore we know how to behave towards others. We also know how we can expect others to behave towards us. With the impacts of colonisation, the world became unsafe... In traumatised populations, lore collapses. (Atkinson, 2002, p.45)

Atkinson highlights how inextricably linked safety is with a worldview made real in culture and the practices of lore. To her, safety is found in the obligations and responsibilities that individuals share with each other in relation to their behaviour, the way they raise children, the way they tend to and manage their land, the connections they experience with their ancestors. Safety is at the heart of community relationships around children.

In their chapter, Kickett, Chandran and Mitchell emphasise how trust and safety are bedrock qualities of the relationships that support and offer healing to Aboriginal children being looked after by their kinship network. The practice of *Kaadininy* or 'listening and learning' is also similar to Atkinson's description of *Dadirri* as

> a knowledge and consideration of community and the diversity and unique nature that each individual brings to the community...a reflective non-judgemental consideration of what is being seen and heard; and, having learnt from the listening, a purposeful plan to act, with action informed by learning, wisdom and the informed responsibility that comes with knowledge. (Atkinson, 2002, p.16)

In this circular form of praxis, listening and acting with responsibility is at the heart of a culturally strong approach to Therapeutic Care. For people who have been dispossessed of their land and had their culture denied, giving voice and life to their stories of resistance, survival and strength, having them heard, understood and validated, is, in and of itself, a deeply embedded relational therapeutic process. The integration of an understanding of the pain of intergenerational trauma as it weaves through these stories provides additional resources for meaning-making and experiences of interdependence that allows hope to emerge. Helping kinship carers and the family network, with patience and openness, is an effective way to support Aboriginal children with the multiplicity of cultural, individual and relational needs they carry with them.

Reference

Atkinson, J. (2002). *Trauma Trails: The Transgenerational Effects of Trauma in Indigenous Australia*. North Melbourne: Spinifex Press.

8

Children in Kinship Care

Promoting Their Mental Health and Well-Being

ELAINE FARMER AND MEREDITH KIRALY

Introduction

Kinship care (where children are brought up by members of their extended family or friends) has a long history and is widely used in many countries, including Australia, New Zealand, the US and the UK. Although in each country the legal dispositions used and financial allowances (if any) vary, many issues for caregivers and children cross national boundaries.

The living circumstances of children in kinship care have a number of unique features which set them apart from children living with their parents or with non-kin foster carers. In this chapter we discuss these aspects of their lives and the implications for intervention and therapy.

Australia defines children in kinship care on care orders as being in statutory or formal kinship care. In the UK, children on care orders who are in a kinship care placement are described as being in kinship foster or formal care. In Australia 47% of all children in statutory care are currently in kinship care (AIHW, 2018). In the UK 17% of children in foster care were placed with relatives or friends in 2017 (Department for Education, 2017), but many children are instead placed with kinship carers under private law orders (e.g. Special Guardianship or Child Arrangement Orders). In this chapter we consider all children in kinship care whether under care orders, informally arranged, or placed, as in the UK, under a private law order.

Robust models of intervention to improve children's mental health and well-being specific to kinship care are fairly rare and usually broadly follow well-evaluated approaches to working with children in foster care. An example is the KEEP (Keeping Foster and Kinship Carers Supported) training programme for foster and kinship carers developed by the Oregon Social Learning Center in the US (Price *et al.* 2009). However, the foundation for any interventions needs to be a full awareness of a range of practice issues, some of which are shared with foster children and others of which are specific to (or greatly heightened in) kinship care.

There have been few large-scale kinship care research studies in Australia to date (e.g. Gibbons and Mason, 2003; Kiraly and Humphreys, 2016), although several relatively large Australian studies have focused on grandparent carers (COTA, 2003; Dunne and Kettler, 2008; Brennan *et al.*, 2013).

The authors will therefore draw in particular on two UK studies of kinship care which shed light on a number of key practice issues. The first was a study that included an analysis of census data from 2001 which showed the prevalence and characteristics of full-time care by relatives in the UK (Nandy *et al.*, 2011). This has since been updated by an analysis of the 2011 census data (Wijedasa, 2015). The second part of the study (Selwyn *et al.*, 2013) involved interviews with 80 informal kinship carers and 80 children they were raising aged 8–18. It used some standardised measures which enabled comparisons to be made with the general population. In this study, 61% of carers were grandparents, 20% were aunts and uncles, 13% were friends of the family or more distant relatives, and 6% were sibling carers. As informal kinship carers, these carers did not have an entitlement to financial or other support from the local authority.

The second of these studies (Wellard *et al.*, 2017) examined the experiences and outcomes of 53 young adults (aged 16–26) who had lived in kinship care for at least two years, and compared their outcomes with those of care leavers[1] and also their peers in the general population. All 53 young people were interviewed, as were most of their kinship carers. The General Health Questionnaire (GHQ) (Goldberg and Hillier, 1979) was used to determine the young people's psychosocial functioning, and the Parental Bonding

1 In the UK, the term 'care leavers' excludes children in formal kinship care.

Instrument was used to examine the parenting they felt they had received from their kinship carers (Parker, Tupling and Brown, 1979).

The chapter begins with some of the crucial features of kinship care. It is followed by a discussion of key issues for the children and their carers and implications for practice.

Key features of kinship care

Characteristics of kinship carers: Types of carers

Analysis of the 2011 population (census) data for England (Wijedasa, 2015) showed that half (51%) of the children were growing up with relatives in households headed by grandparents, and 23% were being raised in households headed by a sibling. The remainder were in households headed by another relative, such as an aunt, uncle or cousin. To date, Australia lacks comparable data (Kiraly, 2018). Typical research samples over-represent grandparent carers and under-represent sibling carers (Kiraly, 2015).

Kinship care in Indigenous and ethnic communities

In Australia, Indigenous children are ten times more likely than non-Indigenous children to be in out-of-home care (AIHW, 2018). In the UK, the prevalence rate of kinship care for black, Asian and minority ethnic children is twice the rate of white children (Wijedasa, 2015). In the US, African-American children are again disproportionately represented among those cared for by relatives (see e.g. Hegar and Scannapieco, 1999; Ehrle and Geen, 2002). The ethnic or Indigenous demographics of kinship carers can have an effect on predominant placement characteristics. For example, a high proportion of older lone African-American (and to a lesser extent Hispanic) grandmother carers in the US are on incomes below the poverty level (Hegar and Scannapieco, 1999), and high levels of poverty and deprivation are also seen among Indigenous Australian kinship carers (ABS, 2008; Brennan *et al.*, 2013; Kiraly, James and Humphreys, 2015). Important as these issues are, space prevents further discussion of them in this chapter.

Health

A considerable literature shows the poor health of many kinship carers, partly but not exclusively because many are grandparents (Wijedasa, 2015). In Selwyn *et al.*'s large qualitative study (2013) more than 70% of all the kin carers had a long-standing health condition or disability and over one-third (37%) of the carers' lives were restricted by pain (affecting all types of carers except siblings). Two-thirds of the carers were clinically depressed on the measure used, although only 27% had been diagnosed as such. These findings support previous research (Minkler *et al.*, 1997; Hughes *et al.*, 2007; Brennan *et al.*, 2013) showing that grandparent kinship carers were more likely to have poorer physical health and to be depressed than those without this caring responsibility.

Poverty

Wijedasa's (2015) population data analysis showed that in 2011 more than three-quarters (76%) of children being brought up by relatives were living in a deprived household (classified in terms of unemployment, low levels of education, poor health or overcrowded/shared housing). Selwyn *et al.* (2013) found that many informal carers lived in grinding poverty, reducing their quality of life. Similarly in Australia, kinship carers are known to experience significant levels of financial hardship (McHugh and Valentine, 2010; Brennan *et al.*, 2013). Carers' financial stress was often a *consequence* of caring for the kinship children – many had given up good jobs to take the children (see also Gautier and Wellard, 2012; Brennan *et al.*, 2013) or, in the case of retired carers, had only their pensions or limited savings to live on. Some carers pay substantial legal costs to secure the child's placement with them. Kinship families also often live in overcrowded conditions.

In Australia and the UK, care allowances (when they are made) are set at relatively low levels, and may be below those provided for children in non-kinship foster care. The majority of kinship children are not under a legal order and their (informal) carers will therefore not receive a care allowance (McHugh and Valentine, 2010; Nandy *et al.*, 2011; Wijedasa, 2015).

Kinship children: Exposure to adversities

Many children who move into kinship care (informal or formal) have been abused or neglected. For example, in Wellard *et al.*'s (2017) study, 66% of the children were thought by their carers to have been maltreated, and the figure in Selwyn *et al.*'s (2013) study was 88%.

In the UK, children in non-kin foster care and in kinship care have been found to be remarkably similar in terms of their characteristics and the kinds of adversities they have experienced prior to placement (Farmer and Moyers, 2008). That study found that similar proportions of children in both kinds of placement had parents who experienced domestic violence (52% both), had mental health difficulties (44% kin and 45% non-kin care) or had misused drugs or alcohol (60% kin and 51% non-kin care). Although there is as yet no definitive Australian comparison data, anecdotal evidence suggests that the Australian situation may be similar. Recent studies in the UK show that the proportion of children in kinship care because of parental misuse of drugs and alcohol is particularly high (68% in Wellard *et al.*, 2017); this proportion may be even higher in Australia (Patton, 2004).

Looked at overall, then, children enter kinship care having experienced a variety of adversities, and many grow up in poverty and with carers in poor health. Financial pressures can affect children's well-being by limiting access to recreational activities, educational opportunities and clothes and goods similar to other children (Hunt and Waterhouse, 2012).

Benefits of kinship care

In spite of the challenges outlined, children in kinship care generally experience greater placement stability than those living with non-kin carers, as shown in a systematic review of over 100 research studies (Winokur, Holtan and Batchelder, 2014). Many studies show that kinship children usually make close relationships with their carers who show high commitment and rarely give up on them, even when their behaviour is very challenging. Growing up, they see more of the extended family than other children in care, and often maintain these supportive family relationships into adulthood (Kiraly and Humphreys, 2016; Wellard *et al.*, 2017). In addition, young people usually stay with their kinship carers as long as they wish, and their carers support them when they leave home and encourage their educational aspirations (Wellard *et al.*, 2017).

Outcomes of children and young people in kinship care

Overall, the outcomes of young people who grow up in kinship care have been found to be better than for children in foster or residential care on a range of dimensions (Winokur *et al.*, 2014; Wellard *et al.*, 2017). Nevertheless, given their pre-care adversities, it is not surprising that a significant minority have enduring difficulties. About one-third of children in kinship care have been shown to have significant emotional and behavioural difficulties on the Strengths and Difficulties questionnaire (see e.g. Holtan *et al.*, 2005; Farmer and Moyers, 2008; Selwyn *et al.*, 2013). Although this proportion is lower than for children in non-kin foster care in the UK (45%–74%) (see e.g. Meltzer *et al.*, 2003; Sinclair, 2005), it is higher than in the general population (10%). Similarly, a New South Wales study (Tarren-Sweeney and Hazell, 2006) found high rates of mental health difficulties on the Child Behavior Checklist (CBCL) (Achenbach, 2001) and the Assessment Checklist for Children (Tarren-Sweeney, 2007) in kinship care and non-kin foster care, with higher rates for the latter group.

Thus, despite the generally better outcomes in kinship care, the parenting of some kin children still presents many challenges, and their kinship carers may struggle to manage them. We now turn to considering some of the particular issues relevant to mental health intervention that arise for children in kinship care.

Issues for children

Children's lack of understanding of their past and unanswered questions

Children who have been traumatised may struggle with feelings of unresolved loss and self-blame, and may have difficulty in recognising and expressing their emotions. Research suggests that open family communication is a very important element of reparenting children who have suffered traumatic life experiences (Cook *et al.*, 2003; Cohen, Mannarino and Deblinger, 2006). It is therefore important for kinship carers to talk to children about their experiences and help reduce any guilt and confusion they might feel. Their understanding of past events and ability to integrate painful memories into a coherent story depends largely on what their carers tell them.

However, it has been found that many kinship carers have some difficulty in communicating openly with the children they care for. This is because the carers may have strong feelings about the reasons parents could not bring up the children, and sometimes feel responsible for these difficulties (Crumbley and Little, 1997). As a result, children may not broach the past with their carers because they do not want to upset them. In the Selwyn *et al.* (2013) study, only nine (11%) children said that their carers regularly spoke to them about their past, whereas almost half of the carers (45%) avoided the topic. This left some children feeling troubled by matters in their past which they did not fully understand. As one young person in Wellard *et al.*'s (2017) study said:

> I'd get angry and I would start throwing stuff…because I didn't really understand why I wasn't with my mum…at school I would see everyone's mum picking them up. Everyone would ask me, 'Why are you with your aunt?' I was like 'I don't know'. (p.39)

Selwyn *et al.* (2013) found that one in five children had unanswered questions about why they had not been able to stay with their parents, and were troubled by what they saw as 'secrets', events that they did not fully understand or questions that they had been unable to ask:

> I'm not completely sure of the proper reason [I live in kinship care]. I still find it hard to understand, just hard to get my head around and stuff. (16 year old living with aunt) (p.21)

> I don't know why I'm not living with [my parents]. (9 year old living with grandmother) (p.21)

Some children wanted to know about the nature of their parents' difficulties (such as alcohol misuse) or to understand more about a parent's death:

> I want to know [how my mother died] but I just live on with life and try and put it behind [me]…not [let it] get the best of me. (14 year old living with grandmother) (p.22)

Some children, especially boys, wondered who their father was, or were concerned about what they saw as the secrecy surrounding their father's identity. Even if family matters have been discussed with children briefly when they were younger, as they mature they usually want more detailed information about their personal history (Wade *et al.*, 2014).

Loss, repeated rejection and feelings of responsibility

Loss of parental care

On joining kinship carers, children often feel relief from the maltreatment and uncertainties of home life, but they also report feeling anger, sadness, anxiety, isolation and rejection (Selwyn *et al.*, 2013). Some feel abandoned or responsible for the circumstances that had led to the kinship arrangement. These feelings of loss and guilt are aggravated when children do not understand why they are not living with their parents (Wellard *et al.*, 2017).

Loss heightened by repeated rejection

Rushton and Dance (2003) reported that children in adoptive or foster care who were preferentially rejected by their parents when they lived at home tend to make poorer progress than those who were not. In Selwyn *et al.*'s (2013) study, more than a quarter (26%) of the children had been particularly overtly rejected or abandoned by a parent *before* their move to kinship care, with parents telling these children that they were unwanted and in two cases dropping a child at the kinship carer's front door and driving off. For a number of children, feelings of rejection were compounded because their parents continued to bring up their siblings, later-born babies or the children of a new partner, particularly when the parents did not maintain contact with them.

Unlike children in non-kin foster care, many children in kinship care remain living in the same neighbourhood as their parents (Hunt, 2009). Although proximity makes it easier for parents to visit, it can make it harder for children to understand when parents openly ignore them or contact is unreliable. In the Selwyn *et al.* (2013) study, one-fifth of the children were exposed to episodes of repeated rejection while in kinship care:

> [His mother] doesn't come over, although she comes past [the house]. I know at one time I found Max crying on the door and I said, 'What's the matter?' He said 'Mum has just gone up the road in a car and she didn't even wave to me'. (Grandparents bringing up 15 year old) (p.30)

> It's hard...because I see my mum picking [my brother and half-sister] up [from school] and I think 'Why couldn't that be me?' (10 year old living with aunt) (p.30)

Such repeated rejection can have a severe impact on children and may also affect their educational progress. Some children take their anger out on their kinship carers or their distress emerges in difficult behaviour at school.

Separation from siblings

There has been growing recognition of the importance of siblings to children who live away from their parents (Kosonen, 1996; Mullender, 1999; Dunn, 2007; Meakings, Coffey and Shelton, 2017). This is equally true for children in kinship care. In Kiraly and Humphreys' (2016) study, kinship carers emphasised the importance to children of contact with these separated siblings:

> They get so excited to see each other. (p.234)

> They miss their youngest sister who is in foster care. (p.232)

In the Wellard *et al.* (2017) study, three-quarters of the young people had been separated from a sibling at some point, but most had some contact with at least one separated sibling (see also e.g. Burgess, 2010), particularly when their siblings were placed with other relatives. However, Wellard *et al.* (2017) also found that a fifth of the young people had lost contact with a sibling or mourned the loss of closeness with a sibling where contact was only occasional. The young people also spoke of their continuing concern for siblings after separation. Some had been 'parental' children who had looked after and helped their younger siblings in the context of their parents' deficiencies. If a younger sibling was subsequently harmed by their parents or placed for adoption, these young people often felt responsible and guilty, thinking that they should have prevented this happening. Their strong feelings were sometimes reflected in challenging behaviour.

Kinship carers are not always aware of the depth of the young people's feelings about their siblings, including loss, feeling responsible for them, self-blame or feeling singled out for rejection (Wellard *et al.*, 2017). They may need advice about the importance to children of sibling contact and how to help children talk about these feelings. They may also need assistance in maintaining contact with siblings whenever possible.

Loss of connection to relatives and others important to the child

Kinship placements that involve a geographical move may result in disconnection from other relatives and children's friends. These relationships become particularly significant to children separated from their parents (Messing, 2006). In reviewing previous studies of children's perspectives on kinship care, Kiraly and Humphreys (2013a) reported:

> An overwhelming theme in all the studies was the importance to children of their contact with their siblings and wider family, including cousins, aunts, and uncles. (p.316)

Stigma, feeling different and being different

Feeling different – stigma and being bullied

Young people in kinship care spoke of how angry they had felt as teenagers, sometimes linking this to feeling 'different' to their peers because of not living with their parents (Wellard *et al.*, 2017). Although some studies have suggested that kinship care is perceived by children as less stigmatising than non-kin foster care (Broad, Hayes and Rushforth, 2001; Messing, 2006), Farmer, Selwyn and Meakings (2013) found that more than a third (36%) of the children in their study reported being subjected to hurtful remarks because they were not living with their parents (see also Hislop *et al.*, 2004). A teenager in this study explained:

> People that I've just met have been quite insensitive and…be like, 'It's a bit weird you don't live with your parents. Do they hate you?' (17 year old with grandparents) (p.28)

Some children were also affected by the shame associated with their parents' reputations and behaviour (see also e.g. Kroll, 2004) – for example, being subjected to taunts about parents who were drug or alcohol dependent, who solicited sex or who were in prison.

Being different - children's own caring responsibilities

Some children in kinship care take on extra responsibilities that alter their lives and would not be replicated in non-kin care (see e.g. Hunt, Waterhouse and Lutman, 2008). For example, in the Selwyn *et al.* (2013) study, 10% of the children had caring responsibilities for someone in their kinship family. These children prepared food for their carers, helped them to mobilise, completed household chores, kept their carers company and helped with medication regimes. This had an impact on the children's opportunities to maintain a broad social network, especially when they did not wish to leave their carers alone, or where they lived at a distance from friends. Many of these young carers had close relationships with the kinship carers they helped look after and did not resent the restrictions this placed on them. However, a few felt more acutely that they were missing out on opportunities for leisure activities and spending time with friends.

Other children help to care for their younger siblings. In the Wellard *et al.* (2017) study, there was a connection between children who had high levels of responsibility for younger siblings and kinship families where there were particular challenges, related to the carers' youth or disability and/or the number and difficulties of the children. These young people could be weighed down by the responsibility for their siblings and felt they had not had the opportunity to be like 'normal teenagers'.

Impact of relationships with parents

Reviews of the kinship care literature suggest that relationships between parents and kinship children are more likely to be maintained in kinship care than when children are placed with non-kin foster carers (Flynn, 2002; Hunt, 2003; Cuddeback, 2004). Contact with parents is usually arranged informally and supervised where necessary by the carers (Ehrle and Geen, 2002; Farmer and Moyers, 2008; Kiraly and Humphreys, 2016). However, parental contact is quite often fraught with difficulties and is not always beneficial for the children (Aldgate and McIntosh, 2006;

Farmer and Moyers, 2008; Hunt *et al.*, 2008). Of course, contact is considerably more complex when children are in kinship care because of the prior history (and often relationship) between the parents and the kin carers, proximity of the parents in many cases and because supervision is usually left to the carers. Managing positive and safe contact between the children and their parents (nearly always without professional support) is a major task for kinship carers, and one they frequently find extremely difficult and emotionally draining (Hunt, Waterhouse and Lutman, 2010; Kiraly and Humphreys, 2016). Some carers explicitly link the associated stress to their feelings of depression (Selwyn *et al.*, 2013).

Difficulties in parental contact

Kinship carers make great efforts to protect children from parents who place them at risk through exposing them to substance misuse, involving them in criminal activities or looking after them inadequately, and most carers manage this very well (see e.g. Farmer and Moyers, 2008; Selwyn *et al.*, 2013). In a study of formal kinship care in Australia, about half of the carers reported difficulties with children's parental contact (Kiraly and Humphreys, 2016), and Selwyn *et al.* (2013) and Wellard *et al.* (2017) had similar findings. As noted earlier, persistently difficult contact typically involved parents who were unreliable in keeping in touch and also those who frequently let young people down or who had lifestyles that exposed children and young people to inappropriate or risky situations.

> [The children's mother] would say that she was coming. The girls would be sitting there waiting and she'd never turn up. Out of 79 contacts [arranged], she actually took 11 of them up and 5 of them she was late with. (Step-grandparent bringing up 13 year old) (Selwyn *et al.*, 2013, p.37)

> All I remember is like just waiting at the window for her to pull up and she never came. (Tessa, 17) (Kiraly and Humphreys, 2013b, p.322)

When contact does occur, children may be exposed to their parents' difficulties, especially alcohol and drugs misuse (Selwyn *et al.*, 2013; Kiraly and Humphreys, 2016). One girl in Selwyn's study said it was 'pretty good' when she saw her drug-using mother at weekends and they 'hung out' together. The grandmother was concerned that the girl would be drawn into using drugs or end up becoming her mother's carer, taking over the grandmother's role.

Threats and aggression from parents

Some parents who realise that they are unable to provide adequate care are nonetheless overwhelmed with feelings of anger and resentment against the relatives who have stepped in to look after their children. They may accuse the carers of 'stealing' the child or of being too indulgent or too strict. They or their partners sometimes threaten, harass or physically assault the carers. In a few cases, if child welfare services intervention is not provided, such behaviour can put the placement at risk of disruption (see e.g. Farmer and Moyers, 2008).

Parents who undermine kin placements

Other parents criticise the carers to the child or countermand their discipline, in this and other ways undermining the kinship placement. One grandparent said:

> Her mum stirs things up against us…for instance Phoebe said to me only yesterday morning 'No wonder mum can't stand you, you never ever stop going on'. I can well imagine that's what mum's been saying…I suppose she has a loyalty to her mum. Her mum puts her pennyworth in about how controlling we are. (Grandparents bringing up 16 year old) (Selwyn *et al.*, 2013, p.35)

It is not unusual for children to become critical of their carers following contact with a parent, especially when parents give them much more freedom than they have in the carer's home.

> He would say: 'Oh mummy's better than you…mummy will let us do this'. (Grandmother bringing up 10 year old) (Selwyn *et al.*, 2013, p.35)

Contact that is difficult to control with parents who are dependent on the carers

Just under a third of the kin carers in Selwyn *et al.*'s (2013) study (mostly grandparents) were still supporting the children's parent in some way. Many of these carers were in effect parenting two generations simultaneously. Four-fifths of these children had parents with ongoing problems with addiction:

> [My daughter] still expects me…to do things for her all the time. She wants me to look after her and she's ill a lot and she's not ill because of the HIV, it's usually because of the drugs. (Grandmother bringing up 8 year old) (p.37)

Some such parents relied on financial support from the carers even when the carer's budget was stretched. They visited the kinship carers to get their own needs met, sometimes with little regard for their own children who lived there. These visits could be difficult to control and very upsetting for both the carers and children. For example, one father in the Selwyn *et al.* (2013) study who misused alcohol often went to his mother's (the carer's) house at night, drunk, shouting and banging on the door to be let in. This was so stressful for the carer and child that the grandmother said that she sometimes wished her son was dead.

Divided loyalties for children

Children have particular difficulties and poorer outcomes when they feel torn between wanting to stay with their parents and being with their carer (Selwyn *et al.*, 2013; Wellard *et al.*, 2017). Indeed, one in five kinship carers in Selwyn *et al.*'s (2013) study thought that the quality of their relationship with the child was affected by the child's relationship with, or feelings about, a parent, and the children concerned were found to be significantly less well attached to their carers than others. Sometimes these difficulties occurred because children felt continuing responsibility for helping parents with mental health or substance misuse difficulties, and felt guilty about leaving them when they moved out. Their divided loyalties could make it difficult to build close relationships with the kinship carer, whom they sometimes blamed for the move.

> I used to always want to live with my mum. I used to always think my grandma was trying to take me away from my mum…then it was hard for me and my grandma to get a bonding. (20 year old young woman living independently reflecting on being bought up by her grandmother) (Wellard *et al.*, 2017, p.17)

Children who witness arguments between their parents and their carers can feel caught in a conflict of loyalties to their parents and their carers:

> Sometimes she [mum] gets angry…she argues with grandma…it's hard. (16 year old young man living with his grandmother) (Selwyn *et al.*, 2013, p.38)

Impact of parental death

Arguably, there has been insufficient recognition of the significance and impact of bereavement in kinship care, especially when the care is informal. Just over a third (34%) of the children in Selwyn *et al.*'s (2013) study of informal kinship care had moved to their kinship carers because a parent had died. Parental death is less often reported in studies of formal kinship placements in the UK, where the incidence ranges between 4% and 13% (Aldgate and McIntosh, 2006; Farmer and Moyers, 2008; Hunt *et al.*, 2008). In addition, by the time children in kinship care reach adolescence and young adulthood, a considerable proportion (38% in Wellard *et al.*'s (2017) study) have experienced the death of one or both parents, often as a result of suicide or a drug overdose.

As well as dealing with their own loss, the young people are usually living with carers who themselves are grieving. Research has shown that a carer's well-being following the death of a child's parent is a significant predictor of the child's well-being, since the carer's ability to resolve their own grief can affect the child's overall functioning (Sandler *et al.*, 2010; Melhem *et al.*, 2011).

Many kinship carers have difficulties in talking with bereaved children about their parents and the past, especially when they are struggling to deal with their own feelings about the parent's death. So although some kinship families are able to support one another through their loss, in other families young people remain unable to seek comfort from their carer, or unable to talk to them about their late parent, and consequently sometimes remain angry (Wellard *et al.*, 2017). Bereaved children who do not have the opportunity to talk about the past may have some difficulty in resolving their own feelings of loss. In addition, children whose *parents* have died are significantly more likely than others to worry about the health of their *carers*, and about their carers dying (Selwyn *et al.*, 2013).

Children's worries about the future

Expressing and managing emotions

Selwyn *et al.* (2013) found that on a standard measure of children's emotional and behavioural difficulties – the Strengths and Difficulties Questionnaire (SDQ) (Goodman, 1997) – the greatest area of difficulty for kinship children was in their ability to express and manage their emotions, where as many as 39% scored in the abnormal range. In responses to the SDQ, kinship carers stated that the children had many fears, were easily scared, often complained of headaches or stomach aches, and were often unhappy, downhearted or tearful.

Worries about death, illness and the future

In the Selwyn *et al.* (2013) study, the children were also asked to write down what they worried about. Nearly half (44%) of the kin-placed children recorded a worry that was related to death or illness, and many worried that their parents or carers might have an accident, be hurt or die. This compares with between 16% and 23% of children in the general population who worry about ill health or death (Henker, Whalen and O'Neil, 1995; Silverman, La Greca and Wasserstein, 1995; Muris *et al.*, 1998). Given the older age and poor health of some carers and the risky lifestyles of many parents, the children's worries were not unfounded. Typical worries included:

> If something would happen to my nanna – I don't want to lose her like I lost my mum. (Selwyn *et al.*, 2013, p.25)

> If my granny and grampy die, where will me and [my sister] go? (p.25)

Some children in the Selwyn *et al.* (2013) study were concerned about who would look after them if their carer died. One teenager, for example, started to complain of 'tummy ache' and diarrhoea. Medical investigations were inconclusive. In talking to a psychologist, the child was able to express her fears openly. Her carer explained:

> [The psychologist] thought she was worrying about certain things and actually, as it turned out it was right, because I'd had an accident. I had to go into hospital and Zoe actually said 'Mummy died overnight and I was frightened that was what was going to happen to you and where would I go?' (Grandmother bringing up 14 year old) (p.26)

Not surprisingly, children often found it difficult to share their worries about their carers' poor health and their own future with the carers themselves.

Contingency plans

Just under half (49%) of the kinship carers had made a contingency plan about who would care for the children if they died or became too ill to care for them. However, these plans had rarely been shared with the children (Selwyn *et al.*, 2013). It is obviously important for children to know about such plans and to receive reassurance about future arrangements for them in the event that they are needed.

Now that a range of issues which can affect children's mental health have been addressed, we turn to consider the experiences of kinship carers.

Parallel experiences and challenges for kinship carers

Relatives and friends experience a sudden and unexpected change in their life course when they become carers, with a resulting loss of freedom to enact their life plans. Many older carers, rather than looking forward to a leisurely retirement, return to an earlier stage in their life cycle as they take on childcare responsibilities for a second time. In contrast, sibling carers and young aunts and uncles may be thrust forward into an accelerated transition to parenthood and miss out on further education, friendships and partnerships.

Thus, although kinship carers are generally deeply committed to bringing up the children, they incur major losses in doing so. Crumbley and Little (1997) suggest that, at the start of intervention, counsellors should help kin carers to make an inventory of their losses in order to help them to move on.

Losses for kinship carers and changed relationships

Kinship carers experience a sequence of losses in parallel with those of the children. They not only have to develop a new kind of (parental) relationship with the children (which can sadden those who had valued their former role of indulgent grandparent or aunt), but they may also feel guilt at taking over the parent's role (Crumbley and Little, 1997). They also have to establish very different relationships with the child's parents, who are often their adult children or siblings. Many kinship carers also experience dual loyalties as they continue to support the children's parents but know they have to put the children's needs first. As has been seen, if a parent has died, they may be struggling to come to terms with this loss when the kin children are also grieving.

Whereas kinship children may be sad about a lack of contact with siblings, kinship carers in turn may feel guilty if they cannot take a whole sibling group or a baby who is born later to the parents (Kiraly, 2011).

Loss of friendships, risks to partnerships, and lack of extended family support

At the very time when kinship carers need support, they often lose friendships. For grandparents, their peers have often retired and embarked on a more carefree life when the carers are starting to rear children again. Sibling carers and young aunts/uncles often take on the parenting role so early in their lives that they lose friends who are moving into tertiary education or employment, and lose opportunities for an age-appropriate social life. In addition, kinship carers often give up their jobs to look after the children or reduce their working hours, leading to loss of affiliation at work, as well as reduced finances and later retirement income.

Taking on kinship children can also cause tensions in the family. Selwyn *et al.* (2013) found that, for 58% of the kinship carers, caring for the child had caused serious difficulties in partner relationships, and 23% of couples had separated as a result. Carers' adult children may also be critical, fearful of the burden on the carers, or feeling that their own children are not getting enough attention (Selwyn *et al.*, 2013). Importantly, although it is often thought that kinship carers benefit from extended family support, some do not, and carers can become quite isolated (Selwyn *et al.*, 2013). Yet when kin carers turn to child welfare services and ask for help for the children or themselves, they are often refused (Wellard and Wheatley, 2010; Aziz, Roth and Lindley, 2012; Hunt and Waterhouse, 2012).

Occupying a devalued role

While non-kin foster carers occupy a valued role in society, kinship carers occupy a much more ambiguous role, and they are sometimes held responsible for the parents' difficulties. Echoing children's experience of feeling stigmatised, over a third of the carers in Selwyn *et al.*'s (2013) study had been the butt of critical remarks from members of the public because they were kinship carers.

Difficult relationships with the children's parents, feelings of guilt and blame

As described earlier, relationships with the child's parents are often complex and immensely difficult for carers. Kinship carers often describe particularly stressful relationships with parents who are misusing drugs or alcohol (Kroll, 2004, 2007; Selwyn *et al.*, 2013). This is a key area affecting children's well-being where help for kinship carers falls far short of what is needed.

Kin carers may carry feelings of guilt if they have involved child welfare services in order to safeguard the children. Grandparent carers may also feel partly to blame for the parents' difficulties since they had brought them up. Kinship carers often also feel ashamed of the parents' behaviour (e.g. if they are misusing drugs or alcohol, are in prison or involved in prostitution). They may feel saddened or angry that their own adult children (or siblings) have turned out to be poor parents (Barnard, 2003).

Multiple caring roles

It is not uncommon for kinship carers to have the responsibility of caring for other family members such as their partners, their own elderly parents and sometimes another vulnerable child in addition to the kinship children (Pitcher, 1999, 2002; Wellard and Wheatley, 2010).

Children with behavioural and emotional difficulties

Parenting children is tiring and physically demanding, especially for carers in poor health. In addition, a significant minority struggle to cope with children who have complex and severe behavioural difficulties. A grandmother in Selwyn *et al.*'s (2013) study linked her poor health with the child's disruptive behaviours:

> She's draining all [the energy] out of me. She's draining everything I've got. [Her disruptive behaviour] goes on for hours... [I am] just run down with all the carry-on and I've been taking really bad headaches, but I think that's just stress, because I'm not sleeping. (Grandmother bringing up 12 year old) (p.49)

The findings from both national and international studies are clear: a number of children raised by kinship carers are likely to need additional help if they are to achieve their potential (Hunt, 2018). However, studies consistently find that children and their carers receive insufficient help. For example, Selwyn *et al.* (2013) found that a quarter of the children with abnormal SDQ scores had received no help at all with their difficulties.

Issues for intervention

Implications for practice related to the issues discussed relate to assessment, preparation, training and follow-up support for carers, and direct assistance for children. Three areas in particular need to be highlighted. First, attention needs to be drawn to the importance of providing assistance at the initial transition into kin care, since this is likely to have long-term benefits in anticipating and mitigating some of the issues that may follow. Second, we need to listen more carefully to the views of children about what they need and to ensure children have opportunities to share their feelings and worries with their kinship carers or others whom they trust. Third, it is important to recognise the significance of bereavement and loss in kinship care.

Realistic assessments and the need for information and training

Assessments need to be made using a strengths-based model focusing on the family in its particular context in order to help families to identify their strengths and resources and to investigate, in partnership with them, what supports would be needed to enable them to care (see e.g. Doolan, Nixon and Lawrence, 2004; Broad and Skinner, 2005; Aldgate and McIntosh, 2006). Time needs to be allowed for prospective kinship carers to consider and fully understand the children's support needs and what their own needs might be as a new family group. This will include the challenges of managing ongoing family relationships and contact with parents; these should be fully addressed and supported both at the outset and as circumstances change.

When an assessment takes place with a child who is already living with kinship carers, this should not prejudice the decision as to whether the care provided is suitable in the longer term. Where necessary, a discussion needs to take place with both carers and children to allow them to plan for a child's move to longer-term care in a way that reduces the chance of either carer or child feeling inadequate or rejected.

In addition, few kin carers have the benefit of the information sessions and training available to non-kin foster carers and residential workers. Opportunities to attend training/information sessions on key issues in kinship care and on the impact of trauma on children are likely to be helpful (Kiraly, 2018).

Advising children what to tell others about themselves, and dealing with bullying

From the outset, it is important for children to be given advice on how to manage information about where they live, including, where appropriate, developing a cover story (see e.g. Fahlberg, 2004). They need to be encouraged to speak out both at school and at home about bullying. School policies about bullying should include information about how kinship children may be targeted. Where the reputation of children's parents is used against the children by other children (e.g. as drug users or prostitutes), some may benefit from a change of school.

Recognition and awareness of support needs

Kinship carers without strong support from their wider family and those whose social support networks are limited (Farmer, Moyers and Lipscombe, 2004; Selwyn *et al.*, 2013; Wellard *et al.*, 2017) need to be recognised as having a greater need for support. These carers should be prioritised for help from kinship services. A realistic assessment of financial and other needs is also required so that kinship carers are not pushed into poverty, reducing their ability to provide optimal care for children (Wellard *et al.*, 2017). Respite care or occasional child care may need to be arranged.

Where the carers are grandparents, children may become carers for their grandparents as they age. Such young people need to be recognised and supported as young carers, and understanding of their situation at school is required. Some of these kinship families may need help from adult services to assist carers with health problems, so that the caring burden does not all fall on the children's shoulders. Where children are providing a great deal of care for their younger siblings, this may be because the original assessment by child welfare services did not take full of the account the amount of support that would be needed by these kinship carers and had not provided sufficient help for them. A new assessment of need may be required to obtain more help from child welfare services.

Help with special needs

Given the high proportion of kinship children with additional needs, there needs to be good communication with schools so that children receive appropriate help and support with their schoolwork, and are offered help from counselling or mental health services in relation to their psychological difficulties. Without such help, their experience of being different may be magnified as they fall behind with their schoolwork and try to cope with feelings of anxiety, anger and depression.

Open communication

Kinship carers need advice both at the outset of care and later on about how to talk sensitively to children about their past and their parents' difficulties, and some carers may need active assistance to facilitate this. Explanations need to underline that the child is not to blame for the move and is not responsible for their parents' actions. There will also be some children who need life story work (Rose, 2012) to help them make sense of their lives and move on from their past experiences.

Given the extent of overt and ongoing rejection that many children experience from their parents, some carers would benefit from advice about how to help children deal with this. Children may need the opportunity to talk about their feelings about parents who have rejected them, yet are nonetheless bringing up their siblings or a partner's children. In some cases, intervention from a professional in individual or family sessions might help parents to understand the effect of their behaviour and help them to modify it.

Relationships with parents, separated siblings and other significant people

Although most kinship carers manage contact with parents very well, there is clearly a need for kinship carers to have access to advice and support when contact becomes problematic. This could be from child welfare services, a therapist or peer support from other experienced kinship carers. Sadly, many kin carers are unable to access such help (see e.g. Hunt *et al.*, 2010; Selwyn *et al.*, 2013; Kiraly and Humphreys, 2016). There are times when contact needs to be supervised or curtailed to safeguard children and their placements. Counselling for children regarding their feelings about their parents and kin carers may sometimes also be helpful.

Children's own views about visits with their parents need to be sought regularly to ascertain what is and is not working for them in relation to frequency, location and supervision of visits. Children's views are likely to change over time as they mature and parents' circumstances change. This can be a particular problem where a court has set contact conditions at the time of proceedings, which over time may become outdated or inappropriate to the child's needs.

When parents actively undermine placements, they may need assistance to help them come to terms with the new arrangements, guidance on what can be said to the children, and sometimes restrictions on contact so that the stability of the placement is not undermined.

Arrangements for sibling contact need to be made at the start of placements and carers encouraged and, if necessary, assisted to keep this contact going. The child may also benefit from continued contact with other relatives such as cousins, aunts, uncles or grandparents whether through direct contact or by phone or social media. Likewise, if the placement has resulted in a change of location and/or school and children miss their friends, they should be asked how they would like to maintain these connections.

Bereavement and plans for the future

There needs to be more awareness of the impact of bereavement in kinship care, and readier access to bereavement or counselling services for both the kinship carers and children affected. Children also need permission to grieve and to be given clear, honest and accurate information about parents who have died, with opportunities provided for children to talk about their parents and ask questions about them. Some kinship children may need direct intervention to help them with their grief and loss.

If a parent becomes ill or dies, children may need reassurance about their carers' health. They need to know what contingency plans their carers have made for them if they become too unwell to continue to care. Professionals should encourage carers to make and share contingency plans. If carers are isolated and cannot make such plans, they might be helped by talking this through with a social worker who could explain how the children would be cared for if they could no longer live within the extended family.

Help for children with serious emotional and behavioural difficulties

The minority of children in kinship care who have serious emotional and behavioural difficulties present particular challenges for kin carers, who have been neither prepared nor trained to cope with such troubled and sometimes angry children. Many carers struggle valiantly to bring order to their own and the children's fragmented lives. Robust assessment and more assistance for children with serious emotional and behavioural difficulties are called for, as are advice and help for their kinship carers. Carers need information about how to source help when needed – for example, from children's mental health services or school counsellors.

Conclusion

Overall, the outcomes for children in kinship care are notably better than for children in non-kin care. Nonetheless, there needs to be much greater recognition of the particular needs of kinship children by schools and among the range of professionals they encounter. A considerable amount could be achieved by improved preparation, advice and help for kinship carers and children at the outset and during placements. In particular, more assistance and advice is needed about managing contact and talking to children about their backgrounds. This can help children develop a coherent narrative about their lives and manage ongoing relationships with one or both parents, rather than continue to be distressed by their parents' circumstances and behaviours. Help needs to be much more timely and accessible for the substantial minority of children with severe and enduring emotional and behavioural difficulties. Lack of intervention is likely to have major consequences for their psychological, educational and economic outcomes in adulthood.

References

ABS (Australian Bureau of Statistics) (2008). *National Aboriginal and Torres Strait Islander Social Survey*. Canberra: ABS.

Achenbach, T.M. (2001). *Child Behavior Checklist (CBCL)*. ASEBA, University of Vermont.

AIHW (Australian Institute of Health and Welfare) (2018). *Child Protection Australia 2016–17*. Canberra AIHW.

Aldgate, J. and McIntosh, M. (2006). *Looking After the Family: A Study of Children Looked After in Kinship Care in Scotland*. Edinburgh: Social Work Inspection Agency.

Aziz, R., Roth, D. and Lindley, B. (2012). *Understanding Family and Friends Care: The Largest UK Survey*. London: Family Rights Group.

Barnard, M. (2003). Between a rock and a hard place: The role of relatives in protecting children from the effects of parental drug problems. *Child and Family Social Work*, 8(4), 291–299.

Brennan, D., Cass, B., Flaxman, S., Hill, T. *et al.* (2013). *Grandparents Raising Grandchildren: Towards Recognition, Respect and Reward.* Sydney: Social Policy Research Centre, University of New South Wales.

Broad, B., Hayes, R. and Rushforth, C. (2001). *Kith and Kin: Kinship Care for Vulnerable Young People.* London: National Children's Bureau.

Broad, B. and Skinner, A. (2005). *Relative Benefits: Placing Children in Kinship Care.* London: British Association for Adoption and Fostering.

Burgess, C., Rossvoll, F., Wallace, B. and Daniel, B. (2010). 'It's just like another home, just another family, so it's nae different.' Children's voices in kinship care: A research study about the experience of children in kinship care in Scotland. *Child and Family Social Work*, 15(3), 297–306.

Cohen, J.A., Mannarino, A.P. and Deblinger, E. (2006). *Treating Trauma and Traumatic Grief in Children and Adolescents.* New York, NY: Guilford Press.

Cook, A., Blaustein, M., Spinazzola, J. and van der Kolk, B. (eds) (2003). *Complex Trauma in Children and Adolescents.* Los Angeles, CA/Durham, NC: National Child Traumatic Stress Network. Accessed on 5/1/2019 at www.nctsn.org/resources/complex-trauma-children-and-adolescents.

COTA (Council on the Ageing) (2003). *Grandparents Raising Grandchildren.* Canberra: Commonwealth Department of Family and Community Services.

Crumbley, J. and Little, R.L. (eds) (1997). *Relatives Raising Children: An Overview of Kinship Care.* Washington, DC: Child Welfare League of America.

Cuddeback, G.S. (2004). Kinship family foster care: A methodological substantive synthesis of research. *Children and Youth Services Review*, 26(7), 623–639.

Department for Education (2017). Children looked after in England (including adoption), year ending 31 March 2017, SFR 50/2017, 28 September 2017. Accessed on 5/1/2019 at https://assets.publishing.service.gov.uk/government/uploads/system/uploads/attachment_data/file/664995/SFR50_2017-Children_looked_after_in_England.pdf.

Doolan, M., Nixon, P. and Lawrence, P. (2004). *Growing Up in the Care of Relatives or Friends: Delivering Best Practice for Children in Family and Friends Care.* London: Family Rights Group.

Dunn, J. (2007). Siblings and Socialization. In J. Grusec and P. Hastings (eds), *Handbook of Socialization.* New York, NY: Guilford Press.

Dunne, E.G. and Kettler, L.J. (2008). Grandparents raising grandchildren in Australia: Exploring psychological health and grandparents' experience of providing kinship care. *International Journal of Social Welfare*, 17(4), 333–345.

Ehrle, J. and Geen, R. (2002). Kin and non-kin foster care: Findings from a national survey. *Children and Youth Services Review*, 24(1–2), 15–35.

Fahlberg, V. (2004). *A Child's Journey through Placement.* London: BAAF.

Farmer, E. and Moyers, S. (2008). *Kinship Care: Fostering Effective Family and Friends Placements.* London: Jessica Kingsley Publishers.

Farmer, E., Moyers, S. and Lipscombe, J. (2004). *Fostering Adolescents.* London: Jessica Kingsley Publishers.

Farmer, E., Selwyn, J. and Meakings, S. (2013). 'Other children say you're not normal because you don't live with your parents'. Children's views of living with informal kinship carers: Social networks, stigma and attachment to carers. *Child and Family Social Work*, Special Issue, Rediscovering Family and Kinship: New Directions for Social Work Theory, Policy and Practice, 18(1), 25–34.

Flynn, R. (2002). Kinship care: Research review. *Child and Family Social Work*, 7(4), 311–321.

Gautier, A. and Wellard, S. (2012). *Giving up the Day Job? Kinship Carers and Employment*. London: Grandparents Plus.

Gibbons, L. and Mason, J. (2003). Challenges posed by kinship care: A study focussing on New South Wales. *Children Australia*, 28(4), 12–18.

Goldberg, D. and Hillier, V. (1979). A scaled version of the General Health Questionnaire. *Psychological Medicine*, 9(1), 139–145.

Goodman, R. (1997). The Strengths and Difficulties Questionnaire: A research note. *Journal of Child Psychology and Psychiatry*, 38(5), 581–586.

Hegar, R. and Scannapieco, M. (eds) (1999). *Kinship Foster Care: Policy, Practice and Research*. Oxford: Oxford University Press.

Henker, B., Whalen, C.K. and O'Neil, R. (1995). Worldly and workaday worries: Contemporary concerns of children and young adolescents. *Journal of Abnormal Child Psychology*, 23(6), 685–702.

Hislop, A., Horner, B., Downie, J. and Hay, D. (2004). *The Perceived Experiences of Children and Adolescents Living with Their Grandparents: 'Why Living with My Grandparents is So…Good'. A Report to the Commonwealth Department of Health and Ageing*. Bentley, Western Australia: Centre for Research into Aged Care Services, School of Nursing and Midwifery, School of Psychology.

Holtan, A., Ronning, J.A., Handegard, B.H. and Sourander, A. (2005). A comparison of mental health problems in kinship and nonkinship foster care. *European Child and Adolescent Psychiatry*, 14(4), 200–207.

Hughes, M.E., Waite, L.J., LaPierre, T.A. and Luo, Y.L. (2007). All in the family: The impact of caring for grandchildren on grandparents' health. *The Journals of Gerontology Series B: Psychological Sciences and Social Sciences*, 62(2), 108–119.

Hunt, J. (2003). *Family and Friends Carers: Scoping Paper Prepared for the Department of Health*. London: Department of Health.

Hunt, J. (2009). Family and Friends Care. In G. Schofield and J. Simmonds (eds), *The Child Placement Handbook*. London: BAAF.

Hunt, J. (2018). Grandparents as substitute parents in the UK. *Contemporary Social Science*, 13(2), 175–186.

Hunt, J. and Waterhouse, S. (2012). *Understanding Family and Friends Care: The Relationship between Need, Support and Legal Status. Carers' Experiences*. London: Family Rights Group.

Hunt, J., Waterhouse, S. and Lutman, E. (2008). *Keeping Them in the Family: Outcomes for Children Placed in Kinship Care through Care Proceedings*. London: BAAF.

Hunt, J., Waterhouse, S. and Lutman, E. (2010). Parental contact for children placed in kinship care through care proceedings. *Child and Family Law Quarterly*, 22(1), 71–92.

Kiraly, M. (2011). Commentary: The ties that bind – complexity and challenges in the kinship care family. *Children Australia*, 36(2), 43–45.

Kiraly, M. (2015). A review of kinship carer surveys: The 'Cinderella' of the care system? Child Family Community Australia (CFCA) information exchange, Australian Institute of Family Studies, Melbourne.

Kiraly, M. (2018). *Fairy Godparents and Fake Kin: Exploring Non-Familial Kinship Care ('Kith Care')*, Diversity in Kinship Care, Research Series Report 1. Melbourne: University of Melbourne.

Kiraly, M. and Humphreys, C. (2013a). Family contact for children in kinship care: A literature review. *Australian Social Work*, 66(3), 358–374.

Kiraly, M. and Humphreys, C. (2013b). Perspectives from young people about family contact in kinship care: 'Don't push us – listen more'. *Australian Social Work*, 66(3), 314–327.

Kiraly, M. and Humphreys, C. (2016). 'It's about the whole family': Family contact for children in kinship care. *Child and Family Social Work*, 21(2), 228–239.

Kiraly, M., James, J. and Humphreys, C. (2015). 'It's a family responsibility': Family and cultural connection for Aboriginal children in kinship care. *Children Australia*, 40(1), 23–32.

Kosonen, M. (1996). Maintaining sibling relationships: Neglected dimension in child care practice. *British Journal of Social Work*, 26(6), 809–822.

Kroll, B. (2004). Living with an elephant: Growing up with parental substance misuse. *Child and Family Social Work*, 9(2), 129–140.

Kroll, B. (2007). A family affair? Kinship care and parental substance misuse: Some dilemmas explored. *Child and Family Social Work*, 12(1), 84–93.

McHugh, M. and Valentine, K. (2010). *Financial and Non-Financial Support to Formal and Informal Out-of-Home Carers: Final Report*. Sydney: Social Policy Research Centre.

Meakings, S., Coffey, A. and Shelton, K.H. (2017). The influence of adoption on sibling relationships: Experiences and support needs of newly formed adoptive families. *British Journal of Social Work*, 47(6), 1781–1799.

Melham, N.M., Porta, G., Shamseddeen, W., Walker, M. and Brent, D.A. (2011). Grief in children and adolescents bereaved by sudden parental death. *Archives of General Psychiatry*, 68(9), 911–919.

Meltzer, H., Gatward, R., Corbin, T., Goodman, R. and Ford, T. (2003). *The Mental Health of Young People Looked After by Local Authorities in England*. London: The Stationery Office.

Messing, J. (2006). From the child's perspective: A qualitative analysis of kinship care placements. *Children and Youth Services Review*, 28(12), 1415–1434.

Minkler, M., Fuller-Thomson, E., Miller, D. and Driver, D. (1997). Depression in grandparents raising grandchildren. *Archives of Family Medicine*, 6(5), 445–452.

Mullender, A. (ed.) (1999). *We Are Family: Sibling Relationships in Placement and Beyond*. London: British Agencies for Adoption and Fostering.

Muris, P., Meesters, C., Merckelbach, H., Sermon, A. and Zwakhalen, S. (1998). Worry in normal children. *Journal of the American Academy of Child and Adolescent Psychiatry*, 37(7), 703–720.

Nandy, S., Selwyn, J., Farmer, E. and Vaisey, P. (2011). *Spotlight on Kinship Care: Using Census Microdata to Examine the Extent and Nature of Kinship Care in the UK at the Turn of the Twentieth Century*. Bristol: University of Bristol. Accessed on 5/1/2019 at www.bristol.ac.uk/sps/research/projects/completed/2011/rj5314/finalkinship.pdf.

Parker, G., Tupling, H. and Brown, L. (1979). A parental bonding instrument. *British Journal of Medical Psychology*, 52(1), 1–10.

Patton, N. (2004). *Parental Drug Use: A Recent Phenomenon*. Melbourne: The Mirabel Foundation.

Pitcher, D. (1999). *When Grandparents Care*. Plymouth: Plymouth City Council Social Services Department.

Pitcher, D. (2002). Placements with grandparents: The issues for grandparents who care for their grandchildren. *Adoption and Fostering*, 26(1), 6–14.

Price, J., Chamberlain, P., Landsverk, J. and Reid, J. (2009). KEEP foster parent training intervention: Model description and effectiveness. *Child and Family Social Work*, 14(2), 233–242.

Rose, R. (2012). *Life Story Therapy with Traumatized Children: A Model for Practice*. London: Jessica Kingsley Publishers.

Rushton, A. and Dance, C. (2003). Preferentially rejected children and their development in permanent family placements. *Child and Family Social Work*, 8(4), 257–267.

Sandler, I.N., Ma, Y., Tein, J.-Y., Ayers, T.S. *et al.* (2010). Long-term effects of the family bereavement program on multiple indicators of grief in parentally bereaved children and adolescents. *Journal of Consulting and Clinical Psychology*, 78(2), 131–143.

Selwyn, J., Farmer, E., Meakings, S. and Vaisey, P. (2013). *The Poor Relations? Children and Informal Kinship Carers Speak Out*. Bristol: University of Bristol/Buttle UK.

Silverman, W., La Greca, A. and Wasserstein, S. (1995). What do children worry about? Worries and their relation to anxiety. *Child Development*, 66(3), 671–686.

Sinclair, I. (2005). *Fostering Now: Messages from Research*. London: Jessica Kingsley Publishers.

Tarren-Sweeney, M. (2007). The Assessment Checklist for Children – ACC: A behavioral rating scale for children in foster, residential and kinship care. *Children and Youth Services Review*, 29(5), 672–691.

Tarren-Sweeney, M. and Hazell, P. (2006). Mental health of children in foster and kinship care in New South Wales, Australia. *Journal of Paediatric Child Health*, 42(3), 89–97.

Wade, J., Sinclair, I., Stuttard, L. and Simmonds, J. (2014). *Investigating Special Guardianship: Experiences, Challenges and Outcomes*. London: Department for Education.

Wellard S., Meakings, S., Farmer, E. and Hunt, J. (2017). *Growing Up in Kinship Care: Experiences as Adolescents and Outcomes in Young Adulthood*. London: Grandparents Plus.

Wellard, S. and Wheatley, B. (2010). *Family and Friends Care: 'What If We Said No?'* London: Grandparents Plus.

Wijedasa, D. (2015). *The Prevalence and Characteristics of Children Growing up with Relatives in the UK: Characteristics of Children Living with Relatives in England Part 1*. Bristol: University of Bristol.

Winokur, M., Holtan, A. and Batchelder, K.E. (2014). Kinship care for the safety, permanency, and wellbeing of children removed from the home for maltreatment: A systematic review. *Campbell Systematic Reviews*, 10.

PRACTICE REFLECTION

Joe Tucci, Janise Mitchell and Ed Tronick

The structure of the chapter by Farmer and Kiraly in itself highlights the insight they have gained in their ongoing research about kinship care. They methodically describe the experiences of children in kinship care and the kinship carers themselves. The themes they have drawn together reflect a number of key issues in the practice of Therapeutic Care with all types of carers, but in particular with kinship or relative carers.

First, kinship carers are family to the children they are looking after. In one study they cite, more than half of the kinship carers were grandparents and a quarter were being looked after by siblings. These are relationships with pre-existing histories of significance and differing levels of intimacy. Dynamics between children, their parents (from whose care the children were removed) and the kinship carers are bound over time with layers of meaning, which makes caring for children in kinship care in many ways more complicated than caring for children by non-related carers.

These dynamics weave together past activations of heightened arousal and fractured implicit memory systems that have become associated with tension, conflict, shame, responsibility. Some of these act to prevent their resolution in the present, leaving children and carers compromised in being able to move forward. For example, children and carers find it difficult to talk about why children are no longer in the care of their parents. These interactions loom large as secrets that obstruct trust being formed and experienced for both.

Therapeutic Care orients some of its effort into understanding the individual narratives of kinship carers, including the strengths and challenges they have experienced. These are the stories that integrate their own trauma with their own acts of courage and determination into their identity. Understanding the themes that replay in the lives of carers also provides some insight into how and why they may react to the children in their care in particular ways. This is an important setting-off point for engaging them in reflective practices that bring these unconscious processes slowly into their awareness, which then enables them to be more adaptive in their responses to their children's needs. Often, this process is facilitated by the Therapeutic Specialist after they have spent time together and built a relationship that affirms the intentions and commitments of the carers to their children. Carers are invited by the Therapeutic Specialist to softly review their history of relational experiences, finding points in which they felt resourced and points in which they felt compromised. As they do this, they become more available to the affective states of their children, sharing with them the implicit experiences of relational rupture, repair and safety that they hold in common.

Therapeutic Care also recognises the need for active mediation of the role of parents in the lives of kinship carers and their kinship children. Because of the previous histories that they hold in relationship to the kinship carers, parents are often able to exert differing levels of disruptive influence over what happens with children, sometimes resulting in a perpetuation of the abusive or neglectful attitudes that led to children being removed from their care in the first place. It is the role of the Care Team to ensure that there is enough protective buffering around the kinship carer and children to avoid what can be a detrimental impact by parents. Equally, it highlights that with targeted effort with the parents, there is an opportunity for the relationships between parents, kinship carers and children to be reconstructed so that children are able to be safely raised but continue to connect with their parents. These are important outcomes in the life-course view of children in out-of-home care, as many continue to feel the pull of these original loyalties to parents as they mature, at times causing stress on the kinship care arrangement and destabilising it. Forewarned processes of planning enable children in out-of-home care to not be forced into sharp impossible choices about whom to explicitly love or by whom they should want to be cared for. It allows children to relate to important people in their lives in ways that enable the continuity of relationships over time and with relevant meaning.

Second, it is almost as if experiences of loss are multiplied by the shared history and experiences of children and kinship carers. Children grieve for the loss of their parents, their friends, their school, their pets. Kinship carers may also come to grieve the loss of their relationships with their own children who may sever ties with them because of their decision to become carers to their children. Equally, the death of a parent leaves kinship carers and children experiencing such deep grief that they may not always be able to be comforted. Kinship carers and children can often work it out on their own. But as the intensity of these mutual and sometimes contingent experiences mount, they need support to help navigate the undercurrents that circle around them, keeping them separate.

Third, Therapeutic Care must address the disadvantage that kinship carers often find themselves in. As Farmer and Kiraly point out, many kinship carers experience financial hardship as a consequence of caring for children. There is little therapeutic opportunity when carers are themselves struggling to meet basic requirements such as housing, clothing and food. This is an important point to consider in programs that are part of the state's mandate to fund and manage. The context in which care is provided requires a solid brace which meets the basic needs for children and their carers in order to achieve the more therapeutic goals of stability and healing.

Finally, there is the reminder in this chapter of the need for planning to be considered and carefully executed for children in all forms of care, but again in particular in kinship care. Children need to be actively supported to maintain relationships with siblings. Children need to be actively supported to fulfil their cultural obligations. Children need to be actively supported to maintain connections with members of the broad family network and clan. All of this is what any parent would do for and with their children. They plan. They talk. They deliberate. They decide. Therapeutic Care holds this position for children in out-of-home care. It recognises the need for this kind of decision-making to occur with people who are in roles that have significance in the care, education and development of children.

Planning is essential. Ensuring that plans for children are implemented well and reviewed to account for children's changing and evolving needs is critical.

Although Therapeutic Care has a more established presence in foster care and residential forms of care, it is less well conceptualised in the context of kinship care. Indeed, the field is still evolving models of kinship care and support as a unique discipline. As so potently highlighted by Farmer and Kiraly, the needs of kinship carers are often quite discrete to non-family-based foster care. Debate still exists as to the nature of support that should be available to family members caring for other family members versus the autonomy and responsibility of family to their own.

It is clear that kinship care is a preferred form of care for children who are unable to live with their parents in many countries today. It is also clear that the majority of children living in 'statutory' or 'formal' kinship care arrangements have experienced similar levels of trauma, disruption and disadvantage to their peers in non-kin foster care and residential care, while their carers receive less training and support compared with carers in non-kin foster care or residential care and can have a range of additional vulnerabilities and stressors. Thus the need to develop and evaluate effective therapeutic care models of kinship care and support is imperative.

Effective therapeutic care approaches to kinship care must pay attention to the uniqueness of kinship care. To respond to the unique challenges facing kinship carers identified in this chapter, therapeutic models of kinship care and support will benefit from:

- giving specific attention to intergenerational trauma and its consequences
- taking a family systems approach, rather than a traditional 'placement support approach', thus actively engaging all key family members across generations
- utilising processes such as family group meetings or conferences to support the extended family to come together around all family members in ways that empower the family to find their own solutions and address each other's needs.

9

Therapeutic Care Teams

Horizontal Teams in the Vertical World of Out-of-Home Care

NOEL MACNAMARA

Introduction

Therapeutic Care Teams are at the very heart of the Australian Childhood Foundation (ACF) work with children and young people in therapeutic foster and kinship care. ACF provides Therapeutic Specialists to support children, young people and the networks of relationships that care for and support them in out-of-home care (OOHC) across Australia. The Therapeutic Specialists provide clinical leadership within the Therapeutic Care Teams.

The objective underpinning of Therapeutic Care Teams is the establishment of holistic arrangements that are explicitly geared to the needs of children and young people, drawing on theory, evidence of what works, practice wisdom and a focus on making a real and sustainable difference. This objective is not new. The impetus to bring together services to meet the perceived needs of children, rather than around the administrative or professional structures of service provision, has been discussed in academic and professional circles since the 1970s (O'Brien *et al.*, 2009).

Foster and kinship care are complex settings in which to provide therapeutic interventions due to the high rates of difficulty, poor outcomes and high number of professionals and carers involved (Kinsey and Schlösser, 2012).

In a review of foster care, Bromfield and Osborn (2007) found:

> [T]he task of caring is more demanding, stressful and complicated today than at any other time in history. Increasingly, children in out

> of home care present with a complex matrix of needs and challenges that are often not well understood or responded to, resulting in their poor psychological, emotional, social and academic functioning. (p.6)

In 2018, 16,932 children and young people were in foster care and 20,943 children were in kinship care in Australia (AIHW, 2017). Foster care is a form of OOHC where the caregiver is authorised and reimbursed by the state/territory for the care of the child. Kinship care is a form of OOHC where the caregiver is a relative (other than parents) who is reimbursed by the state/territory for the care of the child. For Aboriginal and Torres Strait Islander children, a kinship carer may be another Indigenous person who is a member of their community, a compatible community or from the same language group (SNAICC, 2017).

The complexity of treatment needs for children and young people who have experienced developmental trauma is now well recognised. Despite this recognition, there is limited published information available about practice responses that address the complex needs of children and young people who have been placed in OOHC. The Therapeutic Care Team approach is one which draws from multiple theoretical perspectives, and is multidisciplinary and multifaceted in implementation.

This chapter will review the benefits and potential limitations of integrated working practice across both health and welfare fields of practice. After looking at the prevailing literature, the Therapeutic Care Team approach, developed and implemented in Victoria, Australia, will be presented as a model that is demonstrating some promising results.

Background: Integrated working

There is now substantial theoretical and research literature espousing the benefits of multidisciplinary practice in the health and social welfare sectors (Caw and Sebba, 2014; Frederico *et al.*, 2017; Hammick *et al.*, 2009). Integrated working for children's outcomes has been described as 'the holy grail of policy and services' (Canavan, Dolan and Whyte, 2009, p.385). Integrated working (e.g. child protection, OOHC, child welfare services, youth justice) has become increasingly recognised as important for policy to support children in OOHC. The focus is to share information to avoid duplication of effort and fragmentation, shared assessment and coordinated plans, integrating delivery of services, strategy and governance.

This documentation reveals a developing awareness of the important contribution to practice that a well-coordinated, cohesive professional response to complex problems may offer.

In the learning disability field, for example, where children and young people are frequently identified as having 'complex needs', a singular approach is rarely seen as adequate. Multidisciplinary groups of professionals are sometimes referred to as care teams (Limbrick, 2011, 2016). Such teams offer opportunities for integrated, holistic interventions.

The concept of multifaceted support teams is underpinned by a theoretical foundation supporting early intervention, which 'recognises the interconnections of all aspects of infant activity and honours the infant as a whole being' (Limbrick, 2011, p.13). This thinking has more recently been extended to claim the power of citizens working with professionals to incorporate the role of team activism and advocacy in respect of persons living with a disability (Limbrick, 2016).

In the health field, patient care has a long-established multidisciplinary tradition (Frykholm and Groth, 2011; Opie, 1997). This approach differs from those in the welfare sector, with an assumed hierarchical team where medical professionals ordinarily have a leadership role. This, in part, reflects the medical nature of the field of practice and the operational hierarchy within hospitals and allied health care settings. It may also, however, reflect a particular view of the value of knowledge. In health, it is often the case that a traditional, positivist view of evidence is tightly held, so that alternative forms of professional knowledge, including practice wisdom and cultural knowledge, may not be highly valued in practice. The impact of this worldview may in turn result in a limited view of patients' needs, restricted to a medical diagnosis and response. Despite the potential limitations of health care multidisciplinary teams, some authors suggest that the potential efficacy of health Therapeutic Care Teams may offer substantial practice benefits, including enhanced quality of care and more comprehensive and fully informed care plans, and thus more holistic care experienced by the service user (Frykholm and Groth, 2011; Opie, 1997).

Turning to the mental health field and that of adolescent mental health in particular, a chorus of authors are in furious agreement as to the resounding benefits of effective collaborative practice (Kelly *et al.*, 2003; Lamers *et al.*, 2015; Palmer, 2012). What is less clear, however, are the actual measures of effectiveness and whether the actual benefits outweigh the potential for additional costs including limited agency resources. In addition, the potential costs or limitations of collaboration are cited as including a lack of role clarity within the team, failure to orientate new members to the team, ongoing inter-professional mistrust and the tendency for one discipline to dominate the team discourse. As Bendall *et al.* (2018) state:

> The siloed nature of health and human services delivery in Australia, along with limited resources and capacity and competition for policy prioritisation and funding, has presented many road blocks to services working together in a collaborative way. (p.572)

While acknowledging the importance of the therapeutic alliance between multidisciplinary teams and parents or carers, in adolescent mental health, there is limited research examining the parent–team relationship, or indeed the team itself (Lamers *et al.*, 2015).

Children and young people in out-of-home care

Children and young people who have been placed in the OOHC system are arguably among the most vulnerable groups. It is suggested that many of these children and young people have complex mental health needs that are inadequately serviced by traditional approaches, including traditional hierarchical multidisciplinary approaches (Golding, 2010). Standard case formulation practice based on traditional models of mental health clinical conceptualisation may not capture the unique needs of children and young people who have experienced complex trauma (Golding, 2010; Tarren-Sweeney, 2010). An alternative conceptual paradigm is proposed by Tarren-Sweeney (2010), based on research evidence that children and young people in OOHC are likely to have mental health difficulties, with approximately half of this population reported to have clinically significant problems requiring treatment.

It has been well established in Bronfenbrenner's (1979, 1994, 2005) groundbreaking bioecological theory that children's development is influenced by overlapping and connected levels of influence extending from individual child factors through the family and other relevant individuals (such as peers) to the wider society. It has also been established by Rutter (1987) and by Sameroff and colleagues (Sameroff and Fiese, 2000) that the most disadvantaged children, who face multiple risks, are the most likely to have poor outcomes.

Multiple and diverse risks are likely to be evident at several levels of influence simultaneously (e.g. individual, carer and environmental living conditions) (Hanson and Carta, 1995), and in order to intervene successfully, services need to be offered at all the necessary levels, which will be accomplished most effectively by integrated working (Davidson, Bunting and Webb, 2012).

Ten principles for responding to children and young people in OOHC are proposed and presented ecologically, over three levels: at the practice level, at the service model design level and finally with respect to the wider society (Tarren-Sweeney, 2010). This multidimensional, multifaceted approach seeks to respond to the child in the context of her lived experience and environment. It incorporates practice and system design that is multidisciplinary and collaborative, and integrates specialist clinical services for these children and young people with the case work offered by care organisations (Golding, 2010; Tarren-Sweeney, 2010). The ten key principles for guiding the design of services for children and young people in care (Tarren-Sweeney, 2010) are summarised below as including:

1. specialised knowledge and skills
2. clinical/psychosocial – developmental scope of practice
3. advocacy
4. primary–specialist care nexus and universal assessment
5. preventative, long-term engagement and monitoring
6. integral part of social care milieu
7. active ownership

8. normalisation strategies
9. service engagement
10. whole of government accountability. (Tarren-Sweeney, 2010, p.617)

These ideas transform the concept of multidisciplinary working to one which is created to provide an integrated service to the child. On the basis of these proposed principles, therapeutic services are fully integrated with care and casework approaches.

Collaboration: Rhetoric versus reality

Although collaborative and team approaches to practice have been documented as making an important contribution, it is appropriate to consider the limitations of collaboration. Some identify the importance of collaboration but warn that the rhetoric may not always resemble the practice, in the context of budget cuts and depleting resources. These authors suggest that pitfalls occur when collaborative practice is mandated in response to a critical incident or unfavourable publicity.

> Where this kind of collaboration is ordered and at times legislated, it is unlikely that a detailed analysis of the problem situation will have taken place and that, as a result, the 'new' way of working may become just another procedural requirement. In these situations, there is a potential risk of a focus on procedural solutions rather than attitudinal change. (Horwath and Morrison, 2007, p64)

A hierarchy of collaborative practice is conceptualised as ranging from communication across disciplines or agencies to full integration. In summary, the levels of collaborative practice include:

1. More communication across disciplines and agencies;
2. Some level of co-operation, which may focus on a particular situation or case;
3. Interagency and multidisciplinary coordination, where key stakeholders shared;

4. Forming a coalition is identified as a means of capturing motivated and informed key stakeholders in collaborative working relationships with a specific focus on agreed goals;
5. Service integration is described as the penultimate in collaborative practice and is where both formally mandated practice, service system design and skilled and motivated individuals work together to enhance service delivery. (Horwath and Morrison, 2007)

For collaboration to be effective, a high level of trust, strong relationship-based networks and attention to critical 'people issues' are required as part of the implementation process.

Therapeutic Care Teams

Having identified a plethora of literature in relation to multidisciplinary and collaborative practice, the scholarly literature documenting Therapeutic Care Team practice in child welfare is sparse. An emerging discourse outlining 'wraparound' interventions delivered by multidisciplinary teams identifies primarily social workers, nurses and psychologists in various settings, including a mental health unit and various community settings (Kinsey and Schlösser, 2012). Much of the literature here, while contemporary, is in the form of grey literature describing various programs and the incorporation of the Therapeutic Care Team concept in the program design. The Government of Western Australia is one example where the statutory child protection authority has outlined a 'Therapeutic Care Team Approach' to practice, described as a model that evolved from partnership practice (Government of Western Australia, 2016). The practice framework describes the Therapeutic Care Team as a central and integrated element of the approach to working with children and young people and their families in Western Australia. However, there is no evaluation of the operationalisation of this policy position.

Also in the field of OOHC, and foster care in particular, Core Assets in the United Kingdom and Key Assets in Australasia have documented what they describe as a 'team parenting' approach (Caw and Sebba, 2014). The approach involves a multidisciplinary team around the child to ensure that the child's complex needs are assessed and met, and their resilience developed. In this model, carers play a key role in understanding and responding to the child's difficulties and are offered specialised training and support (Caw and Sebba, 2014). Each member of the therapeutic team has a clearly defined role, with the child's therapist described as a core member.

In Victoria, Australia, two foster care programs have documented and evaluated their Therapeutic Care Team approach to the provision of therapeutic foster care (Frederico *et al.*, 2017; McPherson *et al.*, 2018). What follows is a detailed examination of the features of these Therapeutic Care Teams, along with a case study presentation demonstrating the approach in practice.

What is a Therapeutic Care Team?

The Therapeutic Care Team approach has integration of a holistic approach at its heart and is a planned and coordinated way of supporting a child or young person and their carer. It is based on the principle that all the professionals and others who have a significant relationship with the child or young person are equal and are working towards agreed goals, and it promotes an understanding of different roles and responsibilities and the need to review progress and the changing needs of the child or young person. The focus is on the need to work together to one therapeutic plan in an integrated way towards best outcomes. As Judith Herman (1992) said:

> Recovery cannot occur in isolation. It can take place only within the context of relationships characterized by belief in persuasion rather than coercion, ideas rather than force, and mutuality rather than authoritarian control – precisely the beliefs that were shattered by the original traumatic experiences. (p.23)

The Therapeutic Care Team approach is built on a commitment to relationship-based practice and adherence to the principles of trauma-informed practice. A framework of physical, emotional and psychological safety is essential to enable the child or young person to address the issues that have brought them into the OOHC system. It has been argued that the relationships with people who care for and about children are the golden thread in children's lives, and 'the quality of a child's relationships is the lens through which we should view what we do and plan to do' (Care Inquiry, 2013, p.2). A key process in helping them come to terms with their experiences is the development and experience of safe, trusting, stable and nurturing relationships (Happer, McCreadie and Aldgate, 2006; Munro, 2011).

A Therapeutic Care Team is a network of professionals, parents, caregivers and any other significant adults who have been gathered around the child and young person and charged with the responsibility of providing quality nurturing care and the coordination of service delivery. The Therapeutic Care Team is responsible for setting the direction of the child's treatment, delivering the intervention, managing the ecological impacts, promoting a collaborative approach to influencing children's multiple environments and overseeing any statutory requirements – essentially building and coordinating a flexible network of services to meet the multiple and changing needs of children who have suffered trauma and loss. This is to counter the challenges the children face in the OOHC system:

> I know that I can't live with my mum and dad but I would like to find a place that I can stay in forever rather than moving all the time and feeling more and more unhappy and not really understanding what's going on and why things keep changing, just as I get used to new people and a new place. I just want adults to see how hard it is for me not having one person in my life that really knows me, understands me and stays with me. This means adults keep making mistakes, getting confused, missing things and making me angry. Sometimes I get so angry that I explode like a volcano with no way of stopping until all the lava inside is out. (Robert, eight years old, residential care) (Therapeutic Specialist, Australian Childhood Foundation, 2016)

The composition of a Therapeutic Care Team will vary depending on the issues and needs of the individual child or young person and those who care and support them. However, it will always include the Therapeutic Specialist, child protection practitioner, the child's case manager, the placement agency case worker, caregiver(s) and, where appropriate, the parents or other family members and those with a significant relationship to the child or young person. The Therapeutic Care Team may also be extended to include personnel from any other agencies involved in the child's treatment, such as drug, youth justice, disability and mental health services.

The main distinction between a Therapeutic Care Team and other meetings or forums (such as case conferences, professionals' meetings or planning meetings) is the development of the Therapeutic Care Team as a working group which promotes an attitude of partnership, collaboration and information sharing. A Therapeutic Care Team is a relationship in which all parties feel equal and share responsibility for the success of their common purpose: the best interests of the child and the well-being of the carer.

When a Therapeutic Care Team is fully relationship-based it will map out the key partnerships that are required between roles and build the team that seeks to resource and support the network of relationships of care and support around the child. This shifts the focus of organising from individual roles to relationships between roles, and forces the team to map out the key relationships required for the collaboration to function effectively. Tasks such as goal setting and resource allocation then work through the partnerships, not prescribed roles.

Although Therapeutic Care Teams are groups, they are also made up of individuals. In addition to behaviours that facilitate the function of the Therapeutic Care Team, certain personal values are necessary for individuals to function well within the Therapeutic Care Team. The following are five personal values that characterise the most effective members of high-functioning Therapeutic Care Teams in the OOHC system.

1. **Honesty:** Therapeutic Care Team members put a high value on effective communication within the Therapeutic Care Team, including transparency about aims, decisions, uncertainty and mistakes. Honesty is critical to continued improvement and for maintaining the mutual trust necessary for a high-functioning Therapeutic Care Team.

2. **Discipline:** Therapeutic Care Team members carry out their roles and responsibilities with discipline, even when it seems inconvenient. At the same time, Therapeutic Care Team members are disciplined in seeking out and sharing new information to improve individual and Therapeutic Care Team functioning, even when doing so may be uncomfortable. Such discipline allows Therapeutic Care

Teams to develop and stick to their standards and protocols even as they seek ways to improve.

3. **Creativity:** Therapeutic Care Team members are excited by the possibility of tackling new or emerging problems creatively. They see even unanticipated bad outcomes as potential opportunities to learn and improve.
4. **Humility:** Therapeutic Care Team members recognise differences in training but do not believe that one type of training or perspective is uniformly superior to others. They also recognise that they are human and will make mistakes. Hence, a key value of working in a Therapeutic Care Team is that fellow Therapeutic Care Team members can rely on each other to help recognise and avert failures, regardless of where they are in the hierarchy. In this regard, effective Therapeutic Care Team work is a practical response to the recognition that each of us is imperfect, and no matter who you are, how experienced or smart, you will fail.
5. **Curiosity:** Therapeutic Care Team members are dedicated to reflecting upon the lessons learned in the course of their daily activities and using those insights for continuous improvement of their own work and the functioning of the Therapeutic Care Team.

The impact of putting these values into practice is well captured by this carer:

> If I had still been a generalist carer, it would have been 'game over' for me – I could not cope with that level of stress on my own. If you have a child in your home who creates secondary trauma, you are much more likely to give up without the support of the therapeutic specialist and the therapeutic care team. (Frederico *et al.*, 2014, p.213)

A Therapeutic Care Team is not a treatment *per se*; it is a *process*. As such, it aims to achieve positive outcomes through several mechanisms, such as:

- undertaking a comprehensive therapeutic assessment

- developing therapeutic plans that are designed to meet the identified needs of children, young people and their caregivers
- addressing a range of life areas (placement, school, community, family contact)
- being culturally responsive
- recognising the strengths of children, young people and their caregivers
- support children and young people's rights
- employing evidence-based treatments within the process
- monitoring progress on measurable indicators of success and changing the plan as necessary
- focusing on, and being accountable for, outcomes.

The impetus for creating a Therapeutic Care Team surrounding a child or young person is the desire to provide individualised services that are truly holistic and coordinated. The spirit of creating a Care Team includes making the commitment to serve, treat and maintain a child or young person within their placement for the duration of their stay and beyond.

Practice principles for Therapeutic Care Teams

The following nine practice principles are essential to understanding the Therapeutic Care Team process:

1. **Safety and well-being:** The safety and well-being of the child is always paramount.
2. **Child and carer's voice:** Child and carer perspectives are sought and prioritised during all phases of the placement.
3. **Team-based:** The members that comprise the care team must have a strong commitment to the child or young person's well-being.
4. **Collaboration:** Each team member must be dedicated to the team, the team's goals and the therapeutic plan. The plan

reflects the assessment and a merger of team members' perspectives and resources.

5. **Culturally respectful:** The care team process respects the values, preferences, beliefs, culture and identity of the child or young person and their community.
6. **Individualised:** The therapeutic plan is tailored to the needs and wants of the child or young person.
7. **Strength-based:** The process and the therapeutic plan hone in on and build upon the capabilities, knowledge, skills and assets of the child and carer, their family and community, and other team members.
8. **Persistence and flexibility:** There is a commitment to achieving the goals set out despite challenges. The care team persists in working toward the goals included in the therapeutic plan.
9. **Outcomes-focused:** Outcomes must be determined and measured for each goal established with the child and carer as well as for those goals established at the program and system levels.

Functions of the Therapeutic Care Team

The key functions of the Therapeutic Care Team are:

- agreeing what needs to be put in place based on an up-to-date assessment
- creating a therapeutic plan, which has clear, achievable milestones
- resolving what actions individual members of the care team will carry out, and agree timescales
- liaising, as appropriate, with other services
- agreeing and working towards the same outcomes, with members taking responsibility as individuals for specific actions

- identifying any challenges and taking steps with the child and family to address and overcome them
- monitoring and reviewing the therapeutic plan.

Therapeutic Care Team: Case study

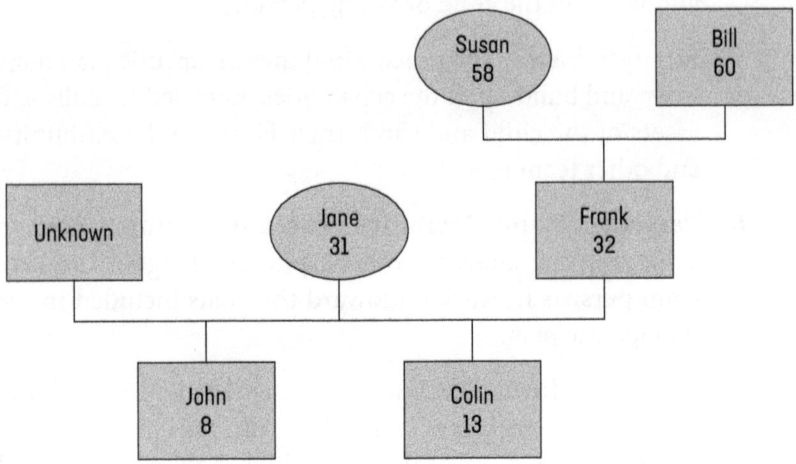

Figure 9.1 Genogram

Colin is 13 years old and he has been in care for 11 years. Colin's family have been known to child protective services since his birth. Both of his parents had drug and alcohol problems. Colin's father was also violent and a habitual criminal. Colin's needs were of low priority in the chaotic home environment and his parents would often spend their income on drugs and alcohol rather than food for the family. Colin's father was imprisoned for an assault. While his father was in prison, Colin's mother had a number of unsuitable partners, the last of whom assaulted Colin, resulting in bruising on his face and buttocks. This led to him being removed from his mother's care.

Colin was placed with his paternal grandmother by child protective services. However, it was not known that she also was an alcoholic who suffered from agoraphobia. She received no support, financial or practical, in her care of Colin.

Colin's grandmother's home was kindly but armoured by denial, delusion and a 'no talk' rule. Consequently, Colin did not understand what was happening and, not surprisingly, he believed that it was all his fault. Colin's predominant feeling was overwhelming confusion.

At five years old, Colin started school. Colin complained regularly of being bullied by children at school and he had no friends. Parents of other children complained that he was frightening their children by his 'strange' behaviour and aggressive attitude. The school staff were so concerned about him that they contacted child protective services. Following an investigation Colin was removed from his grandmother's care and placed in temporary foster care.

In foster care, Colin was difficult, aggressive, challenging and volatile, with frequent angry outbursts, verbal and physical aggression toward family members, and multiple indications of arousal (e.g. difficulty sleeping, impaired concentration, edginess and irritability). By the age of nine, he had been in eight foster care placements and was then placed in residential care. Colin experienced many child protection workers during this time. There was no intervention plan or particular direction for Colin and he drifted in the care system.

In residential care, Colin became increasingly aggressive and engaged in sexually inappropriate behaviour with other children. He also experienced difficulties sleeping. During this time, he was diagnosed with attention deficit hyperactivity disorder (ADHD), oppositional defiant disorder (ODD), conduct disorder, anxiety disorder and sleep disorder. He was medicated but received no other interventions. Colin was suspended from school due to his behaviour. He wandered the neighbourhood and was missing for periods of time.

At this point, Colin was referred to our therapeutic foster care program. A Therapeutic Care Team was formed. It consisted of the child protection worker, residential unit manager, the foster care worker, ACF therapeutic specialist and mental health worker. Colin's file was reviewed and the foster care worker and the therapeutic specialist met with Colin.

From the formation of the Therapeutic Care Team it focused on creating a 'shared meaning' and a mutual vision for the work with Colin and his carer. In addition, the Therapeutic Care Team members developed a shared meaning about the terminology and principles of disciplines other than their own. This facilitated a shared understanding and good communication across interdisciplinary boundaries.

Colin was matched with John, a single male. John was a teacher and had been a respite carer for many years. He had cared for Colin for a short time between placements when he was seven years old. John was willing to take extended leave from his employment to help Colin's transition into the placement.

The Therapeutic Specialist provided training for John about child development, disrupted attachment, complex trauma and reparenting children who hurt.

Colin moved into John's home.

The Therapeutic Care Team was expanded to include John and the deputy principal of the school Colin would attend. The Therapeutic Care Team met on a weekly basis. The Therapeutic Specialist conducted a full assessment of Colin and this formed the basis of the therapeutic plan. The assessment found that Colin's presentation was inconsistent with the diagnoses that had been made. The child protection worker arranged for Colin to be reassessed.

The Therapeutic Specialist provided the school with training about trauma-informed care for children in the classroom. The Therapeutic Care Team coordinated all of the activities and planning. All interventions were integrated, meaning that transition between disciplines and other services was as 'seamless' as possible. Although not all Therapeutic Care Team members were involved in direct service delivery for Colin and John, all members were involved in planning and monitoring aspects of intervention. After assessment and planning, the care team met regularly to share information, monitor and review.

Colin had not had contact with his grandmother since entering residential care. The Therapeutic Care Team decided that Colin's grandmother should be assessed to see whether contact between Colin and his grandmother would be appropriate. This proved to be a pivotal event. Colin's grandmother was assessed as suitable, and arrangements were made for her to meet with Colin. She also informed the Therapeutic Care Team that Colin had an aunt who lived quite close to his new placement and she had information about Colin's mother and father.

The Therapeutic Care Team referred Colin to a counsellor for his sexually inappropriate behaviour. The counsellor joined the

Therapeutic Care Team. The Therapeutic Care Team continued to meet weekly.

Within the first six months of his placement with John, Colin's behaviour stabilised. He slept well and his diagnoses for ADHD, ODD, conduct disorder and anxiety disorder were reviewed and he was taken off all medication. He disclosed that he had been sexually assaulted by a cousin when he was in his grandmother's care and in a residential placement by another resident. He started and fully attended school. He was reconnected with his grandmother and an aunt. The Therapeutic Care Team were able to complete some life story work and help Colin understand why he was in care.

Conclusion

The care of children and young people who have experienced abuse, neglect and trauma and who reside in the OOHC system requires a team of resilient professionals and others with a significant relationship with the child who are capable of responding to multifaceted problems that resist simple solutions. At its best, the Therapeutic Care Team addresses these problems by bringing together a flexible and mutually supportive team that can innovate and remain agile to meet the needs of the child or young person and over time shape services to help improve outcomes and change the negative trajectory. It utilises a democratic relational base involving empathy, respect, trust, reflection and information sharing at the child, practice and system levels. These relationships can be facilitated, enhanced and linked to improvements in outcomes for children and young people.

Therapeutic Care Teams are an antidote to this fragmented and uncoordinated care system in which continuity of care is often the victim. Interventions that matrix across the accepted hierarchical structures (horizontally) increase cooperation and communication across the traditional silos and unlock resources that are often inaccessible to the child or young person. They provide a framework that can be systematically applied to better connect and coordinate an array of service providers and points of service delivery, capable of matching flexibly the needs and preferences of children and young people over time and at various stages of their care.

To sum up, the Therapeutic Care Team is a method by which children and young people experience cohesiveness and connectedness of the care system, which provides the foundation for care capable of addressing the promotion of social and emotional well-being in general and trauma prevention and treatment in particular. Therapeutic Care Teams represent a systemic willingness to know about the pain and suffering caused by trauma and begin addressing it in a holistic way that is healing rather than retraumatising.

References

AIHW (2017). *Child Protection Australia 2015–16.* Child Welfare Series No. 66. Cat. No. CWS 60. Canberra: AIHW.

Bendall, S., Phelps, A., Browne, V., Metcalf, O. *et al.* (2018). *Trauma and Young People: Moving toward Trauma-Informed Services and Systems.* Melbourne: Orygen, The National Centre of Excellence in Youth Mental Health.

Bromfield, L.M. and Osborn, A. (2007). *'Getting the Big Picture': A Synopsis and Critique of Australian Out-of-Home Care Research* (Child Abuse Prevention Issues No. 26). Melbourne: Australian Institute of Family Studies, National Child Protection Clearinghouse. Accessed on 7/1/2019 at https://aifs.gov.au/cfca/publications/getting-big-picture-synopsis-and-critique-austra.

Bronfenbrenner, U. (1979). *The Ecology of Human Development.* Cambridge, MA: Harvard University Press.

Bronfenbrenner, U. (1994). Ecology models of human development. *The International Encyclopedia of Education*, 2nd Edition [online], 3, 36–43.

Bronfenbrenner, U. (2005). *Making Human Beings Human*, 1st Edition. Thousand Oaks: Sage Publications.

Canavan, J., Dolan, P. and Whyte, L. (2009). Privileging practice: Facing the challenge of integrated working for outcomes for children. *Children & Society*, 23, 377–388.

Care Inquiry (2013). *Making Not Breaking: Building Relationships for Our Most Vulnerable Children.* London: House of Commons.

Caw, J. and Sebba, J. (2014). *Team Parenting for Children and Young People in Foster Care: A Model for Integrated Therapeutic Care.* London: Jessica Kingsley Publishers.

Davidson, G., Bunting, L. and Webb, M.L. (2012). *Families Experiencing Multiple Adversities: A Review of the International Literature.* Belfast: Barnardo's Northern Ireland.

Frederico, M., Long, M., McNamara, P., McPherson, L. and Rose, R. (2014). The way all foster care should be: The experience of therapeutic foster carers in the Victorian Circle Program. *Children Australia*, 39(4), 211–215.

Frederico, M., Long, M., McNamara, P., McPherson, L. and Rose, R. (2017). Improving outcomes for children and young people in out of home care: The role of therapeutic foster care. *Child and Family Social Work*, 22(2), 1064–1074.

Frykholm, O. and Groth, K. (2011). References to personal experiences and scientific evidence during medical multi-disciplinary team meetings. *Behaviour and Information Technology*, 30(4), 455–466.

Golding, K. (2010). Multi-agency and specialist working to meet the mental health needs of children and young people in care and adopted. *Clinical Child Psychology and Psychiatry*, 15(4), 573–587.

Government of Western Australia (2016). *Therapeutic Care Team Approach Practice Framework: Working Together to Support Children and Young People in Out-of-Home Care to Improve Their Future Outcomes*. Accessed on 7/1/2019 at www.dcp.wa.gov.au/Resources/Documents/Policies%20and%20Frameworks/Care%20Team%20Approach%20Practice%20Framework.pdf.

Hammick, M., Freeth, D., Copperman, J. and Goodsman, D. (2009). *Being Interprofessional*. Cambridge: Polity Press.

Hanson, M.J. and Carta, J. (1995). Addressing the challenges of families with multiple risks. *Exceptional Children*, 62(3), 201–212.

Happer, H., McCreadie, J. and Aldgate, J. (2006). *Celebrating Success: What Helps Looked After Children Succeed?* Edinburgh: Social Work Inspection Agency.

Herman, J. (1992). *Trauma and Recovery: The Aftermath of Violence – From Domestic Abuse to Political Terror*. New York, NY: Basic Books.

Horwath, J. and Morrison, T. (2007). Collaboration, integration and change in children's services: Critical issues and key ingredients. *Child Abuse and Neglect*, 31(1), 55–69.

Kelly, C., Allan, A., Roscoe, P. and Herrick, E. (2003). The mental health needs of looked after children: An integrated multi-agency model of care. *Clinical Child Psychology and Psychiatry*, 8(3), 323–335.

Kinsey, D. and Schlösser, A. (2012). Interventions in foster and kinship care: A systematic review. *Clinical Child Psychology and Psychiatry*, 18(3), 429–463.

Lamers, A., Delsong, M., van Widenfelt, B. and Vermeiren, R. (2015). A measure of the parent–team alliance in youth residential psychiatry: The Revised Short Working Alliance Inventory. *Child Youth Care Forum*, 44(6), 801–817.

Limbrick, P. (2011). Holistic interventions in complex care. *Nursing Children and Young People*, 23(10), 123–134.

Limbrick, P. (2016). *Caring Activism: A 21st Century Concept of Care. A Proposal for Citizens to Join Together to Support Vulnerable Children, Teenagers, Adults and Elderly People*. London: Interconnections.

McPherson, L., Gatwiri, K., Tucci, J., Mitchell, J. and Macnamara, N. (2018). A paradigm shift in responding to children and young people who have experienced trauma: The Australian Treatment and Care for Kids Program. *Youth Services Review*, 94, 525–534.

Munro, E. (2011). *Munro Review of Child Protection: Final Report – A Child-Centred System*. Accessed on 7/1/2019 at www.gov.uk/government/publications/munro-review-of-child-protection-final-report-a-child-centred-system.

O'Brien, M., Bachmann, M.O., Jones, N.R., Reading, R. *et al.* (2009). Do integrated children's services improve outcomes? Evidence from England's Children's Trust Pathfinders. *Children and Society*, 23(5), 320–335.

Opie, A. (1997). Thinking teams thinking clients: Issues of discourse and representation in the work of health Therapeutic Care Teams. *Sociology of Health and Illness*, 19(3), 259–280.

Palmer, K. (2012). Outcomes for youth with severe emotional disturbance: A repeated measures longitudinal study of a wraparound approach of service delivery in systems of care. *Child Youth Care Forum*, 41, 407–425.

Rutter, M. (1987). Psychosocial resilience and protective mechanisms. *American Journal of Orthopsychiatry*, 57(3), 316–331.

Sameroff, A.J. and Fiese, B.H. (2000). Transactional Regulation: The Developmental Ecology of Early Intervention. In J.P. Shonkoff and S.J. Meisels (eds), *Handbook of Early Childhood Intervention*. New York, NY: Cambridge University Press.

SNAICC (2017). *Understanding and Applying the Aboriginal and Torres Strait Islander Child Placement Principle*. Melbourne: SNAICC.

Tarren-Sweeney, M. (2010). It's time to re-think mental health services for children and young people in care, and those adopted from care. *Clinical Child Psychology and Psychiatry*, 15(4), 613–626.

PRACTICE REFLECTION

Joe Tucci, Janise Mitchell and Ed Tronick

In his chapter, Macnamara has elucidated, perhaps for the first time, a framework for conceptualising the function and practice of Therapeutic Care Teams. As he points out, it is underpinned by democratic principles of decision-making with a unified purpose of understanding, planning for and organising to meet the present and future needs of children in out-of-home care.

Sitting at this collective table, members of Therapeutic Care Teams are not there to represent their discipline or even the organisation that employs them. They are there to draw on their individual expertise with humility and respect for each other's points of view in order to find common frames and shared strategies that serve children's interests, healing their past and preparing them for the course of their lives.

Effective Therapeutic Care Teams have the mandate to hold a structure around children and their most immediate intimate relationships, in particular their carers and siblings, and at times their school. In this sense, this structure performs the role of priming those relationships to attend, in everyday moments, to opportunities for regulatory repair that children in out-of-home care are in need of. The Therapeutic Care Team buffers and resources carers and children as they learn about each other and begin to share moments of physiological, sensory and narrative attunement. It helps to integrate systemic influences in ways that are manageable for carers and children. For example, the return of matters to court can often disrupt children's sense of stability with their carers. The Therapeutic Care Team works to understand when court appearances are scheduled to occur, hypothesise the reasons why children may react in the ways they do and make plans with the carer and other important adults in the network about how best to respond so that children experience not only the activated stressed states triggered by court but also the predictable comforting reactions offered to them in a systematised way by those important to them.

This is the power of Therapeutic Care Teams – the amplification of the resources offered to children resulting from intentional coordination of the relationships around children.

The world of the traumatised child is most often characterised by chaos and confusion, undermining a sense of safety derived from understanding who is in your world, what to expect and how and when things happen in your life. Too often the formal systems around children, designed to protect, support and care for them, serve to further amplify their experience of confusion and chaos. We know that all children do well when their world is characterised by predictability, consistency and routine across all their relationships and the different environments within which they live, learn and play.

Many children in foster and kinship care present with high-level needs and complex behaviours that challenge the adults and systems around them to know how best to understand and respond to their needs. The definition or frame given to a need or a problem is often dependent on the perspective of the individual, their background and own history, and their training, role or organisational mandate. How a need or problem is defined shapes the way it is responded to. As such, it is not uncommon for trauma-based behaviours to be understood and responded to in a range of different, sometimes contradictory ways. At times these responses may be less about the actual needs or behaviours themselves than the capacity of adults and systems around the child to address them effectively.

Through this chapter, Macnamara offers an important reminder that effective care for children extends beyond their placement. Even more critically, the mechanism of a Therapeutic Care Team affords opportunities for confusion to be minimised and intentional steps taken collectively towards an integrated, holistic and congruent response to children's needs across multiple relationships and settings.

10

Defining the Conceptual Maps That Resource the Day-to-Day Interactions between Carers and Children to Become More Therapeutic

DANIEL HUGHES AND JONATHAN BAYLIN

Children develop stories of their day-to-day lives, stories that represent how they make sense of yesterday, that guide their perceptions and responses today, and anticipate what will occur tomorrow. Stories emerge from embodied experiences with other people, and children's first stories emerge from their positive and negative experiences with caregivers. Children traumatized by their parents or first caregivers make stories involving shame and terror, vigilance and mistrust, hopelessness and survival. For caregivers to influence these children in positive ways, they need to help them have experiences that are radically different from the frightening and painful kind they had with their first caregivers. These new experiences of feeling safe, accepted, comforted, and enjoyed provide the experiential base for the child and caregiver to co-construct new stories, stories that include being valued by a trustworthy adult.

In order to help maltreated children develop new stories, caregivers also need to develop stories that support their readiness and ability to provide trustworthy care for children who do not trust care. We all need stories to give direction to our lives (Zak, 2012). The story of the trustworthy caregiver includes their ability to understand their child's story and to understand their role in helping the child develop a new one. The caregiver's story includes the ability to generate trust with a defensive child by not becoming defensive themselves, facilitating their child's emotional regulation skills by remaining regulated themselves, and increasing their child's reflective skills by parenting with reflection, not reaction. The caregiver's story involves the ability to engage in safe, reciprocal relationships with a child who is often initially unable and unwilling to engage in such relationships. The caregiver's story needs to serve as an invitation to the child to engage in a similar story with the caregiver, where both caregiver and child cherish mutual respect and delight, cooperation and reciprocity, engagement and repair. The caregiver's story includes the awareness that she is neither perfect nor invincible and that she needs care from other adults who understand and support her. The caregiver's influence comes from holding on to a hopeful, compassionate story that invites the child to lift the wall of disengagement and share in the construction of a new story that is deeply meaningful to both, where trust and care are experienced and embodied by the child in ways that are both healing and transformative.

Let's begin by mentioning two traumatized children who are being raised by caregivers who are trying to understand their story and guide the development of a shared story:

- Six-year-old Jack insisted on deciding everything in the home – where he sat at dinner, if his foster mom could smile at him, when he would go to bed, what they were allowed to talk about while in the car.
- Ten-year-old Ruth might scream and cry for long periods of time when she was not allowed to do something that she wanted to do.

Jack and Ruth were now in seemingly safe, predictable, caring families, with caregivers who provided reasonable expectations, encouragement, affection, and consequences. And they had been in their homes for 6–12 months without giving any signs that things might be different in the months ahead. Why? Their repetitive, defensive, behaviors which are confusing and frustrating to caregivers.

These behaviors and many others are the ongoing effects of the trauma on the child, part of the child's habitual, mindless, trauma-driven survival strategy. Inevitably, these behaviors are inherently more asocial than pro-social. Confronted with these 'negative' behaviors, caregivers have a natural tendency to speak sternly and defensively with the child about these behaviors in an effort to get the child to 'behave better'. Typically, efforts to target these behaviors with instruction, reminders, and consequences are ineffective. Patiently repeating these interventions tends to create no lasting changes. One time the behavior might stop (though sometimes only after a tantrum), only to return an hour or a day later.

Addressing the behavioral manifestations of trauma-driven mistrust does not address the core incentive for this defensive behavior: survival in a harsh, uncaring world. The child's reflexive defensiveness is not influenced by immediate circumstances or incentives to change, but rather by the child's deep mistrust of the motives and future behavior of adults who try to get close to them. The more confusing or frustrating is the behavior, the more likely we are seeing how the trauma is still daily expressing itself. These behaviors often reflect the traumatic story that is guiding the child's life. Unless we are able to change this story to one that is more conducive to a life characterized by caring and safety, the behaviors are likely to occur again and again in spite of our best efforts to reduce or manage them.

When young children have experienced abuse and neglect within the relationships that they had with their parents, they are left with a legacy which is the conceptual map – the story – for the nature of who they are and what a family is. With that story – a story of shame, terror, mistrust – the legacy creates the extreme difficulty that such traumatized children have in being able to heal and thrive within the relationships present in their new homes. It is left to their new caregivers – foster carers, relatives, adoptive parents – to relate with them in ways that will show them that this family is different, that they are different, and that a new story – a story of hope, discovery, comfort, and joy – can develop. We are guided by theories and research in the fields of attachment, intersubjectivity, and neurobiology in understanding how caregivers might be able to assist these children in creating new stories. From these fields of knowledge we have developed the principles and interventions of

Dyadic Developmental Psychotherapy (DDP) and DDP-Influenced Parenting (Baylin and Hughes, 2016; Hughes, 2011). Now we will first describe the stories of traumatized children that prevent them from trusting their new caregivers and make it very difficult for these caregivers to provide them with the care that they need.

Blocked trust: Going it alone

Children exposed to early-life adversity survive by adapting neurobiologically to living with undependable, untrustworthy caregivers (Belsky, 2005; Teicher *et al.*, 2003). This adaptation requires suppression of the development of the social engagement system, the brain system that would typically be developing in a supportive environment (Porges, 2011, 2017). Instead, poor care promotes a developmental trajectory favoring the self-defense system, a brain circuit devoted to surviving through self-care, rapid deployment of the fight, flight, freeze reactions, and emotional detachment (Sapolsky, 2017). By using the self-defense system, the child learns to disengage emotionally while having to stay in physical proximity to an adult. Instead of Plan A, trusting in an adult to provide comfort, protection, and pleasure, these children go with Plan B: mistrusting adults while learning to maintain sufficient proximity to them to get basic survival needs met. We call this adaptation to poor care *blocked trust*. Blocked trust consists of both a strategy for managing the emotional pain of exposure to poor care and a behavioral strategy for meeting survival needs in spite of poor care.

Social pain, social buffering, and state-specific story construction

In order to survive without a trustworthy caregiver, children have to somehow manage their *social pain*, the intensely negative feelings of being alone without someone to turn to for help, for comfort. Neuroscientists who study social pain have shown that the pain of rejection is real pain, pain that activates circuitry in the brain much like physical pain (Eisenberger *et al.*, 2011). In a trustworthy relationship with a caregiver, the child's distress activates the adult's pain system, the neural basis for empathy (Kalin, Shelton, and Lynn, 1995).

The presence of the comforting adult has the effect of turning off the child's distress response, soothing the child while instilling the child's trust in the adult to be responsive to the child's needs. Neuroscientists call this process of co-regulating the child's negative states *social buffering* (Coan, Schaefer, and Davidson, 2006; Tottenham *et al.*, 2012). Literally, the soothing presence of a trusted caregiver quiets the child's neural alarm system, helping to shift the child's internal state from a negative one to a positive one, from a state of dysregulation to a more regulated state conducive to safe social engagement. By experiencing many repetitions of this state-shifting process (interstate travel), the child learns to trust that negative states can be endured, that help is coming. This actually helps the child learn that states of sadness and fear and pain can be endured because help is coming from a responsive, effective co-regulating adult (Tronick, 2017).

In the absence of a socially buffering relationship, the young child needs some way to manage intensely negative states by himself at a time when his brain has not yet developed much capacity for self-regulation. One of the ways that even a very young child may start to regulate negative affect, including regulating the pain of not having a secure comforter, is through the activation of the opioid system (Panksepp, 1998). Opioids (especially endorphins) are analgesic. Releasing them automatically in response to experiencing neglect and abuse enables the young child to partially block the social and physical pain associated with being mistreated. Opioids serve double functions: suppressing pain and suppressing sensory awareness. When the opioid system is strongly activated, it both reduces the subjective experience of suffering and also reduces the level of engagement with the immediate environment. In short, without knowing it, the child initiates a process of automatic, mindless disengagement, a process of habitually going away internally, despite the necessity of staying in physical proximity to a hurtful caregiver to survive. This opioid-driven process is now thought to be the neurobiological foundation for chronic dissociation and reflexive disengagement (Lanius *et al.*, 2010).

While this 'going away' defense is adaptive in the original environment of poor care, chronic disengagement from the immediate environment takes the child's attention away from the immediate experiences of interacting with a new caregiver (Sapolsky, 2017).

This has major consequences for the process of generating a new story to replace the trauma-based narrative. Children who had to dissociate early in life in order to suppress their awareness and subjective experiences of distress often have narratives about being 'gone', even dead or, at least, hardly alive. Story construction is 'state specific', and in a state of deep disengagement, a child's state-driven story would inevitably be one of being unworthy of being alive, of being valued, of being seen and heard and felt.

Besides learning to suppress the social emotions that would typically move a child to approach a caregiver, maltreated children have to develop a behavioral repertoire for strategically managing (through intimidation, manipulation, avoidance, control) their relationship with caregivers. Behaviors which are adaptive for the mistrusting child include 'self-provisioning' or getting things they need when they can (later called 'stealing'); 'self-protective story telling' (later called 'lying'); storing up energy reserves by binge-eating sugary and fatty foods; hiding from caregivers by 'getting small'; and disengaging by downshifting from sympathetic states to parasympathetic states to reduce the probability of drawing negative attention and to reduce the pain of being 'present' while being rejected or abused (later emerging as chronic shame) (Baylin and Hughes, 2016).

Trauma-driven stories and these defensive behaviors block the child's ability to experience the new caregiver as different from the old one. In this way, the originally adaptive defense and the story associated with it contribute to a chronic process of blocking engagement with a new caregiver. This blocked engagement suppresses the potential for change, including the core process of constructing a new story of hope, trust, and safety. The very process the child had to use to block the pain of not having a social-buffering adult now functions as a block to being present enough to experience the difference of living with a safe, trustworthy caregiver.

Without engagement, the child cannot have the intersubjective sensory experiences necessary for building a new story. New experiences of being cared for are grist for the child's story-making process. These experiences are essential for helping the child replace the trauma-driven story with a story about being a worthy child in the care of a trustworthy adult. Without these new experiences, there can be no new story. This is why DDP puts safe-enough engagement front and center as the initial relational goal for laying the foundation for therapeutic care.

The default mode network and the story revision process

Children who start life with undependable or hurtful parents inevitably internalize negative feelings and beliefs that organize poorly around a sense of self that is fragmented, brittle, or chaotic. For example, one child in therapy said when asked why her biological mother mistreated her, ''Cause I'm dirt.' To her, dirt was the embodied experience of who she was, her first version of 'self'.

Recently, neuroscientists have discovered that we have a brain system dedicated to processing information about ourselves. Because this system is active when we are not doing something else, it's called the default mode network or DMN (Raichle *et al.*, 2001). This circuit is now thought to be the brain system we use for self-reflection and for initiating a process of ongoing reappraisal in order to change our self-image based on new experiences with other people (Sajonz *et al.*, 2010).

The DMN appears to be a unique brain circuit that we use to think about ourselves, other people, and our relationships, and to recall autobiographical memories to make better sense of what we have experienced in life. Once the DMN was discovered, studies were done of people with trauma histories, depression, and addictions to see how this 'self' system functions in these different groups (Bluhm *et al.*, 2009). What researchers saw in these studies is that the DMN is underdeveloped and less functional in cases of developmental trauma, substance abuse, and mental illness (Broyd *et al.*, 2009). Certainly, a child who is growing up with a core narrative of 'I'm dirt' wouldn't feel comfortable or safe spending much time thinking about herself or her relationships with other people. In addition, the child who is dealing with external threats from other people has to stay vigilant on the outside environment rather than spending time thinking about herself, her relationships, and the meaning of her experiences. For both of these reasons, it is likely that a child with blocked trust would have an underdeveloped DMN and therefore an underdeveloped sense of self and lack of reflective functioning.

In short, it is now clear that the neurobiology and neuroanatomy that support our sense of self and our ability to change our ways of thinking about ourselves are affected by early experiences of care. With good care, the DMN develops well and organizes a strong sense of self that involves acceptance and pride over who one is. With traumatizing care, the DMN develops poorly, as does the sense of self, and the self that does emerge is vague, limited, and of little value. The DMN is replete with opioid receptors, and the young child could suppress the development of this 'self' system by using the opioid-driven defense system to cope with the pain of early maltreatment.

In developmental terms, a goal for a therapeutic conceptual map is to help children have new experiences of safety which they can use to change their feelings and beliefs about themselves. This means changing their stories, their trauma-driven narratives, from unquestionable stories of being worthless to stories of being valued, stories of resilience. This requires the child first to experience 'felt safety' with a socially buffering, co-regulating adult whose presence provides the child an opportunity to start using the DMN to go inside safely. (The DMN is connected to the medial prefrontal cortex, a brain region chronically underactive during states of defensiveness and negative affect.)

Blocked care and mutual defensiveness

When children have to block their needs for attachment and companionship to survive poor care, they often lack the ability early in the relationship with a new caregiver to send positive signals of pleasure and approachability, communicate distress, and seek comfort. The child's suppression of these typical ways of activating parental caregiving greatly reduces the child's capacity to enter into a trust-based relationship with a parent. Indeed, instead of sending open and engaged requests to the adult for care, the defensive child is often sending messages which implicitly or explicitly communicate 'Stay away or I'll hurt or reject you'.

Instead of triggering the social reward system (oxytocin and dopamine) (Fleming, 1988; Mayes *et al.*, 2009) in the caregiver's brain, the child is likely to trigger the adult's self-defense system, activating chemicals such as norepinephrine and cortisol. This makes the process of becoming a trustworthy, social-buffering presence very challenging, putting the caregiver at high risk for developing *blocked care* (Hughes and Baylin, 2012). When a parent's blocked care meets a child's blocked trust, a dyadic mutual defense state of disengagement forms that can be very difficult to change. Mutual defensiveness suppresses the process of new story construction in both the caregiver and the child, reinforcing the child's shame-driven story and validating the child's negative beliefs about self and adults.

Developing trust

If the child is going to begin to trust their new caregiver, safety needs to be central in the day-to-day interactions between the caregiver and the child who has experienced developmental trauma. These caregivers need to find a way to become a soothing presence that these children need them to be in order to learn to trust and to make new stories. These caregivers need to develop the kind of robust compassion for their child and for themselves that protects them and the child from blocked care and mutual defensiveness, while reducing blocked trust. The mistrustful child is certain to approach new relationships with a self-protective stance of defensiveness. This defensive manner of relating will be evident in his facial expressions, voice, gestures, and movements. These expressions will register in less than a half second in the brain of the caregiver and evoke a similar defensive response from her. Stephen Porges (2011, 2017) calls this unconscious ultra-fast threat detection process *neuroception* to distinguish it from the slower conscious process of perception.

The caregiver's defensiveness will then elicit an even greater defensive reaction in the child, increasing the child's mistrust. This interaction sets the stage for repetitive failure in this new relationship to help the child recover from the effects of relational trauma. When the child mindlessly uses this neuroceptive process to detect threat in the presence of the caregiver, this leads to a split-second 'decision' to carry on with business as usual, where the child is self-reliant and the caregiver is left without a caring role with a rejecting child. For change to occur, it needs to begin in this neuroceptive time frame where the adult's presence is first sensed by the child's brain. In brain terms, this means that the adult has to send safety signals into the child's amygdala where this neuroceptive process is performed in about 50 milliseconds.

Trustful relationships are considered by Porges to be characterized by an open and engaged attitude, not a defensive one.

In such relationships the caregiver and child are open to each other and fully engaged in the interaction. They are having an impact on each other. According to Porges, if the two individuals are not in the same state – if one is defensive and the other is open and engaged – their neurobiological states strive to become synchronized. Since safety is a priority for both, they are likely to both become defensive rather than both become open and engaged. However, if the caregiver is able to inhibit this tendency to become defensive and remain open and engaged, then this same process will evoke a tendency in the child to become open and engaged also. This open and engaged attitude – again expressed in a split second through the face, voice, and gestures of the caregiver – sends neuroceptive signals to the child that he is safe. This person, this relationship, is different. Such a signal is confusing and the child may hesitate to respond. If this caregiver is able to continue to maintain the open and engaged attitude in the face of the child's confusion, the child is likely to move, step by step, toward an open and engaged attitude in return.

How is a parent able to inhibit the natural tendency to respond defensively to a defensive child? Different research programs (Dozier, 2008; Hendler and Feldman, 2017) that study interpersonal neurobiology in parent–child relationships are showing that when a parent can maintain a state of compassion towards a child and can recover this state quickly and effectively when defensive reactions are triggered, the parent provides highly enriched relational experiences for the child, experiences that help the child to develop the capacity for open engagement, empathy, and trusting connections with adults. Conversely, this line of investigation, as shown intriguingly in recent research by Ruth Feldman's group, reveals that parents who spend a lot of time in a state of social defensiveness tend to transmit this negative state of mind to their children over time. In this new brain-based research, we can see how an adult's state of mind towards a child can engender intergenerational effects that either promote children's capacity to trust or cause them to mistrust caregivers.

Compassion for the traumatized child, including his very difficult history, enables the caregiver to understand the meaning of the child's challenging and defensive behaviors, and helps the caregiver to not react with her own defensiveness. She may have difficulty responding with empathy to the child at that time because the child is not showing vulnerability that would activate an empathic response, but compassion, a more reflective mental state, activates the caregiver's positive state of mind toward the child and motivates the caregiver to help the child. A parent of a child with blocked trust could have a hard time being empathic: the child is hiding his pain so the parent does not get a chance to see it, hear it, feel it. A compassionate perception of the child enables the caregiver (helped by knowledge of the details of his traumatic history) to be able to 'see' the pain underneath the child's defensiveness. Helping parents to shift from a behavioral model of parenting to a compassion-based model by adopting a compassionate state of mind is a core process for facilitating change and growth in children with blocked trust.

We have found that caregivers are more likely to be able to inhibit their defensiveness and relate with compassion when they maintain an habitual attitude that promotes an open and engaged state of mind. This is the attitude of PACE, representing playfulness, acceptance, curiosity, and empathy. This attitude enables the caregiver to hold the child's mind alongside their own without rejection, judgment, or indifference. With PACE, the caregiver sends signals of safety to the child's neuroceptive system while the child is in a defensive state. Until the adult's messages to the child's amygdala convey safety more than threat, the child is unlikely to experience the adult's presence as safe enough. If the child's brain detects safety signals in the adult's presence – for example, in the adult's tone of voice (prosody) or the adult's upper facial muscles (genuine Duchenne smile) – then a state shift from defense towards openness and engagement is likely to occur in the child. This state-shifting process in the context of ongoing, moment-to-moment engagement, where the child becomes open to the caregiver's experience and guidance, is central to the development of trust.

Trust and reciprocal conversations

Within a relationship characterized by trust, there are reciprocal conversations where the expressions – nonverbal and verbal – of one strive to be in synch with those of the other. These initiatives and responses – fine-tuned again and again with interactive repair – are evident in the interactions in healthy parent–infant relationships. They are nonverbal – involving the face, voice, gestures. They are synchronized – call-and-response cycles occurring in microseconds. The parent and child form a dyad that is specific to each parent and child. It is within this specific dyad that the child feels safe because he is special to this unique caregiver: she understands him; he matters to her. What makes him unique is seen and responded to in a manner that makes the caregiver unique. This dyad, this moment of interaction, is one of a kind.

Within the safety generated by this dyad, both open and engaged with each other, they are able to influence each other's thoughts, emotions, and behaviors. The parent initiates an interaction, and the child readily engages with her. The child initiates an interaction and the parent readily engages. Or the parent initiates and the child hesitates to engage, so the parent modifies (changes, drops, or has an alternative initiative) and the child engages. Within good parent–infant relationships these synchronizing conversations occur frequently throughout the day, showing us that words are not the central component of conversations. Rather, conversations represent a meeting of minds and hearts, a joining together for developing reciprocal interests and discovering delightful, engaging qualities in each other.

Trust and intersubjective experience

These conversations are the setting for intersubjective experiences where the parent and child's experiences of each other become a template for their experience of themselves. A young child discovers that he is clever, enjoyable, and fascinating because his parent experiences amazement, joy, and fascination when engaged with her child. A parent discovers that she is an interesting, comforting, and loving parent because her young child experiences interest, comfort, and love while engaged with his mother.

These intersubjective experiences affect all areas of the child's developing sense of self. The child is able to identify, regulate, and communicate his affective states because his parent is attuned affectively with these states with synchronized states of her own. The child holds his attention longer on a novel object or event because his mother is also interested in that object or event. A child is motivated to do or learn something because his parent shares the same intention. Thus, the child's affect, cognition, and motivation take form through synchronizing these aspects of his inner life with those of his parent.

Within these conversations, the traumatized child's new caregivers are holding him in their minds. They think about him when planning the day and the days and months of the future. In thinking of him they are aware of where he is and what he is doing, and they know if he needs their assistance in any way. If he might need help, they will be there for him. Beyond issues of safety, they also choose to be with him to share interests and activities, to experience joy together. Along with holding his actions in their minds, they are holding his inner life – his mind – in their minds as well. His perceptions, thoughts, emotions, wishes, memories are in their minds and they consider these in deciding how they need to be with him. His inner life is influencing how they care for him. His inner life has value, just as do the inner lives of his caregivers. Although sometimes they decide for him what behavior is needed and what behavior is limited, they still understand and accept his thoughts, feelings, and wishes that lead to his behavior. And they comfort him when they need to limit a behavior that he wishes that he could do. The attitude of PACE mentioned above is of great value in helping the parent to hold the child's mind in her own mind while she organizes his day to provide optimal therapeutic experiences.

Now the traumatized child is truly learning that her new home is different. When she had been experiencing abuse and neglect, what she thought, felt, and wanted had no influence over the behavior of her parents. They did not seem to care what was important to her but rather focused only on what they thought and what they wanted to do. In her new home, her caregivers are interested in what is on her mind and they are also influenced by it. She matters to them. She can influence them. They truly try to understand what she thinks about what is best for her and, if they agree with her, they change their behavior because they want to do what is best for her. They are not indifferent to her; rather, they want to 'get it right' in providing her with good care.

She is becoming safer, day after day. Within the relationship that is deepening with her caregivers, with this connection she is safe even when they correct her behaviors. She begins to trust that the limits that they place on her behavior are there because they think they are necessary for her safety and happiness.

Trust and interactive repair

But her new caregivers do not always get it right, and, in fact, their relationship would not develop with strength and confidence if they did! Often the parent initiates a conversation and the child hesitates to engage, so the parent modifies (changes, drops, or has an alternative initiative) and the child then becomes engaged. This is known as interactive repair: each – with the parent often taking the lead – contributes to the continuous fine-tuning required for the interaction to have the best possible value for both (Tronick, 2017). These repairs build the strength of the relationship. When the child shows that she does not enjoy or is not interested in the parent's initiative, the parent changes the initiative! The child's response matters! They are truly reciprocal – the thoughts, emotions, intentions of both parent and child are needed for the success of these conversations. They are the building blocks of the relationship and they need to include the intentions and interests of both. This is a defining quality of a family characterized by trust. In such a family, every member – adult and child – knows that their inner life (thoughts, emotions, intentions, perceptions, value, memories) will have a safe place to be accepted, shared, and valued for their contribution to the development of the family and all who live within it.

Interactive repair occurs moment to moment, most often outside of awareness, as our neurobiological system does its job in ensuring the integrity of the intersubjective, synchronized relational engagement. Looking at relationships within a longer time frame, repair is also seen as a central ingredient in maintaining vibrant relationships that are able to accept differences, separations, and conflicts, and find a way forward that respects the inner lives and separateness of both parent and child. No conflict is bigger than the relationship. Conflicts are not ignored. They are not avoided through adopting rigid relationship expectations based on dominance and submissiveness. Rather, conflicts and repair are understood and accepted as a necessary ongoing aspect of all close relationships. It is the responsibility of the caregiver, not the child, to ensure that differences and conflicts are followed by interactive repair. They will be acknowledged and addressed, demonstrating the caregiver's commitment to the relationship. Repair does not require an apology (unless one is warranted). Repair is simply acknowledging the break in the relationship and holding the intention to address the break and find a way for the relationship to stay strong. Such initiatives involving repair are central in the traumatized child's developing trust in the new relationship.

Trust and developing stories

As these synchronized, intersubjective conversations increasingly occur between the traumatized child and her caregiver, new stories begin to emerge. These stories contain new meanings of the events of the past and present, and with these new meanings there begins to develop a new sense of self and other. A new possibility emerges within the mind of the traumatized child that maybe she had been hurt not because she was bad, lazy, or unlovable, but rather because her parents did not know how – or were not able – to care for her in a manner that she needed and deserved. Her prior care left her confused, frightened, sad, lonely, and full of shame. Her prior care failed to show her that she was lovable, capable, enjoyable, and had a good heart and mind. Her new caregivers are providing her with a sense of self that includes these qualities. And her new caregivers are demonstrating that they are committed to getting to know and love her, while doing what they think is best for her, moment to moment, day to day, while also initiating needed repairs in the bargain!

Therapeutic care for traumatized children works to make it safe for kids with blocked trust to reflect on themselves and their lives in order to reappraise who they are, to learn to value themselves. This reappraisal process requires the activation of higher brain regions, regions in the prefrontal cortex that are typically suppressed while these children are living defensively, in survival mode. Therapeutic care has to awaken these higher regions in the child's brain if the child is going to have a chance to reflect upon new experiences that counteract old experiences and learn new things about himself based on these useful disparities. Again, PACE has a vital role in this process. A family atmosphere of lightness and playfulness inspires confidence and a sense of relaxed safety. Conveying acceptance of the child, whether or not her behavior is being evaluated, communicates that she is safe to discover who she is – and was – before she had been traumatized. Curiosity facilitates her discovery of her old story and her possibilities for a new story. Empathy assures her that she is not alone in her sadness or shame. Being assured of comfort, she will be safe enough to feel sad and vulnerable.

Now we would like to provide an example of this process of moving from mistrust to trust, through developing synchronized conversations with a traumatized child leading to co-creating new stories.

Janet, age 9, screamed and threw the game that she was playing all over the living room because her foster mother, Kathleen, told her to put it away before coming to dinner. Mark finished preparing the meal alone while Kathleen went to find out what was happening for Janet. She found Janet pouting on the edge of the couch. Kathleen could tell – from getting to know her over the past seven months – that she might be able to approach her then to find out what made Janet upset. Kathleen quietly sat on the other end of the couch.

'I can never have any fun! You don't want me to be happy!'

Kathleen replied with similar intensity in her voice: 'Oh, honey! You don't think that I want you to be happy! That must be so upsetting for you! No wonder you yelled and threw the game if you think that I don't want you to be happy.'

Janet instantly yelled, 'You don't! You think I'm bad and shouldn't have any fun!'

Kathleen: 'Ah! It seems to you that I don't want you to have fun because I think that you're a bad girl! Ah! That would be so hard for you if you think that! Of course you'd be mad at me if I think that!'

Janet: 'I am mad at you! You're mean to me! I thought that you had to be nice to me!'

Kathleen: 'Oh, Janet! I think you're saying that you don't feel safe with me – so it's hard to like me and like living here if you think that I'd only be nice to you because I had to and did not like you or care for you.'

Janet: 'I don't mean it! Don't make me leave! I want to stay!'

Kathleen: 'How confusing for you. You think that I don't want you to have fun and that I think that you're bad and don't like you. But you worry that because you told me that, I won't want you to keep living with us.'

Janet: 'Can I stay?'

Kathleen: 'Of course you can stay! You're just angry with me and that's OK. I understand why you are. You think that I told you to put the game away because I don't want you to have fun and I'm mean to you probably because I think that you're bad and don't want to be nice to you – don't even like you. Oh, Janet, I'm sorry that this is so hard for you, so confusing.'

Janet: 'I often don't feel like you like me.'

Kathleen: 'I know, Janet, I know. I also know that I do like you and I have to keep working hard to find ways to show that I like you, and want you to have fun, and don't think that you're bad, so that you do feel those things – all of them – most of the time.'

Janet: 'I hope that you can figure out how to do that.'

Kathleen: 'Maybe we can both figure out ways to make it easier for you to know that and for me to show that. And now how about we put the game away together and then get our dinner before Mark eats it all.'

This conversation is not likely to happen easily, and when it does happen it is likely to take place in bits, over a period of days, weeks, or longer. But it does represent a goal – a realistic, though difficult goal – for helping children express their trauma story and begin the process of developing a new story. Janet's story included these experiences: Her foster mother, thinking that she is bad and wanting her to be unhappy, will soon tire of her obligation to take care of her and then she will ask her to leave. Kathleen did not challenge this story by telling her that she was wrong or by reassuring her. She instead expressed understanding, acceptance, and empathy for her difficult feelings, perceptions, and expectations. This response, expressed in an open and engaged manner, created doubts about the meanings of her old story and caused Janet to wonder about something being different. Gradually, she began to think that Kathleen is sad for her difficult life, does want her to be happy, and understands why it is hard for her to live in her home. Kathleen might actually like caring for her and might really want her to stay. Kathleen might think and feel things about her – that she will show her – that her parents never felt or thought. As this new story takes hold – over a course of its writing and rewriting, during a period of months most likely – her behavior will follow in starts and stops. Change can cause anxiety. The new story is so appealing, but so frightening too. It could be based on a lie, a mistake. Beginning to trust and being betrayed would be so much more acutely painful than is the dull pain of a life of mistrust.

This chapter of Janet's developing story – putting away the toys before having dinner – joins several others that develop around events associated with new emotions of joy and pride, new thoughts of worth and competence, and new relationships of sharing, laughter, and love. Gradually, Janet begins to see herself as being a girl similar to how Kathleen sees her rather than as the girl that she had seen during her past abuse and neglect. Janet begins to develop a new sense of self – a self that is integrated and lovable. A self that is coherent enough to contain her anger, fear, confusion, and guilt, and still be accepted as being of worth. If we could look into the processing of Janet's brain while she was walking with Kathleen into the kitchen for a shared meal, we might see a very active DMN, pulling together new intersubjective experiences into a story, a story rich in meanings that further the process of integrating a robust, affirming sense of self. From there, and with many similar experiences with therapeutic care in the months and years ahead, Janet is likely to develop a coherent, comprehensive autobiographical narrative.

Jack and Ruth

Let's return to consider how our day-to-day interactions would look if we were to help the children we met at the start of this chapter – Jack and Ruth – to begin to develop new stories that would guide them in their lives in their new homes.

Jack was six and needed to control everything, including what other members of the family said or did. His caregivers thought that his story included his conviction that he was safe only if he controlled whatever happened. He could not trust that he could relax and enjoy his family life for fear that his foster parents would not notice what he needed to be safe and they would allow something bad to happen. His foster father, remaining open and engaged with him through compassion and PACE, quietly told him that he noticed that Jack liked to decide things and was good at it. He asked Jack to show him how he might decide things too. They took turns deciding what the foster father would do when he walked into a room. They did that for five minutes four times a day. They also played the game 'Father, may I?' and 'Jack, may I?' Finally, Jack would decide which foster parent would decide what they had for dessert. The one who 'won' would jump with happiness to get to decide. Through these day-to-day activities, as well as gently accepting and reflecting on his efforts to control, they were helping Jack to develop a story of collaboration rather than control, of reciprocity rather than dominance. He was learning that they did notice him – who he was and what he needed – and he could trust that they would not forget him. He was learning to trust experiences of connection and repair, and had less need to be vigilant and defensive. He was learning to relax and laugh. He could be a child.

Ten-year-old **Ruth**'s emotional response to frustration was like a much younger child who could not have or do what she wanted. Her story seemed to reflect her rage that the world was a harsh and cruel place and that every disappointment was a sign of indifference or a deliberate effort to make her unhappy. This experience was so intense and pervasive that her caregivers decided that they needed her to see that they understood how hard life was for her at that time. They responded to her distress by matching the affective expression of her emotions to show that they understood her and felt what she was feeling. By matching the energy of how she expressed her anger without being angry themselves, they enabled her to begin to understand and better regulate her anger. Gradually, she engaged in these attuned interactions around lighter, playful, routine events too. Over time she allowed these synchronized conversations also to focus on her vulnerable states, and they were able to comfort her about how hard things were for her, and how hard things have been for much of her life. These new reciprocal conversations were often volatile for Ruth and unpredictable for her foster mom, and they required a great deal of repair until they would 'get it right'. What was challenging for her foster mom was that what it meant to 'get it right' seemed to change day to day and even moment to moment. Within 3–4 months Ruth began to reflect with her foster mother about how she reacted to frustration. Her foster mom told her that it must take a lot of energy and time to get so upset when things do not go well. This was the first time that Ruth sensed that someone had empathy for the distress of her anger rather than simply being angry with her for her anger. In the story that Ruth was developing, her distress over her hard life was understood and she was not alone in her unhappiness. In her new story, she gradually began to notice the opportunities for laughter and happiness that were available to her. And she noticed that these good people – her caregivers – cared for her. She really mattered to them. And they were committed to her care – and to her.

Conclusion

Therapeutic care for traumatized children must be based on safety. Being betrayed or violated by their parents, they do not feel safe in their home. They do not feel safe with those designated to care for them. For these children, traditional child care often does not create safety. Therapeutic care begins to create safety when the caregiver is able to remain open and engaged with their defensive child. By maintaining this open and engaged attitude, the caregiver is able gradually to lead the child into a relational dyad of ongoing synchronizing conversations. This dyad – specific to each unique child and caregiver – enables the child to enter into a rhythmic joint affective state – one that is continuously repaired – that provides both comfort and joy. This dyad enables the child to discover who she is, who her caregiver is, and the true meaning of family. She then, with the support and guidance of her caregiver, is able to write her story of hope, resilience, and growth.

References

Baylin, J. and Hughes, D. (2016). *The Neurobiology of Attachment-Focused Therapy: Enhancing Connection and Trust in the Treatment of Children and Adolescents.* New York, NY: W.W. Norton and Company.

Belsky, J. (2005). Differential Susceptibility to Rearing Influence. In B.J. Ellis and D.F. Bjorklund (eds), *Origins of the Social Mind: Evolutionary Psychology and Child Development.* New York, NY: Guilford Press.

Bluhm, R., Williamson, P.C., Osuch, E.A., Frewen, P.A. et al. (2009). Alterations in default network connectivity in posttraumatic stress disorder related to early life trauma. *Journal of Psychiatry & Neuroscience*, 34(3), 187–194.

Broyd, S.J., Demanuele, C., Debener, S., Helps, K., James, C.J. and Sonuga-Barke, J.S. (2009). Default-mode brain dysfunction in mental disorders: A systematic review. *Neuroscience and Biobehavioral Reviews*, 33, 279–296.

Coan, J.A., Schaefer, H.S. and Davidson, R.J. (2006). Lending a hand: Social regulation of the neural response to threat. *Psychological Science*, 17(12), 1032–1039.

Dozier, M. (2008). Attachment and biobehavioral catchup (ABC): Enhancing children's ability to regulate physiology and behavior. *Development and Psychopathology*, 20, 845–859.

Eisenberger, N., Mastera, S.L., Inagakia, T.K., Taylor, S. *et al.* (2011). Attachment figures activate a safety signal-related neural region and reduce pain experience. *Proceedings of the National Academy of Sciences of the United States of America*, 108(28), 11721–11726.

Fleming, A.S. (1988). Factors influencing maternal responsiveness in humans: Usefulness of an animal model. *Psychoneuroendocrinology*, 13(1–2), 189–212.

Hendler, T. and Feldman, R. (2017). The human coparental bond implicates distinct corticostriatal pathways: Longitudinal impact on family formation and child well-being. *Neuropsychopharmacology*, 42(12), 2301–2313.

Hughes, D. (2011). *Attachment-Focused Family Therapy Workbook*. New York, NY: W.W. Norton and Company.

Hughes, D. and Baylin, J. (2012). *Brain-Based Parenting: The Neuroscience of Caregiving for Healthy Attachment*. New York, NY: W.W Norton and Company.

Kalin, N.H., Shelton, S.E. and Lynn, D.E. (1995). Opiate systems in mother and infant primates coordinate intimate contact during reunion. *Psychoneuroendocrinology*, 20, 735–742.

Lanius, R., Vermetten, E., Loewenstein, R.J., Brand, B. *et al.* (2010). Emotion modulation in PTSD: Clinical and neurobiological evidence for a dissociative subtype. *American Journal of Psychiatry*, 167, 640–647.

Mayes, L., Magidson, J., Lejuez, C. and Nicholls, S. (2009). Social Relationships as Primary Rewards: The Neurobiology of Attachment. In M. de Haan and M. Gunnar (eds), *Handbook of Developmental Social Neuroscience*. New York, NY: Guilford Press.

Panksepp, J. (1998). *Affective Neuroscience*. New York, NY: Oxford University Press.

Porges, S. (2011). *The Polyvagal Theory: Neurophysiological Foundations of Emotions, Attachment, Communication, and Self-Regulation*. New York, NY: W.W. Norton and Company.

Porges, S. (2017). *The Pocket Guide to the Polyvagal Theory: The Transformative Power of Feeling Safe*. New York, NY: W.W. Norton and Company.

Raichle, M.E., MacLeod, A.M., Snyder, A.Z., Powers, M.J., Gusnard, D.A. and Shulman, G.L. (2001). A default mode of brain function. *Proceedings of the National Academy of Sciences*, 98, 676–682.

Sajonz, B., Kahnt, T., Margulies, D.S., Park, S.Q. *et al.* (2010). Delineating self-referential processing from episodic memory retrieval: Common and dissociable networks. *NeuroImage*, 50(4), 1606–1617.

Sapolsky, R. (2017). *Behave: The Biology of Humans at Our Best and Worst*. New York, NY: Penguin.

Teicher, M.H., Andersen, S.L., Polcari, A., Anderson, C.M., Navalta, C.P. and Kim, D.M. (2003). The neurobiological consequences of early stress and childhood maltreatment. *Neuroscience Biobehavioral Review*, 27(1–2), 33–44.

Tottenham, N., Shapiro, M., Telzer, E.H. and Humphreys, K.L. (2012). Amygdala response to mother. *Developmental Science*, 15(3), 307–319.

Tronick, E. (2017). The caregiver–infant dyad as a buffer or transducer of resource enhancing or depleting factors that shape psychobiological development. *Australian and New Zealand Journal of Family Therapy*, 38(4), 561–572.

Zak, P.J. (2012). *The Moral Molecule: How Trust Works*. New York, NY: Penguin.

PRACTICE REFLECTION

Joe Tucci, Janise Mitchell and Ed Tronick

Hughes and Baylin offer a clear way of understanding the pivotal role that carers play in repairing the traumatised physiological states of children in out-of-home care. The themes are self-evident.

Relationships with children are capable of healing the impact of abuse and neglect in the day-to-day moments of mutual interaction.

Children and carers need to move beyond their tendencies to defensiveness in order to experience an openness for change. Carers lead this process by recognising how their own internal reactions are being guided by past activations of hurt and the need to act self-protectively.

Neurobiological safety is the only antidote to the threat-activated internal systems of children and carers. This safety comes to be embodied over time and with consistency of repetition.

Children respond to the messages inherent in the communication from the carer. They hear and experience what the carers say, what they do, and engage with the intentions and motivations they hold for them. As they share in these mutual experiences, children come to feel that their internal states are being received and welcomed into relationships. The templates they use to engage with their own sense of agency are gradually driven by the enlivened accompaniment and interest of the carer and other relationships. Children come to nuzzle into the people around them, permitting them to continue to shape the developmental blocks that trauma has induced in them.

Repair happens not as explicit forms of expression but as implicit co-organisation of synchronous states between carer and children. It occurs after experiences of mismatching states and behaviour, when there is an inbuilt heightened need to regain harmony.

The stories that children and carers carry with them interact in experiences of intersubjectivity. These are the moments in which children and carer see through into the mind of the other – holding at once their history, their strengths, their pain, their needs in the moment and the needs that remain unmet from their past. These stories are embedded in reactions of their neurophysiology, what remains dormant, what is triggered into action, what is shared, what is separate.

Trust and trustworthiness are the core elements of the relationships that characterise Therapeutic Care.

Insight is important for healing, but it is not essential. Stories of change come after safety is embodied in children and carers through their experience of safety in their relationship.

The practice of Therapeutic Care aligns itself with all of the principles of DDP. It also seeks to extend its influence into the frames of reference held by the broader community and the ecosystem of organisations. Therapeutic Care also tackles in an organised way the discourses of inevitable failure and resistance that systems around these children carry with them. This is an important distinction to note: whereas therapeutic forms of care support the renegotiation of children's internal implicit systems, Therapeutic Care requires coordination of therapeutic effort across settings by many people who are engaged in the protection, care and education of children in out-of-home care.

11

Resetting the Fabric of Love

Real-Life Applications That Promote Emotional Connection in the Day-to-Day Experience of Looked-After and Adopted Children and Their Parents

KIM S. GOLDING

Introduction

Junita is cold, hungry and in pain. She whimpers quietly but no one comes. She is alone in the house. Only three months old and Junita is giving up on the need for safe parenting. She has already learned to inhibit her cries. She resists the urge to seek comfort in her mother's face. Junita is taking control of her safety in the only way a small infant can. Junita is learning to do without. It is this self-reliance that will help her to survive despite the scarcity of food and the absence of loving hands. Like many children growing up in a developmentally traumatising early environment, Junita is adapting. She will survive, but this survival will come at a cost. Unconditional love and belonging are not concepts that Junita will understand as she is removed from this home just before her first birthday. It is not something she will experience in the kind but busy temporary foster home she is moved to. It is not something she will recognise when she is eventually adopted by Marisa and Lars at two and a half years of age.

Within this chapter, I will explore Junita's experience with Marisa and Lars. Her difficulty in trusting in unconditional love, when, as a toddler, she is finally offered this. Her difficulty in believing that the boundaries and restrictions placed on her are to keep her safe, and not a threat of abandonment. Her difficulty in building a sense of belonging in this adoptive family. This is a fictional family, but based on a composite of many families I have worked with.

Junita's continual need to control her relationships will prevent her experiencing the reciprocal relationships she developmentally needs. She will compete with her older siblings, the twin birth children of Marisa and Lars, sure that there is not enough love to go around. She feels second best to these siblings who were born into safety and unconditional love. Marisa and Lars will experience the hurt of rejection when they cannot soothe and comfort their daughter, this in turn awakening previous relationship hurts from their past. Despite episodes of blocked care (see Hughes and Baylin, 2012), they will struggle through, supported by caring practitioners and kind family and friends. As they experience connection from others, they will continue to offer opportunities for emotional connection to Junita. They will hold on to the hope that one day Junita will trust in emotional connection and finally discover that she is loved unconditionally, no matter what the difficulties they all encounter along the way.

The nature of love and good enough parenting

Over the decades, child psychiatrists and psychologists have attempted to define the concept of love and to relate this to the notion of good enough parenting. Four decades, the 1950s through to the 1980s, saw four notable thinkers firmly put this topic on to the map. They were instrumental in exploring love and attachment between infants and parents, noting the detrimental effects when these are absent.

Bowlby, during his development of attachment theory, wrote a book which he titled *Child Care and the Growth of* ***Love*** (my emphasis). He drew attention to the poor outcomes when children are deprived of love in their early years, leading to the concept of maternal deprivation. He noticed that a young child needs to experience

> a warm, intimate, and continuous relationship with his mother (or mother-substitute), in which both find satisfaction and enjoyment. A child needs to feel he is an object of pleasure and pride to his mother; a mother needs to feel an expansion of her own personality

> in the personality of her child: each needs to feel closely identified with the other. (Bowlby, 1953, p.13)

Bowlby describes the importance of mutual feelings of belonging, for parents to experience a sense of obligation to the child, and for the child to experience being of value to another person.

A decade later, Winnicott wrote of the ordinary good mother (supported by the father). Winnicott suggests that devotion from parents is a necessary starting point for the child. He writes:

> If human babies are to develop eventually into healthy, independent, and society-minded adult individuals, they absolutely depend on being given a good start, and this good start is assured in nature by the existence of the bond between the baby's mother and the baby, the thing called love. (Winnicott, 1964, p.17)

Winnicott explores the importance of parents treating children as people in their own right. Like Bowlby, he also attributes importance to the continuity of the relationship.

In the next decade, Rutter (1972) added to the discussion, noticing that a child needs an unbroken attachment to the parent, but without the parent being constantly present. Rutter suggests that this, alongside warm family relationships and a stimulating environment, provides the experience of love the child needs.

Bettelheim (1987) followed Winnicott in articulating the idea of good enough parenting. He notes the importance of parental security and self-understanding which gives parents clarity about their children. Parents can then offer children the empathy needed to see and find themselves reflected in the parents' face, as in a mirror. Bettelheim also addresses conflict, noting:

> [T]here are few loves which are entirely free of ambivalence… Not only is our love for our children sometimes tinged with annoyance, discouragement, and disappointment, the same is true for the love our children feel for us. (p.23)

In this the importance of accepting relationship ruptures and providing adult-led repair to help children feel secure is foreshadowed.

Four decades of understanding about love and good enough parenting provided a foundation for continuing research and writing.

Much of this is centred around attachment theory (see Cassidy and Shaver, 2016), with a more recent additional focus on the value of neuroscience (Coan, 2016). Although 'attachment' and 'affectional bonds' have replaced the term 'love', the same ideas of what a child needs for healthy development are reflected in this work. Security (for parent and child), continuity, attachment, empathy, warmth, stimulation, belonging, being held in mind, parental self-understanding and managing conflict provide a template for unconditional love. The child is loved, no matter what, and difficulties as they arise do not diminish this. In recent research these same ideas are reflected in terms such as acceptance and commitment (Dozier and Rutter, 2016).

Much research explores the concept of sensitive parenting and its role in facilitating secure attachment (Feeney and Woodhouse, 2016). A sensitive parent is one that can perceive and flexibly respond to the child's cues for exploration and comfort. Parents thus provide a *secure base* from which children can explore and also a *safe haven* to receive comfort when distressed. Secure attachment is associated with emotional health and well-being, with research highlighting how this is mediated through positive benefits on the child's physiology – for example, child stress reactivity (Bernard and Dozier, 2010) and the child's capacity for emotional regulation (Thompson, 2016).

> Good caregivers must have a genuine understanding and respect for not only individuals' need to grow, learn, discover and accomplish personal goals but also the ingrained need of all individuals for affection, intimacy, and comfort in times of stress. (Feeney and Woodhouse, 2016, p.844)

Unfortunately, Junita did not experience good enough parenting early in life. Her parents were neglectful and abusive rather than sensitive to her needs. Junita developed disorganised-controlling attachments to her parents, relationship patterns associated with increased risk of psychopathology (DeKlyen and Greenberg, 2016). Junita lacked a secure base that allowed her to grow, learn and discover the world. Nor did she have a safe haven offering affection, intimacy and comfort when distressed. Junita learned to be self-reliant and to fear relationships. This impacted on her difficulties managing stress. She was hypervigilant, reactive and prone to episodes of aggressive dysregulation as her emotions overwhelmed her. She expected others to be unavailable and foresaw abandonment in the smallest degree of parental authority offered to her. Her foster carers were unable to provide her with the secure environment she needed to recover. Their commitment to her, although well intentioned, was short-term. When she moved to her adoptive home, she grieved for these carers; her knowledge that parents can be lost was confirmed.

The impact of developmental trauma

Junita is developmentally traumatised by her early experience and the separation and loss that followed. Cook *et al.* (2005) observe that such trauma puts children at high risk of difficulties in seven areas of development. As Junita develops within her adoptive home, all of these are reflected in her functioning.

1. **Attachment:** '[W]hen children experience conditions that are beyond those with which the attachment system is designed to deal, it seems that rigid means of coping (e.g., disinhibited attachment) or a neurobiology that predisposes to later disorder become more likely' (Dozier and Rutter, 2016, p.710). Junita has a disorganised-controlling attachment. She cannot experience security or joy with her caregivers; she struggles to engage in reciprocal relationships; she controls through a combination of coercive, attention-needing behaviours and highly self-reliant behaviours. She will fuss and demand that her parents do things for her, but then is not satisfied when they attempt to meet these demands. When she falls from her scooter and breaks her arm, however, she insists that she is fine and won't let her parents near her.

2. **Biological:** Junita struggles to sleep, remaining awake and alert at bedtime, and quick to wake up at the slightest disturbance during the night. She is also preoccupied with food and rarely notices when she is full.

3. **Affect regulation:** Junita struggles to identify and regulate her affective state, whether positive or negative. This leads

to rapid dysregulation with angry feelings expressed in outbursts of rage, sadness plummeting her into despair, fear quickly rising to terror, and excitement leaving her in a state of pervasive anxiety.

4. **Dissociation:** When Junita experiences circumstances which remind her of her birth parents, she experiences fear which leads to psychological absence and shutdown. For example, she can respond to strangers by falling to the floor and curling up in a foetal position. Her mother notices that men with beards and a smell of alcohol are most likely to lead to this reaction. Less extreme, she sometimes 'spaces out' and seems elsewhere.
5. **Behaviour control:** Junita finds it hard to focus; she is inattentive and active much of the time. She lacks flexibility and is compulsive. For example, she needs her clothes laid out in a particular way and will only eat food items that are not touching each other.
6. **Cognition:** Junita has a poor sense of time and of cause and effect. She also has social cognitive difficulties. She struggles to understand the impact she has on other people and cannot view things from another's perspective.
7. **Self-concept:** Although Junita acts as if she does not care, she is an anxious child who experiences high levels of shame. She has a negative sense of self and lacks expectations that others want to care for her. Shame is often masked by lying and blaming others for things that have gone wrong.

Parenting children who have experienced developmental trauma has a range of challenges. Parents need to be better than good enough if they are to offer the child the experience of security and unconditional love that they need. For example, Dozier (2003) highlights how the idea of sensitive parenting needs to be adjusted for foster carers. Parents need to offer a gentle challenge to the children so that their pre-existing avoidant and resistant patterns do not elicit complementary rejecting behaviours from the carers.

It is not enough to love the child; parents also have to overcome the children's blocked trust (Baylin and Hughes, 2016). Early abuse and neglect leads children to lose trust that parents will meet their physical and psychological needs. They adapt by relying on themselves. This is seen in compulsive, rigid self-reliant behaviours and obsessive preoccupation with and controlling behaviour towards the parents.

Junita rages whenever she is told no, experiences an unexpected change or encounters a boundary to what she wants to do. Her over-sensitive nervous system is hypervigilant to signs of danger; 'You don't love me, I will never be good enough, you are about to get rid of me.' She does not trust that her parents only have good intentions towards her. These appraisals happen fast, as the defensive part of her nervous system takes control. Junita cannot engage socially with her parents; she is not open to their support and cannot use them as a source of comfort to soothe her over-reactive nervous system. She tries to rely on herself instead. Parental presence can regulate stress in children, a process called social buffering (Gunnar *et al.*, 2015). Junita's self-reliance and difficulties in trusting her parents mean this regulation is not available and she remains in a highly dysregulated state.

For Junita, relationships are a source of fear. She constantly miscues her parents about her needs, employing highly coercive and self-reliant controlling behaviours. Junita is unable to enter into reciprocal, intersubjective relationships (Trevarthen, 2001). Opportunities for joint discovery of each other and the world around them are lost as Junita continues to wield control while resisting being open to her parents' influence.

In turn, this impacts on Junita's developing sense of self. She experiences a pervasive sense of shame (Kaufman, 1996). This organises her developing sense of identity as a bad child, who is undeserving of the love and care now on offer to her. This influences much of her behaviour. Although young children experience feelings of shame, the development of feelings of guilt occurs later. With this development the child can experience empathy for others and remorse for what has occurred. This is an important part of the socialisation process aided by parental regulation of shame (Tangney and Dearing, 2002). Junita did not experience this early support and thus the development of guilt was compromised. Her sense of self is shame-based and she cannot notice the impact she is having on others. She sometimes expresses this self-loathing via self-harming behaviours. For example, she will bang her head repetitively. At other times, she defends against these feelings through compulsive lying, blaming others and raging against her parents. She tells them that she hates them and wishes they had never adopted her. She especially targets Marisa in these rages, accusing her of not being a real mother and wishing she would go away. Sometimes after such a rage she will collapse in tears. Now, when Marisa is feeling most vulnerable, Junita is open to some comfort. It is a comfort Marisa finds hard to give, hurting as she is from her daughter's onslaught.

How does developmental trauma impact on the parents?

Junita's earliest experience has left her deeply distrustful and anticipating certain behaviours of her parents. Even when Marisa and Lars try to stay open and responsive towards Junita, she maintains her different expectations. Thompson (2016) suggests that therapy needs to address the child's mental expectations as well as the behaviour of the parents in order for positive change to occur. Junita's adoptive parents are open and engaged, ready to offer companionship, nurture or discipline as needed, but these behaviours provided with the best of intentions are not received in this way. Junita distrusts these good intentions and experiences anxiety that she will again be hurt or separated. She rejects what is being offered and resists parenting. When intersubjective, social engagement is consistently rejected, triggering only defensive responses in the child, parents will struggle to remain socially engaged. They become defensive in turn. Their anger, anxiety or disappointment in the child becomes evident, further reinforcing the child's defensive responses (Porges, 2017).

Often it is the mother, or main nurturer, in the parenting dyad who gets the brunt of the rejection from children with developmental traumas. Offering attachment safety via emotional connection, comfort and nurture triggers alarm for the child, who feels undeserving and anticipates the loss that they believe will follow. The child therefore miscues the parent through a compulsive need for self-reliance or obsessive need for the parent but with a resistance to actually being soothed by her. The parent feels inadequate, hurt and rejected.

Providing parental authority via discipline can be equally problematic. The discipline, whether in the form of boundaries, consequences or praise, all trigger for the child the belief that she is not loved unconditionally. She ignores the discipline, at best, or rages against the parent in a 'meltdown' that seems wholly out of proportion to the discipline being provided. Either way, the parents are left feeling ineffectual. This places them at risk of blocked care, a neurobiological state described by Hughes and Baylin (2012) within which they no longer experience parenting the child as rewarding and have a strong urge to avoid rather than approach the child. Parents no longer want to understand the child and will often interpret actions of the child as being negative – 'it is because she hates me'. Although the parent continues to fulfil their responsibility to the child, helped by a robust executive functioning, they no longer experience any joy in this.

The parent is at increased risk when they have experienced a difficult attachment history themselves. Parents with a good upbringing will approach parenting with a resolved attachment state of mind. They perceive the child's difficulties as related to their difficult early experience rather than failures in themselves. This is similarly true when parents have resolved for themselves any difficulties from their past – what attachment researchers call 'earned security' (Hesse, 2016). When parents have an unresolved attachment state of mind, they are more likely to raise children with disorganised attachment relationships. When children are living in non-birth families, the picture is more complex. For example, Dozier and Rutter (2016) report research which suggests that foster parents with dismissive attachment states of mind also tend to care for children who develop disorganised attachment relationships. They conclude that 'children who have experienced early adversity are especially in need of nurturing care' (p.704), with commitment to the child being more important than sensitivity in this parenting.

Parenting children with developmental trauma

In this section I will follow Marisa and Lars's story of trying to help Junita. The parenting approach being used is based on that recommended by Dan Hughes (Hughes, Golding and Hudson, 2019), in a model of intervention called Dyadic Developmental Psychotherapy, Parenting and Practice. Dyadic Developmental Parenting is explored further in Golding (2017a, 2017b).

Support and self-care

When Marisa and Lars began their preparation for adoption, they had high expectations. They considered themselves good parents to their two birth children, Karl and Kirsten, both early adolescents. Marisa, who came from a large family, had always expected to have a third child, but she respected Lars's ethical beliefs about world population and had not pursued this. When her young people became more independent, her desire to parent another child returned. Adoption seemed to be a good solution; both felt that they had a lot to offer a child who had had a difficult start in life. They also felt that they had a good support network of family and friends.

Indeed, the network was initially supportive. They celebrated the new entry to the family, and even offered to baby-sit so that Marisa and Lars could get an occasional night out. Sadly, this did not continue. As the challenges that Junita presented became more apparent, friends and family became reluctant to help. Additionally, some family members felt that Marisa and Lars were too soft with Junita; they believed she needed boundaries and a firm hand. Even Karl and Kirsten could not understand why Junita got away with things they would never have imagined doing! Marisa and Lars had a deepening sense of failing. In addition, Marisa, who worked in the public sector, began working longer hours as it became apparent that her job was at risk. Lars tried to fit his own work schedule, as a freelance illustrator, around caring for Junita. They also wanted to support Karl and Kirsten, as they moved to high school, with typical struggles with their peer group and increased academic demands. Their time together was becoming less frequent.

When Junita was six, her behaviour was becoming increasingly challenging. She moved out of a nurturing reception class at school into a larger and more structured class. She seemed to be coping, but at home her behaviour was increasingly controlling, with rages that could last for several hours. Marisa and Lars were struggling, and although they were reluctant to seek support, this is what they needed. They were embarrassed to ask for help; it felt as if they were letting down those who had approved them to adopt. Finally, they called the adoption support team. The social worker who came to see them, Hannah, was kind. She sat down with Marisa and Lars and listened as they told her how their lives had become one big battle to survive. Hannah did not judge them. She seemed to understand. She helped them to review how little support they had. Caring for Junita, Karl and Kirsten meant that their own self-care had slipped to the bottom of a very large pile. At first they resisted making changes: they were too busy; they wanted someone to help Junita, maybe therapy would be the answer; they had to attend to work, the family income needed to be earned; they couldn't go out, Junita just could not cope if they left her; they couldn't turn to friends, no one would manage Junita. Hannah listened. She accepted their fears and doubts. She also began to gently challenge their beliefs.

Gradually, Marisa and Lars made some changes to their lives. The biggest of these was joining a local support group and discovering that they were not alone with the challenges that they were experiencing. Marisa agreed to come home from work early one night a week so that Lars could go to the gym, and he encouraged Marisa to pick up again with some old friends that she had lost touch with. It was a relief to get out and not talk about the children! They even managed an occasional evening out together, supported by Marisa's sister, Isabel.

Gradually, Hannah's support shifted towards helping them to think about Junita, and the challenges of parenting her.

Regulation and mentalisation

Together, Hannah, Marisa and Lars revisited Junita's history. Hannah helped them to understand how this made sense of the challenging behaviours that Junita displayed, and why this especially focused on rejection of Marisa. Marisa and Lars became interested in finding some different ways of parenting her. They joined a parenting group set up for adoptive parents.

Marisa and Lars came to understand the importance of their own regulation so that they could connect with Junita and help her to feel more secure. They noticed how easy it was to lose their calm when they experienced Junita as manipulative and angry. Lars would tend to retreat to his workroom, using his drawing to help soothe himself back into a regulated state. This would leave Junita unsupported at a time when she needed him most. Marisa was more quick to anger as she became defensive in the face of the highly rejecting behaviour that appeared aimed at her. She would shout at

Junita, a side of herself she did not recognise. They also noticed how their family culture contributed to this. Both Marisa and Lars came from families where parents were seen as strong, even authoritarian, and children were expected to be obedient. When Junita was defiant, this added to their sense of failure and increased their struggle to remain regulated. Hannah helped them with mindfulness so that they stayed present to Junita, without getting lost in their own sense of failure and helplessness.

Marisa and Lars also noticed how their ability to reflect reduced when they were stressed. It became hard to notice and connect with their own fears and worries, and to remember the anxiety, fear and terror hidden under Junita's most challenging behaviours. Both parents had good reflective function, which meant that they had strong mentalising skills, being able to understand the mind of another, and to make sense of behaviour based on this understanding (Fonagy *et al.*, 2002). When Karl was caught shoplifting, it didn't take long for them to work out that he was struggling with feeling accepted by his peer group. As they empathised with his fears, they could address the shoplifting sensitively, providing a clear message that this is not acceptable while understanding that he needed to experience approval from his peers. They were able to guide him to achieve this without having to break the law! With Junita these abilities seemed to vanish as they became overwhelmed with their own inner fears and failures.

As they discovered ways to stay better regulated, they were able to notice and have more compassion for this inner experience. This in turn helped them to reflect on Junita's inner life. For example, Junita came home from school one day very excited about inviting her parents to the dress rehearsal of the school play. Lars's heart sank when he realised the timing of this was going to be impossible for either himself or Marisa because of prior commitments. He explained this to Junita while assuring her that they would make sure to see the play on another occasion. Junita seemed OK as she settled down to watch her favourite TV programme. It wasn't until later that evening that she started to be difficult. She kept winding up Kirsten, who was becoming irritated with her. She refused to eat, announcing that she did not like butter on her jacket potato and she would not eat sausages that were touching the beans. Marisa was becoming increasingly frustrated, which just evoked a stronger reaction from Kirsten.

Lars could see a full-scale meltdown approaching. He also noticed his own anxiety and desire to withdraw to his workroom. He thought back to Junita's excitement about the school play and he realised what he needed to do. Loudly and with some animation, he said to Junita: 'You have had such a hard day today, you know what, I have an idea. Come with me to my workroom.' Junita looked interested, so ignoring the surprised looks of the rest of the family, Lars led her away. Once settled, he showed Junita some crayons and asked her which colour she thought was best to paint the train he had sketched earlier that day. She happily started exploring the different colours. While she did so, Lars remembered her disappointment about the school play, and wondered if it felt as if Mum and Dad just did not love her when they could not come to school – maybe even that they loved Kirsten better! Junita cried as she agreed that was just how she felt. She even allowed Lars to cuddle her, just for a short while, before deciding she was hungry and she wanted her tea now! There was no meltdown from Junita that evening.

Attachment history

As Marisa and Lars became more understanding of their own reactions to Junita, they noticed times when they found it easy to stay regulated and to reflect on what might be going on for Junita. There were other times, however, when it felt as if a button had been pushed. This was much more difficult. They realised they needed to revisit their own history of being parented. They had done this thoroughly during adoption preparation, so this was surprising to them. Hannah explained that it is hard to predict what is going to be a button until you have the child actually pushing it.

Marisa noticed that some of Junita's behaviours were taking her back to being one of four siblings. She was the youngest, a bit of a late addition to the family, and temperamentally not as calm as the other three. This is not an easy trait in a family where obedience is valued. She saw herself as a bit of a nuisance and felt jealous of the others. Her eldest sister had always resented Marisa, her arrival coinciding with a time when she wanted to be out enjoying her friends. Instead, she was expected to stay in and help with the baby. She dutifully complied, but her resentment was more subtly expressed in her provocation of Marisa. Marisa came to realise that parenting Junita could take her back to this relationship.

When she got angry at Junita's niggling towards Kirsten, she re-experienced all the unexpressed anger towards her sister, now mixed up with her feelings of frustration and failure towards Junita.

Staying open and engaged to the child

With encouragement and support to look after themselves better, and increased understanding about the importance of regulation and reflection, Marisa and Lars were able to see the world through Junita's eyes. They now understood how her hypervigilant, reactive nervous system was on high alert most of the time. They also got better at spotting the anxiety, fear and terror that lay under the surface of the highly challenging behaviours.

Marisa and Lars were learning to stay open and engaged towards Junita even when she was becoming highly defensive. As Porges (2017) observes, we are a socially connected species at the biological level. When one person is defensive, it will pull the other person there also. On the other hand, if one person stays open and engaged, it is more likely that the other person will reduce their defensiveness and become similarly open and engaged. These moments of insight for Marisa and Lars were offering a door to a different world for Junita. Although her nervous system remained hypervigilant and reactive, she was learning that her parents could support her. The intersubjective world was opening up to her and she was experiencing some moments of safety in emotional engagement. Trust and security were becoming a possibility for Junita.

Emotional connection and PACE

Marisa and Lars now wanted to find a way to increase their emotional connection with Junita. They needed a parenting attitude to anchor themselves so that they could be more consistent. It was timely to be introduced to the attitude of PACE.

PACE is a parenting attitude recommended by Dan Hughes (Golding and Hughes, 2012; Hughes *et al.*, 2019). It invites parents to provide their children with moments of playfulness through relational joy; alongside an attitude of acceptance, curiosity and empathy. Curiosity is a tentative wondering designed to understand the children and their internal experience more fully. With understanding, empathy grows. As this is communicated to the children, they experience themselves, and especially their inner life, as being unconditionally accepted. Discipline and boundaries, focused on helping the children to internalise culturally approved behaviours, are provided alongside this attitude of PACE. The children experience safety because of the emotional connection before, during and after the behavioural support.

At nine years of age, Junita is doing well academically. She loves reading and seems to take numeracy in her stride. Unfortunately, this academic strength is not matched socially. Junita remains emotionally immature, and peers are becoming less tolerant of some of her quirkiness. Her need to sit close to the teacher, to be first in the dinner queue and to sharpen all her pencils before she starts to work are no longer seen as cute and endearing. Potential friends are put off by her controlling manner and her insistence that everything is done her way. Marisa and Lars are therefore understandably pleased when Junita appears to be making friends with Nazia, a new girl to the class. Junita is especially excited to get a birthday party invitation and enjoys a shopping expedition with Marisa for some party clothes the weekend before. Marisa allows herself a rare moment of optimism. It is devastating therefore to get the phone call from school just two days before the party. Junita has made racially abusive comments towards Nazia. Marisa and Lars pride themselves on bringing up their children to be accepting of difference, and this is therefore a double blow.

Marisa reminds herself of everything she has understood about PACE as she waits for Junita in the school playground. She anticipates that Junita will be dysregulated following the day's events. She remembers that Junita is likely to act as if nothing has happened or that she doesn't care. Marisa takes a deep breath as she focuses on understanding what is underneath this hard exterior. When Junita arrives, Marisa lets her know that she has talked with the head teacher and quietly comments that it must have been a hard day today. As expected, Junita laughs and tells her that it is fine. Marisa quietly hands Junita her wellies and tells her they are going home via the woods. Junita looks confused but puts them on. As they walk home, Marisa makes sure that they encounter some deep puddles along the way.

They laugh together as Junita jumps in these and they both get wet in the process. Without being aware of it, Junita is being helped to regulate some of the strong feelings left over from the school day. Once home, Marisa suggests a change of clothes and a cup of hot chocolate to warm them up. While Junita is drinking, Marisa quietly wonders if Junita was feeling especially angry today. Junita shrugs. Marisa wonders if Junita was feeling cross with Nazia. Junita tells her no. Slightly exasperated at her guesses getting nowhere, Marisa asks Junita: 'Well, what were you feeling?' Junita immediately reacts: 'I wasn't feeling anything, OK!' Marisa, too, falls into being reactive: 'You must have been feeling something' she snaps. She notices she is feeling frustrated. She reflects on how hard this is and takes a moment to be compassionate to herself before repairing the rupture between them. She tells Junita that she is sorry; it has been a hard day, and now she is adding to it by expecting Junita to know how she feels. Junita, angry still, agrees that Marisa always wants to know how she feels, and she doesn't know; she doesn't feel anything. Marisa then wonders to herself out loud how hard it must be to have everyone think you know what you feel when you don't. Junita relaxes a little. 'Nazia was just being a pain, all right!'

Marisa takes hold of Junita's hands and quietly rubs them. This is about the only direct nurture from Marisa that she will generally tolerate. Marisa lets Junita know that she understands how hard it is to think you have a friend and then that friend is a pain. How disappointing to be so excited about the birthday party and then to fall out with her. Junita tries to say she doesn't want to go anyway, but then crumples. She allows Marisa to hold her as tears flow. Gradually, she is able to tell Marisa that she was jealous when Nazia was playing with one of the other girls. She tried to get Nazia to play with her and got cross when she wouldn't. Nazia then told her she couldn't come to her party and Junita racially insulted her. Marisa continues to comfort Junita and to understand how hard making friends is.

Marisa is not sure what to say about the racial abuse, so decides to leave this for now and discuss it with Lars later. As it happens, they don't need to do anything. The next day Junita surprises them by taking it upon herself to apologise to Nazia. She chooses not to go to her party as she doesn't think she will cope with it. She had been looking forward to visiting her, so Marisa and Nazia's mother organise a play date for the girls instead. Marisa explains that Junita has some difficulties and Nazia's mother agrees she will keep a close eye on them. Junita gets to wear her new clothes, and Nazia's mother, a hairdresser, helps them both to find new ways to style their hair.

PACE and behaviour support

Marisa and Lars learned that Junita needs a lot more regulation and emotional support than her older brother and sister did. Karl and Kirsten always knew that they were loved unconditionally. Although cross sometimes at their parents' boundaries, they knew that their parents had their best interests at heart. They learned to rely on their parents, to turn to them for regulatory support as needed and to make sense of the world with them. As they matured, the emotional connections forged when younger stayed with them, and their parents could focus on guiding and supporting them to behave well in the world. Junita does not have this intrinsic trust in her parents; she doubts their intentions and is quick to experience shame. Her developing abilities to regulate and reflect are fragile and quickly break down under stress. Marisa and Lars learn the importance of building emotional connections with Junita, alongside the behavioural support that she needs to remain safe and accepted in the world.

When they first began to incorporate PACE into their parenting, Marisa and Lars were disappointed that Junita was getting worse. She was more rejecting of them and even quicker to anger. They discussed this at the support group and took on ideas not to expect too much. They learned to 'wonder about' without expecting that Junita could wonder with them. They also made their empathy a little more matter-of-fact while Junita became used to experiencing the resultant connections with them. This helped a little, but they were still concerned that progress was slow. The group facilitator wondered how Junita was when they put in boundaries and discipline. Marisa and Lars realised that they had not been paying too much attention to this, so focused were they on getting their PACE right. In fact, on reflection they realised that they were anxious to provide any discipline in case it provoked a meltdown!

Junita was not experiencing the safety that boundaries and discipline can provide. It was time to reflect on the other hand of parenting.

Marisa and Lars had learned how to help Junita tolerate the warmth and nurture she needed but resisted. They had helped Junita to rely on them, while also supporting her developing autonomy in slow steps. Hand one supported their use of PACE as their curiosity opened up the door to empathy and acceptance, and Junita learned to enjoy moments of fun and joy with them.

With their second hand, Marisa and Lars now learned how to help Junita manage the structure and boundaries she needed to be safe and healthy. They also adjusted these in response to often rapidly shifting levels of emotional maturity, providing increased structure when Junita was stressed and emotionally younger. They learned to provide connection before, during and after behavioural support to reduce the shame that was so quickly triggered with discipline. They also discovered that connection helped Junita to reflect on her behaviour, and to experience remorse. Consequences could be used collaboratively as they figured out together how she could make amends.

Therapy

Marisa and Lars were hopeful that therapy would help Junita to recover from early developmental trauma. They saw this as a first resort, but quickly learned that without therapeutic parenting, therapy was unlikely to make the difference they were hoping for. Unfortunately, the hard work begins with them, although a therapist, Paul, was very helpful in supporting them with this both before and once Dyadic Developmental Psychotherapy started.

When therapy sessions began with Junita, supported by Marisa and Lars, they were surprised that these did not focus on Junita's behaviour. They discovered that therapy is not about fixing the child's behaviour, but helps the child to feel safe within intersubjective relationships. The immediate aim of Paul was to achieve an emotional connection with Junita. Behaviour change is needed, but if this is to be an integrated change, internalised by Junita, then it has to stem from the trust and security that emotional connection can bring. Paul's goal, beyond getting to know Junita, and supporting Marisa and Lars, was to help them all relate and communicate more safely, in a connected way. This emphasis on safety and relationship is important for developmentally traumatised children. It builds their capacity for emotional regulation and reflective function. Children are then able to respond to both current experience and memories of past experience flexibly. Behaviour change then becomes possible, based on stronger, more secure relationships.

Paul helped Junita to talk about how she felt, what she feared, the almost nameless terror which stemmed from her lack of worth, and the certainty she felt that she should not invest in this family, as one day it would be lost too. Marisa and Lars were supported to respond with PACE, the very same approach they were working so hard to bring in at home. Marisa, Lars and Junita were given an experience of a relationship with Paul which helped them to explore and co-construct Junita's subjective experience at a deeper level. Paul provided co-regulation of the increased arousal that the exploration of experience created. This in turn helped Junita to discover new meanings about her experience which she was helped to communicate to her parents. She discovered that they could accept her perception of herself as bad and worthless while also holding hope that she would not always feel this way – that one day she would see herself as they saw her. The creation of meaning together built safety for Junita as she learned to trust in new relationship experience. Junita's identity is slowly being rewritten as she develops the trust and security that was deprived to her as her birthright.

Afterword

Junita is now 15 years old. Karl and Kirsten are both away at university, and Junita is enjoying being the only child. Vacation times when they are home again can be challenging for Junita, but generally she is managing change and transitions better now. Marisa and Lars remember how vulnerable she is when she sees her successful brother and sister, and offer a bit more emotional support at these times. Junita does not always tolerate boundaries – she is a teenager after all! Marisa and Lars are learning to recognise the normal adolescent behaviours that she needs some guidance and support with and distinguishing these from areas where it is harder to keep her safe. Her tendency towards self-reliance makes it hard to help her. Navigating mobile phones and social media is particularly tricky. Junita cannot see how vulnerable she is making herself. This is especially true when Junita becomes more interested in her birth story and discovering who her birth parents are. Luckily, Marisa and Lars find out before she goes to a meeting she has set up with a birth relative. With their persistence, she is able to let them slow her down and do this more gradually. Challenges remain, but there is room for optimism as well. Marisa and Lars feel hopeful that Junita will be able to become who she was always meant to be.

References

Baylin, J. and Hughes, D.A. (2016). *The Neurobiology of Attachment-Focused Therapy: Enhancing Connection and Trust in the Treatment of Children and Adolescents* (Norton Series on Interpersonal Neurobiology). New York, NY: W.W. Norton and Company.

Bernard, K. and Dozier, M. (2010). Examining infants' cortisol responses to laboratory tasks among children varying in attachment disorganization: Stress reactivity or return to baseline? *Developmental Psychology*, 46(6), 1771–1778.

Bettelheim, B. (1987). *A Good Enough Parent*. London: Thames and Hudson.

Bowlby, J. (1953). *Child Care and the Growth of Love*. Harmondsworth: Penguin Books.

Cassidy, J. and Shaver, P.R. (eds) (2016). *Handbook of Attachment: Theory, Research and Clinical Applications*, 3rd Edition. New York, NY: Guilford Press.

Coan, J.A. (2016). Towards a Neuroscience of Attachment. In J. Cassidy and P.R. Shaver (eds), *Handbook of Attachment: Theory, Research and Clinical Applications*, 3rd Edition. New York, NY: Guilford Press.

Cook, A., Spinazzola, J., Ford, J., Lanktree, C. *et al.* (2005). Complex trauma in children and adolescents. *Psychiatric Annals*, 35(5), 390–398.

DeKlyen, M. and Greenberg, M.T. (2016). Attachment and Psychopathology in Childhood. In J. Cassidy and P.R. Shaver (eds), *Handbook of Attachment: Theory, Research and Clinical Applications*, 3rd Edition. New York, NY: Guilford Press.

Dozier, M. (2003). Attachment-based treatment for vulnerable children. *Attachment and Human Development*, 5(3), 253–257.

Dozier, M. and Rutter, M. (2016). Challenges to the Development of Attachment Relationships Faced by Young Children in Foster and Adoptive Care. In J. Cassidy and P.R. Shaver (eds), *Handbook of Attachment: Theory, Research and Clinical Applications*, 3rd Edition. New York, NY: Guilford Press.

Feeney, B.C. and Woodhouse, S.S. (2016). Caregiving. In J. Cassidy and P.R. Shaver (eds), *Handbook of Attachment: Theory, Research and Clinical Applications*, 3rd Edition. New York, NY: Guilford Press.

Fonagy, P., Gergely, G., Jurist, E.L. and Target, M. (2002). *Affect Regulation, Mentalization, and the Development of the Self*. New York, NY: Other Press.

Golding, K.S. (2017a). *Foundations for Attachment Training Resource: The Six-Session Programme for Parents of Traumatized Children*. London: Jessica Kingsley Publishers.

Golding, K.S. (2017b). *Everyday Parenting with Security and Love: Using PACE to Provide Foundations for Attachment*. London: Jessica Kingsley Publishers.

Golding, K.S. and Hughes, D.A. (2012). *Creating Loving Attachments: Parenting with PACE to Nurture Confidence and Security in the Troubled Child.* London: Jessica Kingsley Publishers.

Gunnar, M.R., Hostinar, C.E., Sanchez, M.M., Tottenham, N. and Sullivan, R.M. (2015). Parental buffering of fear and stress neurobiology: Reviewing parallels across rodent, monkey, and human models. *Social Neuroscience*, 10(5), 474–478.

Hesse, E. (2016). The Adult Attachment Interview. In J. Cassidy and P.R. Shaver. (eds), *Handbook of Attachment: Theory, Research and Clinical Applications*, 3rd Edition. New York, NY: Guilford Press.

Hughes, D.A. and Baylin, J. (2012). *Brain-Based Parenting: The Neuroscience of Caregiving for Healthy Attachment.* New York, NY: W.W. Norton and Company.

Hughes, D.A., Golding, K.S. and Hudson, J. (2019). *Healing Relational Trauma with Attachment-Focused Interventions: Dyadic Developmental Psychotherapy with Children and Families.* New York, NY: W.W. Norton and Company.

Kaufman, G. (1996). *The Psychology of Shame: Theory and Treatment of Shame-Based Syndromes*, 2nd Edition. New York, NY: Springer.

Porges, S. (2017). *The Pocket Guide to the Polyvagal Theory: The Transformative Power of Feeling Safe* (Norton Series on Interpersonal Neurobiology). New York, NY: W.W. Norton and Company.

Rutter, M. (1972). *Maternal Deprivation Reassessed.* Harmondsworth: Penguin Books.

Tangney, J. and Dearing, R.L. (2002). *Shame and Guilt.* New York, NY: Guilford Press.

Thompson, R.A. (2016). Early Attachment and Later Development: Reframing the Questions. In J. Cassidy and P.R. Shaver (eds), *Handbook of Attachment: Theory, Research and Clinical Applications*, 3rd Edition. New York, NY: Guilford Press.

Trevarthen, C. (2001). Intrinsic motives for companionship in understanding: Their origin, development, and significance for infant mental health. *Infant Mental Health Journal*, 22(1–2), 95–131.

Winnicott, D.W. (1964). *The Child, the Family and the Outside World.* Harmondsworth: Penguin Books.

PRACTICE REFLECTION

Joe Tucci, Janise Mitchell and Ed Tronick

Golding's chapter is full of generous translations of her body of work inspired by DDP. She highlights how both carers and children need to be open to change in order for children to experience the benefits of an embodied sense of love. As she poignantly traces the story of young Junita, Golding gives us a direct insight into how carers come to pin their hopes on therapy for the child to be the panacea for change that will lead to a reduction in children's trauma-based behaviour and an improvement in the experience of connection in the family:

> Marisa and Lars were hopeful that therapy would help Junita to recover from early developmental trauma. They saw this as a first resort, but quickly learned that without therapeutic parenting, therapy was unlikely to make the difference they were hoping for. Unfortunately, the hard work begins with them… When therapy sessions began with Junita, supported by Marisa and Lars, they were surprised that these did not focus on Junita's behaviour. They discovered that therapy is not about fixing the child's behaviour, but helps the child to feel safe within intersubjective relationships. The immediate aim of Paul was to achieve an emotional connection with Junita. Behaviour change is needed, but if this is to be an integrated change, internalised by Junita, then it has to stem from the trust and security that emotional connection can bring.

Golding's chapter provides a critical reminder that therapeutic care must focus on the meaning of behaviour as a form of communication about what a child needs, and not only respond or react to the behaviour itself. So often carers are seeking therapy for children to 'fix' their behaviours. Golding provides a timely reminder that the key to the recovery of children from traumatic experiences of the past is consistent and attuned relationships, within which they are able to have their needs understood and responded to.

This is the heart of what Therapeutic Care aims to achieve. It invites carers and others to consider how connection provides the means through which trust emerges in the systems of children waiting for it to be matched by the openness and trustworthiness of the carers and other adults. This experience occurs in micro-opportunities in the everyday.

As children and carers experience each other in mutually co-organised ways, the bank of co-regulated opportunities experienced by children and carers builds and builds. As it mounts, the internal states of children and carers begin to believe that this is more the norm than the exception. They begin to experience the predictability of their attuned connection. At this moment, children are offered what their internal states need from relationships in order to experience the calm and the comfort they have craved. Change is compelled because of the sheer weight of evidence to show that self-protection can be let go of and the softness of love be allowed in.

12

Expressive Arts Therapy as Self-Regulatory and Relational Interventions with Children and Caregivers

CATHY MALCHIODI

Introduction

Children may be in therapy for a variety of reasons. In my experience as a trauma-informed expressive arts therapist, they often have experienced various acute traumas such as the death of a parent, a serious accident, or loss of their home or possessions due to disaster. Many have endured multiple traumatic events during their young lives or were subjected to chronically stressful situations such as abuse, neglect, or multiple foster care environments. Although some children are not permanently affected by these experiences, others may suffer serious symptoms that interfere with normal emotional, cognitive, or social development. Children who survive these events often feel helpless, confused, or ashamed and are afraid to trust others or their environment, including caregivers. In some cases, caregivers themselves may have contributed to the level of children's distress due to their own actions, including neglect or abuse, and are equally in need of intervention.

Helping professionals who encounter these children in therapy or other situations often must help them overcome the impact of traumatic events, intrusive memories, and dysregulated emotions; they must also form a safe, therapeutic relationship with them to enable them not only to revisit painful experiences, but also to strengthen resilience and to help them find hope. In order to reach them effectively, practitioners must use both developmentally appropriate methods and interventions that address sensory memories and provide emotional relief.

There is now wide agreement that many psychosocial challenges children face as a result of adverse events result in physiological reactions that create secondary psychological responses (Perry and Szalvitz, 2009). This recognition has reframed how we intervene with children who are emotionally dysregulated and it acknowledges that these symptoms are the body's adaptive reactions to distressing events. There is an increasing consensus that intervention must not only utilize evidence-based practices in psychotherapy with children, but must also employ techniques that focus on the sensory impact of trauma.

This chapter provides a foundation for understanding why sensory-based, creative interventions such as expressive arts therapy are effective and often necessary in work with children and their caregivers. For readers who are not familiar with this approach, a brief description of expressive arts therapy is offered along with key strategies to support two factors essential to reparation and recovery: (1) enhancing self-regulation and (2) supporting relationships through sensory-based attunement.

Defining expressive arts therapy

Expressive arts therapy capitalizes not only on a helping relationship between a practitioner and individual, but also on children's imagination and creative self-expression as central to the process of reparation and recovery. It is an approach that is action-oriented and sensory-based and may include imitation, role play, enactment, sharing, showing, and witnessing (Malchiodi, 2005, 2012, 2015), and often novel relational experiences for children as well as caregivers.

Expressive arts as methods of therapy have been formalized through the disciplines of art therapy, music therapy, dance/movement therapy, drama therapy or psychodrama, and poetry therapy. Each discipline has been applied in psychotherapy and counseling with individuals of all ages, particularly children, and they are often referred to as 'creative arts therapies' because of their roots in the arts and theories of creativity. These therapies and others that utilize self-expression in treatment are also called 'expressive therapies' (Malchiodi, 2005, 2013, 2014a). Additionally, expressive therapies are sometimes referred to as 'integrative' when purposively used in combination in treatment. While play is often part of expressive arts approaches, play therapy is systematic use of a theoretical model to establish an interpersonal process wherein therapists use the therapeutic powers of play to help clients prevent or resolve psychosocial difficulties and achieve optimal growth and development (Crenshaw and Stewart, 2014). Specifically, expressive arts therapy is the integration of two or more creative methods in work with individuals, families, or groups, and is based on a variety of orientations, including arts as therapy, arts psychotherapy, and the use of arts for traditional healing (Knill, Levine, and Levine, 2005); they also may be combined with many theoretical frameworks including, but not limited to, psychodynamic, humanistic, cognitive, developmental, systems, narrative, solution-focused, and others (Malchiodi, 2005, 2011).

Often helping professionals wonder if expressive arts and other creative interventions such as play have a focus only on the 'nonverbal'. In fact, expressive arts include both verbal and nonverbal components because verbal communication of thoughts and feelings is a central part of therapy in most situations. There are, of course, also creative interventions that specifically focus on verbal communication and self-expression as part of treatment, such as drama therapy, creative writing and poetry therapy, and bibliotherapy.

Expressive arts therapy and self-regulation

Self-regulation is a term used to describe the capacity not only to control one's impulses, but also to soothe and calm the body's reactions to stress. It is the ability to modulate affective, sensory, and somatic responses that impact emotions, physiological responses, and cognition. The term self-regulation also refers to the brain's executive capacity to delay actions if necessary and initiate them if necessary, even if one does not want to. In other words, individuals who are self-regulated can delay gratification and suppress reactions in order to become mindful of their action's consequences or to consider alternative, appropriate responses.

Perry (2016) refers to self-regulation as a core strength in children and one that is key to the healthy development of a stress response capability. He explains self-regulation through a continuum of five states of regulation to dysregulation in the following order: calm, aroused attention, alarm, fear, and terror. Goleman's (1996, 2015) concept of 'emotional intelligence' and what he calls the 'emotional hijack' is somewhat similar to Perry's framework. According to Goleman, dysregulation takes the mind on an 'emotional hijack' in response to distress.

These responses are immediate, overwhelming, and at times inappropriate in relation to the nature of a perceived threat; in other words, they are faster than the thinking brain (executive functioning).

Expressive arts interventions have the potential to enhance self-regulation in children and their caregivers who are experiencing distressful physical sensations and hyperactivation such as alarm, fear, or terror. In brief, the kinesthetic-sensory qualities such as rhythm, movement, touch, and sound that are relevant to lower brain functions such as heart rate and respiration can be mediated through various expressive arts approaches. They can also address the right hemisphere dominance found in both expressive arts and the experience of trauma while capitalizing on body-based experiences found in creative activities. In work with children in particular, expressive arts offer many unique dimensions that can enhance self-regulation, but in particular they support the following two areas: (1) *grounding and anchoring*, and (2) *mirroring and entrainment* (summarized from Malchiodi, 2016). By understanding these two areas, practitioners can help children as well as caregivers experience and practice the self-regulatory skills needed to reduce the emotional hijack and sensations of alarm, fear, and terror that increase distress and disrupt positive attachment.

Grounding and anchoring

Grounding is one way we can help children stop or at least slow down stress responses and emotional or physiological dysregulation. Grounding techniques generally refer to ways for individuals to focus on some aspect of external reality and often involve using the senses to reinforce being in the here-and-now and to interrupt anxiety, panic, dissociation, or attention lapses. Grounding techniques can be as simple as shifting attention to external senses, such as identifying things that one can see, hear, or smell in the present (Rothschild, 2010). For example, 'The walls are light green, there are three brown folding chairs, there is a cinnamon smell coming from the next room, there are sounds of cars passing by outside.' One simple example of this strategy is to have a child move around the immediate environment and describe that environment in detail using all one's senses. Another common variation is often referred to as the 'five senses' or '5-4-3-2-1'. In brief, it involves looking around for five things one can see (a table, a chair, a photo of a cat, a stuffed bear, a cup); four things one can feel by paying attention to the body (I feel the cushion I am sitting on); three sounds one can hear; two things one can smell (or name two favorite smells); and one thing one can taste (or name a favorite taste). In applying any grounding technique, it is important to have children rate their experiences before and after to understand whether or not they perceive it as effective; templates with faces showing 'happiest' to 'saddest' for children are common subjective instruments.

The advantage of using expressive arts as a means of grounding is that they are not just sensory-based experiences, they are also creative ones tailored to developmental, cultural, and personal preferences and relevance. In contrast to simply asking children to name a grounding experience, which can be a difficult task when highly stressed, expressive arts can help increase focus on something other than distressing implicit reactions or memories or can serve as an immediate distraction if necessary.

One simple art-based grounding technique involves what is commonly called *bilateral drawing*. By the simplest definition, bilateral simply means 'involving two sides'. Sensory integration is often associated with bilateral techniques found in occupational therapy that assist individuals in organizing specific sensations. In the process of reparation from psychological trauma, various forms of bilateral stimulation or movement seem to be effective in engaging cross-hemisphere activity in the brain (Shapiro, 2017); in art therapy, the process of bilateral work may help reconnect and integrate 'thinking' and 'feeling' via the sensory-based processes involved in art making (Malchiodi, 2011). In brief, it is important to engage children in regulating movements that go beyond the use of the hands to engage the whole body in natural, self-soothing rhythms; these rhythmic movements can be practiced in the air, later transferring them to paper with drawing materials.

This concept is somewhat reflective of Shapiro's model of Eye Movement Desensitization and Reprocessing (EMDR) (2017) treatment that involves dual attention stimulation and consists of a practitioner facilitating bilateral eye movements, taps, and sounds as sensory cues with an individual; in expressive arts, the focus is on movement and eventually translating those movements to drawing on paper. Elbrecht (2018) also proposes that the sensorimotor qualities of this approach provide self-regulatory experiences for children and adults.

Bilateral drawing is particularly useful as a grounding technique because it is an active, focused, and non-threatening experience for most individuals. In work with children's trauma reactions, it is particularly useful for hyperarousal or with children who are susceptible to responding to stress with a freeze response. These individuals often need experiences that involve movement in order to reduce their anxiety or panic or to decrease sensations of feeling trapped, withdrawn, or dissociated. Making marks or gestures on paper with both hands also creates an attention shift away from the distressing sensations in the body to a self-empowered focus, capitalizing on large muscle movements and body-based experiences that are self-soothing. For example, Jenny, a 13-year-old complex trauma survivor, frequently responded to environmental cues with dissociation, alternating with hyperarousal in the form of severe anxiety. I introduced the idea of bilateral gestures in the air, asking her to pretend she was drawing on a large invisible piece of paper. I then invited her to transfer those marks and gestures on large paper with chalk and oil pastels; plain brown wrapping paper is especially good not only because of its size and durability but also because individuals can use white or light-colored chalk pastels.

This simple art activity became a relaxing and regulating experience for Jenny at the beginning of each meeting, and we experimented with several variations of the method including using a 'favorite color' and an 'unfavorite color' to have a visual conversation with each other on large paper. In other sessions, I introduced playful suggestions such as draw 'energized', 'angry', 'sad', 'calm', and other mind–body states, asking Jenny to choose colored chalks in both hands to quickly sketch her sense of each emotion. If she felt stuck, she could simply draw in the air, moving her hands, wrists, shoulders, and then her entire body. In brief, bilateral work in the form of drawing in the air and on paper can be used at the beginning of any expressive arts session in order to help individuals 'loosen up' for other creative expression including movement, play, or dramatic enactment.

Anchoring is another term that is sometimes used to describe the process of using specific cues or experiences to bring one's attention to the present moment or shift sensations from anxious to calm. It is similar to grounding, but in using expressive arts approaches, an anchor usually involves some sort of sensory cue (sound or music) or an object (specific art expression). It is also something that the individual can return to for self-regulation. Goleman (2015) describes a powerful example of anchoring used as part of 'Breathing Buddies' in the New York City public school system, a part of the Inner Resilience Program, a curriculum established after the World Trade Center attacks on September 11, 2001. In brief, the program includes an anchoring ritual involving sound (a bell's chime) and holding stuffed animals while experiencing deep belly breathing as a method of anchoring with children. While a variation of mindfulness breathing is involved, the children are provided several sensory-based anchors including sound and a special toy to reinforce relaxation. The goal is self-regulation which, when achieved, supports children's success in classroom learning by increasing attention, comprehension, and problem-solving.

For individuals who do not have a self-soothing object or strong positive memory, I often invite them to create something that can be used for the purpose of anchoring themselves in the present moment and for use outside the therapy session. With children, this can involve making a tactile object such as a stuffed toy or other small object; sometimes even a simple art expression can be helpful if it is relevant and meaningful to the child. For example, Bonnie, an eight-year-old girl who survived a recreation vehicle accident, had to be hospitalized for several operations and difficult procedures; early in the course of her treatment, she developed fear reactions, insomnia, and claustrophobia during x-ray procedures. We decided to create a 'special friend' who could accompany her during her multiple stays in the hospital and subsequent outpatient visits. The first iteration of this friend was created by Bonnie's thumbprint on an index card; she added various features to the thumbprint to give it a face and personality. On the back of the index card we drew a five-point star and practiced a simple breathing exercise. This form of anchoring worked for Bonnie, and during another session we decided to create a more tactile, three-dimensional version of her thumbprint friend by making a small doll out of pipe cleaners (chenille stems), wrapping it with colorful yarn, and adding various embellishments and a thumbprint face similar to her original creation.

Mirroring and entrainment

Mirroring is another commonly used approach to establish and enhance the relationship between the individual and the helping professional. Within expressive arts therapy, it is generally described as the embodiment or reflection of an individual's movement or nonverbal communications. The goal of mirroring is not only imitation of postures, facial expressions, and gestures, but also includes attunement between the individual and practitioner. The brain's mirror neuron system is believed to be at least one part of these experiences of attunement, empathy (Goleman, 2015), and mirroring. These neurons refer to a special type of cell that fires not only when a person performs an action but also when the person observes someone else make the same movement. For example, when you see someone stub a toe on a concrete curb, you might immediately flinch or shudder with sympathy, sensing what the person's pain or distress is actually like. This is an example of the ability to instinctively understand and respond to what another person is experiencing. Research on mirror neurons and related aspects of neurobiology have also informed the larger domain of interpersonal neurobiology, and although the mechanisms behind these specific brain cells are still not completely understood, they have implications for helping professionals in terms of both mirroring and attuned relationships.

Mirroring is common to almost all expressive arts approaches, but in particular is relevant to dance/movement therapy because of the kinesthetic level of expression and interpersonal aspects involved in movement. For example, expressive arts therapy group sessions, including those for child trauma survivors, often begin with a movement sequence or simple stretches, starting with having everyone reach up to the sky and down to the earth in a rhythmic manner. Participants are simply asked to pay attention to their breathing and their bodily experiences and do as much or as little as they feel comfortable with in terms of movement. For children who are not yet comfortable with moving their bodies or those who find moving in a group overwhelming, I often keep things simple by just inviting participants to 'mirror me', allowing everyone to feel at ease in just following along rather than inventing their own movements. In facilitating this process, I am observing the energy of the group and individual children; for example, is the energy level high, calm, lethargic, or neutral?

Depending upon the nature of the group, children may eventually be invited to demonstrate their own stretches with other participants repeating the movements. The goal is to get group members to move in self-regulating ways and eventually become attuned to each other through movement. Trauma-sensitive yoga is another option that involves specific movements, breathing, and relational dynamics between practitioner and participants that emphasize attunement as a self-regulatory experience. In brief, the overall goal of the application of mirroring in the form of movement is to help children experience their bodies in a safe way as the basis for any additional self-regulating experiences.

A variation of the bilateral drawing activity described in the previous section illustrates another expressive arts approach that capitalizes on mirroring. For example, one of the first things I demonstrate to parent–child dyads who have experienced abuse or interpersonal violence is a simple kinesthetic/sensory activity called the 'scribble chase' or two-way scribble drawing. In brief, both parent and child choose a felt marker or crayon and each has the opportunity to be the leader in a scribble drawing on a large piece of paper. In other words, the child may be the leader of the first drawing, and while he or she scribbles with a pen on the paper, the parent follows the child's lines at the same time with his or her pen. Sometimes we reverse roles and the parent becomes the leader of the scribble with the child following, or in some situations the therapist may be the leader or follower. Although there may be interpersonal goals within this activity, it is also a way to demonstrate ways to mirror each other in a nonverbal way and to attune to another's behavior and nonverbal cues and encourage a caregiver to develop ways to attune to the child.

In coaching a parent to engage in this experience with a child, it is important to help the parent prepare the child for the activity. I often suggest to a mother, for example, that she make eye contact with her child and tell the child that they will be playing a game with crayons on paper. I also may suggest that she make some sort of physical contact with her child, such as a light touch on an arm or upper back, and place their chairs closely as is comfortable for them together at the table. Additionally, I may model the activity with either the parent or child as co-scribbler, asking one of them to be the leader of the scribble drawing while I follow or vice versa. In essence, I am demonstrating expressive arts activities to mirror another's behavior, particularly to sensory-based, nonverbal cues.

A similar approach that capitalizes on mirroring via a simple art-based activity is to introduce a 'two-way conversation on paper'. This two-way conversation can be presented in several ways, but most commonly two people are asked to simultaneously respond to each other's mark-making on paper nonverbally through drawing. This can involve mirroring each other's marks or simply drawing together on the same sheet of paper. I often introduce this approach to parents and children who work on 'conversations' in dyads. While the experience may emphasize mirroring each other's movements on paper, caregivers and children who have attachment difficulties due to multiple traumas may need extra coaching.

For example, although a caregiver may be enthusiastic about mirroring a child's scribbling across the paper, often that caregiver, due to unresolved trauma, can become quickly frustrated and angry with a child when he 'draws over my lines'. Helping the caregiver understand that the child is not necessarily being 'oppositional' or 'defiant' (descriptors sometimes learned from previous evaluations) and that there are other ways to both reframe and redirect the experience is more easily understood through an expressive arts or play activity. For example, when a child becomes overly excited during a scribble chase with a caregiver, I generally reframe the experience within the framework of a trauma-informed lens, emphasizing that the child may be challenged by trauma reactions or developmental issues that the caregiver can help address. I may also serve as an active role model, demonstrating how to communicate with the child through scribble lines, suggesting to the caregiver that she can say, 'I feel really happy when our lines touch. My lines are happy when your lines touch mine in the picture.' The overall goal in this simple art-based conversation on paper or any expressive arts approach that emphasizes self-regulation is to create an experience that not only reinforces positive relationship through tactile, visual, and kinesthetic senses, but also enhances the caregiver's ability to initiate self-regulating responses with their children through mirroring as well as attunement. In brief, both caregiver and child can benefit from sensory-based activities that involve mirroring through movement and sensory-based interaction that supports positive attachment, the foundation of self-regulation throughout the lifespan.

Entrainment is another expressive arts focus that can support self-regulation; sometimes this is also called *rhythmic synchronization*. Entrainment occurs when the rhythm of one experience synchronizes with the rhythm of another. For example, babies hear their first rhythm in utero when listening to their mothers' heartbeats; the natural way to calm infants is to sway, rock, or pat them to the rhythm of a resting heart rate. In expressive arts therapy approaches, heartbeat, motor activity, and brain activity are sources of rhythm and can be influenced to fall into synchronous rhythms not only through the therapist's voice, but by introducing sensory experiences that reinforce resting heart rate (60–80 beats a minute) or slow down or energize individuals.

The group movement experience involving mirroring described in the previous section also underscores elements of entrainment; in other words, the facilitator can entrain group members to synchronize their movements for the purpose of self-regulation. Although other arts-based approaches include aspects of entrainment, music and sound are most often used because rhythm is at the core. Musical entrainment is specifically defined as a process of playing or providing a musical rhythm at a different tempo from the personal tempo of the individual (Wheeler, 2015). In other words, the person's rhythm, whether in the form of respiration or heartbeat, adjusts to the music automatically and unconsciously. There are also specific approaches such as music-assisted relaxation (MAR) to enhance physiological and psychological relaxation (Gardstrom and Sorel, 2015), emphasizing that certain music experiences have a measurable calming effect that decreases agitation. In the field of music therapy, MAR is often combined with progressive muscle relaxation (tensing and releasing muscles throughout the body) or autonomic relaxation (passive focus on heart rate, breathing, or body temperature). Additionally, music listening and singing not only entrain but actually help individuals shift away from hyperarousing memories. Similarly, a therapist's voice can be utilized to promote entrainment via tempo and rhythm, thus promoting self-regulation.

In brief, one way to apply the use of music as entrainment is through its role as an auditory cue to enhance either experiences of calm or experiences of energy. Hyperactivation and dissociation impact how individuals 'keep the beat' internally; one way to address this is to co-create playlists of music for a smartphone, iPod, or a CD device, depending on individual needs. For example, with children who tend toward dissociation and withdrawal, we create playlists of music that would help to ground them when they 'space out' as well as entrain them to feel energized and positive. In contrast, children and caregivers who are experiencing panic reactions benefited from creating a playlist that included gentle instrumental music with rhythms at the beat of a resting heart rate. With all children and adults, it is also important to understand their personal and cultural experiences with music because, of all the expressive arts, music is the one that most quickly stimulates emotional responses and past memories. Because each individual has had specific experiences with music, it is best to approach entrainment by finding out more about preferences, memories of music, and even what level of volume is soothing rather than agitating or unproductive.

Finally, relaxation and stress reduction protocols are popular strategies used to support self-regulation with individuals of all ages and particularly with those who experience post-trauma hyperarousal. There are numerous effective relaxation protocols such as progressive muscle relaxation and stress inoculation (Meichenbaum, 2012). Trauma experts have also developed various specific strategies that help people to decrease uncomfortable physiological reactions. For example, Levine (2015) proposes a series of simple postures to help one's body literally 'slow down' when anxious or fearful; these postures involve various placements of one's hands on the head, heart, and stomach along with rhythmic breathing, and are easily learned by children and caregivers.

'The Four Bs' (brake, breathe, brain, and body) are fairly common techniques that I learned from occupational therapists who use these practices to address sensory integration issues. They are systematic calming methods that can be used with children to help them self-regulate and regain a sense of self-control. While these are movement and body-oriented, I often ask individuals to 'show me through colors, lines, shapes, or mark-making' what the felt (body) sense of the experience is for them; this drawing serves as a visual anchor that can be used as an additional reminder of each practice (Malchiodi, 2012, 2015). These exercises basically are designed to help individuals focus on the body, redirect attention, and facilitate a relationship toward the self that is caring, gentle, and nurturing.

1. **Brake:** When an individual feels out of control, anxious, fearful, or even terrorized, it is important to learn ways to 'put the brakes on'. Rothschild (2010) uses the term 'putting on the brakes' to describe an important practice that helps to keep the hyperarousal at a manageable level. In brief, from a sensory integration perspective, 'putting on the brakes' decreases excess energy and helps release muscle tension. To accomplish this, simply have the individual sit and press the palms of the hands together in front of the chest for 5–10 seconds and repeat this several times to really engage the muscles in the arms and shoulders.

2. **Breathe:** Similar to mindfulness practices, controlled breathing helps a person to regain a sense of body awareness and restore a sense of calm and helps to stabilize and ground the body. To accomplish this, I have the individual take in a breath with hands on the abdomen and breathe deeply into the abdomen. One prompt that helps is following a chart or self-created breathing chart because it orients the individual to breathing in and out by simply following the sides of a drawing of a five-point star or a square (four sides). Similar to 'drawing a breath', children and adults can actually draw their own square or five-point star breathing charts.

3. **Brain:** To create a sense of both alertness and calm, I ask individuals to put their hands on top of their head and press with a light pressure. This not only calms the body but also

activates the brain; it is particularly useful for individuals who dissociate or withdraw during a session by gently bringing them back into the here-and-now.

4. **Body:** Self-regulation and a sense of safety are closely related. In order to approximate a sense of safety, a self-hug (crossing arms in front of the body) with gentle pressure is one approach. The sensation of squeezing pressure on the arms and shoulders not only increases body awareness, but also increases a sense of security, calm, and focus (effective for both hyperarousal and dissociation); with children, including a soft toy as part of the hug experience is also helpful. Levine (2012) uses a similar approach, explaining it as tapping the sense of being 'contained' because the body is essentially the container of all sensations and feelings. In other words, once people can actually feel the container (their bodies), any hyperactivation does not feel as overwhelming. An additional variation that many people find self-soothing and deactivating involves placing the left hand on the head and the right hand on the heart area, focusing on any sensations of energy and temperature change, or observing any energy flow between the hands (Levine, 2012).

The expressive arts relationship: Enhancing attunement

The term *interpersonal neurobiology* (IPNB) (Badenoch, 2008; Schore, 2003; Siegel, 2012) is an overarching theory that includes attachment research, neurobiology, and developmental and social psychology. It is based on the idea that social relationships shape how our brains develop, how our minds perceive the world, and how we adapt to stress throughout the lifespan. IPNB is also based on evidence that indicates that the brain is capable of change (neuroplasticity), especially through positive attachments and relationships; in particular, IPNB practices are particularly relevant to trauma recovery and attachment problems that were once believed to be irreversible.

Siegel (2012) cites the importance of 'critical micromoments' of interaction with individuals that include their tone of voice, postures, facial expressions, eye contact, and motion, which he believes provide clues to the individual's psychobiology. These sensory-based cues become particularly important in identifying and formulating strategies for therapy when applying expressive arts approaches to intervention with children and their caregivers.

Attunement is a key concept within IPNB and is the capacity to be able to read the nonverbal communication and rhythms of others. In other words, it is not only perceiving what individuals say, but also attending to eye signals, facial gestures, tone of voice, posture, and even breathing rate. It is an embodied response because we actually feel a connection to others within our own physiology. Attunement during therapy is also a form of synchronization in which helping professionals become witnesses, seeing and accepting what the individual expresses and perceives, but also presenting themselves in a way that supports self-regulation and decreases stress. Therapeutic relationships that resonate these experiences enhance overall functioning and are believed to actually create new adaptive responses (Badenoch, 2008; Siegel, 2012).

Etcherling and Stewart (2015) note that attunement is predicated upon three action-oriented responses: listening, understanding, and validating (LUV). In other words, when an individual does not feel heard, understood, and accepted, any intervention, including creative ones, will seem like a gimmick or manipulation. This is particularly true when applying expressive arts therapy as trauma intervention because it is not the activity itself that promotes self-regulation; it is the authenticity of both the activity and the relationship between the therapist and individual during that activity that enhances regulatory change. No specific expressive arts or play-based approach will be successful if it is not relevant to the individual and if the therapist does not provide attuned responses.

The unique sensory nature of the 'expressive arts therapeutic relationship', first and foremost, is what makes it different in its impact and role in trauma-informed intervention with children. Attunement operates from 'bottom up' because how we perceive feelings in others involves some of the more ancient parts of the brain – the amygdala, hippocampus, and structures underlying the cortex. The expressive arts therapies emphasize senses, feeling, and nonverbal communication, establishing a different type of attunement between the practitioner and the individual or group less dependent on words. Additionally, specific relational dynamics are present in each expressive art form, and each is characteristically a little different from the others in respect to sensory-based attunement. In art therapy, a therapist is a provider of materials (nurturer), assistant in the creative process, and active participant in facilitating visual self-expression. These are experiences that emphasize interaction through experiential, tactile, and visual exchanges, not just verbal communication, between the client and therapist. Similarly, play therapy, an approach that also involves tactile, visual, kinesthetic, and other senses, reinforces similar experiences of attunement between young clients and helping professionals. Music therapy provides sound and rhythm-based experiences through interaction with music-making; it also has the potential to tap social engagement and communication when collaboration or simultaneously playing instruments is involved. Prosody and vocalizations are particularly effective in stimulating a sense of affiliation and relationship, and experiences involving specific music inherently can calm and self-regulate (Porges, 2011). Drama therapy offers multi-sensory ways to establish relationship through roleplay, modeling, mirroring, and enactment, and often includes other creative arts and play to support and enhance attachment. Intermodal and integrative approaches to expressive arts and play tap possibilities to establish attunement on multiple levels because many different senses may be involved.

In the field of art therapy, one common approach to attunement is often referred to as the 'third hand'. Kramer (1993) is credited with coining the term 'third hand' and demonstrated its applications with children who were challenged by traumatic events. In brief, the third hand refers to the therapist's use of suggestion, metaphors, or other techniques to enhance the individual's progress in therapy and self-expression without being intrusive or imposing values. It also involves the strategic use of the therapist's own active participation through supporting creative expression by mirroring and modeling, and occasionally even redirecting the child's creative process. In work with trauma, I find that the third hand includes being a focused witness to a child's efforts to engage in art and play-based expression and, more importantly, assisting both the child and caregiver in those efforts. The goal is to apply expressive arts and play processes that mimic a healthy neurobiological relationship between a caring adult and child and reinforce self-regulatory skills the child will need to cope with distressful events throughout life.

Third-hand expressive arts and play interventions echo the concept of the 'good enough parent' (Winnicott, 2005) who supports the individual's efficacy experiences during creative exploration and experimentation.

Strategically designed repetitive experiential and self-rewarding experiences that include a positive and attuned witness are central to repairing disrupted attachment and developing a sense of security and confidence (Perry and Szalvitz, 2009). In brief, the expressive arts in therapy can provide reparative enactments of secure attachment experiences, co-created by therapist and client, and are based on interpersonal, creative exchanges. For example, well-attuned parents or caregivers are able to detect what their children are feeling and to reflect those emotions back through sensory means such as facial expressions, vocalizations, touch, and other behaviors; these forms of attuned behavior help children recognize their own feelings and develop the ability to self-regulate (Malchiodi, 2014b). Additionally, being an attuned and focused witness to a child's efforts to complete a hands-on task and assisting those efforts when appropriate mimics the neurobiological relationship between a caring adult and child. For some children, repetitive experiential and self-rewarding experiences that include a positive and attuned witness are central to repairing developmental trauma.

In working with caregivers and their children, my main focus is on strengthening their relationships through positive attunement via expressive arts and play-based approaches. Although a child is often the individual referred for treatment, if possible it is important to get many family members engaged in expressive arts sessions in order to help both the child and caregiver to learn creative ways to establish attunement and thus strengthen attachment as well as parenting skills. Here is one brief example to illustrate key points in the use of expressive arts therapy to support attunement.

Case example: Including the caregiver in expressive arts therapy

Sally, age ten, was referred to therapy after she witnessed her father beating her mother, Marie, on three occasions and for repeated physical abuse by her father. Marie did not report the incidents of physical abuse or domestic violence until protective services removed Sally and her younger brother Tom, age five, from the home when their mother became unconscious due to a drug overdose. Sally found her mother lying on the floor of their apartment and called the police to come to the home while Tom knelt screaming next to his parent's lifeless body. Although their mother recovered, social services felt it was in their best interests to stay at a residential treatment facility for the short term.

When I first met with Sally, she was hypervigilant and unable to concentrate for very long. But she did like to draw and paint and wanted to make a picture of her family because she 'missed her mommie very much'. When I asked Sally to tell me more about the drawing, she said it was a picture of herself, Tom, and 'my mommie'. There were three human figures in the picture, each drawn appropriately for Sally's age range. I asked, 'Is there anyone else in the picture?' Sally replied, 'Well, I forget about my daddy a lot. He was mean to my mommie and hurt her all the time. He hit me and Tom, too.'

From this initial drawing and subsequent sessions, I learned a great deal about Sally's disrupted attachment with her mother and her anger and sense of abandonment due to numerous incidents when Marie passed out from drug overdoses. This disruption was compounded by Marie's neglect, indifference, and non-responsiveness, shattering Sally's trust and reinforcing a disbelief that Marie could protect her from harm. Both Marie and Sally reported that Sally was often anxious, had sleep problems (night-time anxiety and nightmares), and was often impulsive at school. In brief, abuse from her father and the overwhelming sense of abandonment by her mother contributed to a lack of attunement between caregiver and child; in fact, in many situations Sally took on the role of caregiver when Marie's drug addiction prevented normal parenting of Sally and Tom.

In working with Sally, Tom, and Marie, intervention with Sally integrated not only the self-regulatory principles described earlier in this chapter, but also the use of expressive arts to re-establish attunement between Marie and her children. In initial sessions with Sally, I introduced a number of sensory-based experiences designed to recapitulate early attachment experiences. Although she was ten years old, I also introduced a few experiences that I normally use with much younger children, such as listening to various soothing rhythms, playing drums and percussion instruments together, and recalling favorite songs from preschool days. I introduced felt markers with different smells of familiar foods for drawing activities and a variety of tactile materials for art making, taking on the role of someone who provides materials for creative self-expression that is accepted with unconditional regard. At other times, I taught Sally some child-friendly yoga poses, including ones that made us laugh because we enjoyed being 'silly' together. We practiced deep breathing together and I taught Sally several child-appropriate mindfulness activities such as balancing a long peacock feather on the tip of her finger and a colorful, self-created butterfly on the tip of her nose. All of these interventions were selected to support self-soothing experiences; additionally, I was making a 'right-brain-to-right-brain' connection with Sally by communicating with her through hands-on activities rather than words alone (left hemisphere) and using creative interventions to build a relationship.

Before we ended our individual sessions, Marie was allowed to begin to re-establish her parenting role with Sally and was asked by social services to participate in several mother–child creative arts therapies sessions with us. I actually repeated several of the activities I used with Sally with Marie as a participant. Marie herself was in need of self-regulation through other means than drugs; because she was in a violent relationship with her husband for most of their married life, she understandably needed some self-soothing experiences as well. In particular, I focused on some simple self-soothing creative activities that Marie could initiate with Sally and Tom at home, such as quiet times for drawing, creating scrapbooks, and collage work. More importantly, I was able to introduce some experiences of collaborative, attachment-enhancing activities that this family could enjoy at home such as building a dollhouse together from shoeboxes and making puppet families from socks.

Although I use expressive arts as the key approach to intervention when working with caregivers and children, the essential focus of this work is relational. In other words, role modeling as a 'third hand' reinforces the same principles to caregivers as in work with children – how to use creative, sensory-based experiences to self-regulate and to establish positive, attuned connection between caregiving adults and their children. In the case of Marie, the activities I modeled became an important foundation for her own learning to be a role model as well as a more effective parent to her children. Like many caregivers who have been challenged by multiple adverse experiences throughout the lifespan, these sensory-based experiences gave Marie an opportunity to engage in her own self-regulatory self-care and provided strategies that she could practice when confronted by stress and her difficult recovery from addiction. Although I do not know the ultimate outcome of our work together, I do know that Sally, Tom, and Marie were eventually permanently reunited and that Marie, with the help of addictions counseling, has been able to maintain a drug-free existence.

Conclusion

This chapter provides a very brief overview of some of the key principles and concepts to enhance self-regulation and attuned relationship through the expressive arts with children and their caregivers. Although there are many approaches that successfully support self-regulation and attunement in individuals challenged by trauma, expressive arts therapy provides action-oriented strategies that engage children and caregivers in sensory-based activities necessary to reduce hyperactivation, dissociation, and disrupted attachment commonly experienced by survivors when cognitive or solely verbal approaches are ineffective or counterindicated. Most importantly, these strategies are ways to recapitulate a secure relationship with a helping professional that integrates the senses and touches a place where positive attachment is authentically recognized and appreciated.

References

Badenoch, B. (2008). *Being a Brain-Wise Therapist*. New York, NY: Norton.

Crenshaw, D. and Stewart, A. (2014). *Play Therapy: A Comprehensive Guide to Theory and Practice*. New York, NY: Guilford Press.

Elbrecht, C. (2018). *Healing Trauma with Guided Drawing: A Sensorimotor Art Therapy Approach to Body Bilateral Mapping*. Berkeley, CA: North Atlantic Books.

Etcherling, L. and Stewart, A. (2015). Creative Crisis Intervention Techniques with Children and Families. In C. Malchiodi (ed.), *Creative Interventions with Traumatized Children*. New York, NY: Guilford Press.

Gardstrom, S. and Sorel, S. (2015). Music Therapy Methods. In B. Wheeler (ed.), *Music Therapy Handbook*. New York, NY: Guilford Press.

Goleman, D. (1996). *Emotional Intelligence*. New York, NY: Bantam Books.

Goleman, D. (2015). *Focus: The Hidden Driver of Excellence*. New York, NY: Harper.

Knill, P., Levine, S. and Levine, E. (2005). *Principles and Practice of Expressive Arts Therapy*. London: Jessica Kingsley Publishers.
Kramer, E. (1993). *Art as Therapy with Children*. Chicago, IL: Magnolia Street.
Levine, P. (2012). *In an Unspoken Voice: How the Body Releases Trauma and Restores Goodness*. Berkeley, CA: North Atlantic Books.
Levine, P. (2015). *Trauma and Memory: Brain and Body in Search for the Living Past*. Berkeley, CA: North Atlantic Books.
Malchiodi, C.A. (2005). *Expressive Therapies*. New York, NY: Guilford Press.
Malchiodi, C.A. (2011). Art Therapy and the Brain. In C. Malchiodi (ed.), *Handbook of Art Therapy*, 2nd Edition. New York, NY: Guilford Press.
Malchiodi, C.A. (2012). Trauma-Informed Art Therapy and Sexual Abuse. In P. Goodyear-Brown (ed.), *Handbook of Child Sexual Abuse*. Hoboken, NJ: Wiley.
Malchiodi, C.A. (2013). Introduction to Art Therapy in Health Care Settings. In C. Malchiodi (ed.), *Art Therapy and Health Care*. New York, NY: Guilford Press.
Malchiodi, C.A. (2014a). Creative Arts Therapy Approaches to Attachment Issues. In C.A. Malchiodi and D.A. Crenshaw (eds), *Creative Arts and Play Therapy for Attachment Problems*. New York, NY: Guilford Press.
Malchiodi, C.A. (2014b). Art Therapy, Attachment and Parent–Child Dyads. In C.A. Malchiodi and D. Crenshaw (eds), *Creative Arts and Play Therapy for Attachment Problems*. New York, NY: Guilford Press.
Malchiodi, C.A. (2015). Calm, Connection and Confidence: Using Art Therapy to Enhance Resilience in Traumatized Children. In D.A. Crenshaw, R. Brooks and S. Goldstein (eds), *Play Therapy Interventions to Enhance Resilience*. New York, NY: Guilford Press.
Malchiodi, C.A. (2016, 30 March). Expressive arts therapy and self-regulation. Accessed on 8/1/2019 at www.psychologytoday.com/blog/arts-and-health/201603/expressive-arts-therapy-and-self-regulation.
Meichenbaum, D. (2012). *Roadmap to Resilience: A Guide for Military, Trauma Victims and Their Families*. Miami, FL: Institute Press.
Perry, B.D. (2016). Self-regulation: The second core strength. Accessed on 8/1/2019 at http://teacher.scholastic.com/professional/bruceperry/self_regulation.htm.
Perry, B.D. and Szalvitz, M. (2009). *The Boy Who Was Raised as a Dog*. New York, NY: Basic Books.
Porges, S. (2011). *The Polyvagal Theory: Neurophysiological Foundations of Emotions, Attachment, Communication and Regulation*. New York, NY: Norton.
Rothschild, B. (2010). *8 Keys to Safe Trauma Recovery*. New York, NY: Norton.
Schore, A.N. (2003). *Affect Regulation and the Repair of the Self*. New York, NY: Norton.
Shapiro, F. (2017). *Eye Movement Desensitization and Reprocessing (EMDR) Therapy*, 3rd Edition. New York, NY: Guilford Press.
Siegel, D. (2012). *The Developing Mind: How Relationships and the Brain Interact to Shape Who We Are*, 2nd Edition. New York, NY: Guilford Press.
Wheeler, B. (ed.) (2015). *Music Therapy Handbook*. New York, NY: Guilford Press.
Winnicott, D. (2005). *Playing and Reality* (Routledge Classics). New York, NY: Routledge.

PRACTICE REFLECTION

Joe Tucci, Janise Mitchell and Ed Tronick

Malchiodi's chapter is rich with practical strategies that can be used with children and carers to support the expression of reverberating past pain and hurt, and cultivate their engagement in mutually oriented play and curiosity in the present.

Her examples are beautiful in the way they bridge fun, relational activities, opportunities for organised co-regulation and metaphor. It is the higher-order meaning attributed to the engagement of children and carers in therapeutic processes using creative arts that fulfils one of its main ambitions to reorient an appreciation of behaviour merely as behaviour to a form of communication with integrative function.

Children who have reacted in the past by freezing, holding still, restricting their bodies to barely breathing in states of fear are gently invited to move, to experience the changing states that their bodies can go through, feeling the release as muscles enact energetic transfer in motion. Children who have not been flush with experiences of matched states in their past when it involved violation are offered playful opportunities to engage in rhythmic synchronisation – to follow and be followed, to match and be matched.

Throughout, the relationships between therapist–children and therapist–children–carers are the stage through which the efforts made by children and carers to find expressions in new forms of being and behaving are witnessed and acknowledged. It is through this powerful form of recognition that children's previous acts of resistance, no matter how small or ineffective, come to be integrated into sensory and somatic experiences that become imbued with experiences of relational safety.

Shared moments of standing up to the consequences of abuse become part of the mutual narrative of carer and children, facilitated by the therapist in his/her careful tracking of the micro-exchanges of attunement.

Therapeutic Care adopts a role of Therapeutic Specialist as the mediator and interpreter of the relational milieu that surrounds children in out-of-home care. They seamlessly move from individually oriented therapeutic activity with children, to supporting carers to understand children's behaviour, to providing therapeutic resources for carers as they revisit their own self-narratives of relational disruption and relational safety, to advocating on behalf of carers for basic resources required to maintain placements, to engaging the network of important adults in collective and coordinated planning and action. With every function, the Therapeutic Specialists use their own selves as baseline relational capacity for points in the milieu which are compromised and in need of bracing. These are not traditional roles that focus on the implementation of therapeutic practices. Instead, they engage their skills and trauma-informed knowledge base in applications where and when it is most needed.

It is the unique needs of children, the relational capacities of the children's networks and the system's function in authorising care decision-making about children that is the terrain that Therapeutic Specialists cover.

13

Therapeutic Care as it Evolves

JANISE MITCHELL, JOE TUCCI AND ED TRONICK

This year – 2019 – represents the fiftieth anniversary of a book that is still in print. Trieschman, Whittaker and Brendtro (1969) prefaced this seminal exploration of therapeutic management of children and young people in residential care settings with the following words:

> It was our aim in writing *The Other 23 Hours* to bridge somewhat the gap that exists between the theoretical expertise of the professional clinician on the one hand and the very practical, often mundane problems of those who live with the children for the 23 hours apart from the therapy hour. (Preface)

It is in this tradition that Therapeutic Care has evolved. Its ambition is to deliver an organised system of integrated care and therapeutic support for children living in foster, kinship and adoptive care. It is how it comes together that makes a difference to children and the network of important relationships that love, care, educate and support them. For this very reason, Therapeutic Care is still very much a work in progress. It requires more research, more practice development, more conceptualisation and more opportunities for feedback from children themselves as well as those around them.

In this final chapter, some of the spaces that need completing are explored to give direction to all of us who are working hard to offer children in care the reparative experiences they need. It also articulates the need for policy and systemic reform that will be required in order for the ambitions for children that Therapeutic Care holds to be realised.

We need to work more with children's agency in out-of-home care

Bolin (2016) has made the point that although children's participation in out-of-home care decision-making forums is admirable, it is more important to consider how and whether children can actually exert any influence over their lives. Drawing on the work of Kuczynski, Harach and Bernardini (1999), she argues that in order to position children as active agents, children engage in three forms of agency:

- **Meaning construction** is the process through which children come to make sense of their social environment through attending to, evaluating and at times resisting the appropriateness of adults' actions and messages.
- **Intentional action** gives credence to children having their own purpose, goals and strategy underlying their behaviour.
- **Self-efficacy** is the quality that grows in children as they reflect on their actions and the outcomes they are able to achieve through their own planning and actions.

Some research has demonstrated that children can find the experience of participation in planning and decision-making forums in child protection positive and beneficial. However, there are plenty of barriers that get in the way. Knezevic (2017) identified multiple discourses which organise child welfare practices that prevent children from being constructed as active agents. Slightly re-interpreted here, these involve children as defiant (children constructed as unwilling to cooperate in processes that are meant to be for their benefit), children as deficient (children constructed as compromised as a result of exposure to the value and beliefs of their abusive parents), children as immature (children constructed as incapable of participating meaningfully because of the developmental stage or as a result of traumatised experiences affecting their cognitive capacities), children as disloyal (children constructed as being influenced and manipulated by those who pay attention to them) and children as divisive (children constructed as suspicious because they are raised in a different culture that is not the dominant culture perceived to be at play). These discourses are enacted, for example, when children disagree with the views that professionals hold about what is in their best interests (Thomas and O'Kane, 1998). Cossar, Brandon and Jordan (2014) identified that:

> although children value the chance to attend meetings, their attendance at meetings does not guarantee meaningful participation and may be experienced as intrusive or tokenistic. (p.105)

They went on to describe a number of factors identified by children themselves requiring consideration in order to enable them to have any effective influence over decision-making in child protection, including the need for children to:

- trust the workers who they engaged with to help them have their views represented
- not feel as if they are there to be interrogated
- understand the child protection process more fully so they know what is expected of them and when
- not be asked difficult questions that placed them in a bind in front of their parents or carers
- be able to have their meaning of what is happening appreciated regardless of how much it is perceived by adults to contribute to decision-making processes.

The significance of this theme to the practices of Therapeutic Care rests in its contribution to what is meant by child-centred practice. It invites those in relationship around children to build common ground in their deliberations to focus on how to make it possible for children to experience being influential (Hojholt and Kousholt, 2015, Schwartz, 2017). As children do in any family, they come to experience themselves as agents with self-efficacy through *doing with others*. Their engagement in relational actions nurtures their development. They rehearse, role play, practise developmentally appropriate parcels of responsibilities with trusted adults which prepare them as they grow to be able to do more of these on their own. They experience interdependence on their way to independence.

Therapeutic Care will need to incorporate attention on the active agency of children into the evolution of its practice approach. The more adults believe in the right of participation and agency, the more likely it is for children to step into and fulfil this right (Kosher, 2018).

We need to work more on understanding and supporting sibling relationships for children in out-of-home care

In his review of the literature, McCormick (2010) maintained:

> [S]ibling relationships in the foster care experience have historically taken a back seat to other issues, such as the child–caregiver relationship. (p.198)

Like other issues in out-of-home care, there is a difference in perception and reality in practice. McCormick summarised the topic eloquently when he pointed out:

> [T]he majority of child welfare professionals strongly support the idea that keeping siblings together is in their best interest, in most circumstances. The number of siblings in foster care who are separated from one another, however, speaks to the systematic inability to maintain those relationships. It is estimated that more than 50% of youth in foster care who have siblings are not currently placed with any of those siblings… [M]any believe that because of the high levels of separation of siblings in care and the devastating results of these separations, significant change is necessary in the way that children are placed. (p.199)

Stevenson Wojciak, McWey and Waid (2018) identified that, in the US, sibling placements are not even tracked within the foster care system and yet reported that anywhere between 23% and 82% of children are placed without at least one sibling at some point in time while in foster care.

Therapeutic Care is concerned with all the relationships that matter to children in out-of-home care. Children's relationships with their siblings can offer them the sense of permanence of an accompanied other in their lives. For each other, siblings provide the relational means through which a shared history can be experienced, allowing for mutual enjoyment, reflection and opportunities to co-create the meaning of events and experiences that have shaped their identities. They can be a ready-made support group as they travel through changes in environments, such as schools or foster families. They can act as allies when there is a need. They can represent the experience of continuity of love – the sense of belonging over time to relationships that are important. Siblings can provide the means through which children can connect with their family cultural heritage and share in traditions and practices that they have become distant from.

A growing body of research suggests that placing siblings with each other in foster care provides many benefits, including promoting placement stability, adjustment and integration into the foster family, leading to improved educational and developmental outcomes compared with those children who are not placed with their siblings (Affronti, Rittner and Semanchin Jones, 2015; Albert and King, 2008; Barth *et al.*, 2007; Hegar, 2005; Hegar and Rosenthal, 2009, 2011; Leathers, 2005; Miron, Sujan and Middleton, 2013). Taking all this evidence together, Stevenson Wojciak, McWey and Waid (2018) have made the case that sibling relationships of children in foster care is a predictor of resilience and as such supported where it can be.

Of course, this is not the case for all siblings. Stevenson Wojciak (2017) surveyed children who attend a camp specifically designed to reunify them with siblings from whom they have been separated. He found that although for many the sibling relationship offered a range of protective factors to one another, there were tensions for some that needed to be addressed. Many could be resolved by ensuring that more time was allowed for siblings to interact because aspects of the relationship deteriorated as they spent less and less time with each other. Most significant for some, the pain of separating after coming together was significant and made them behave in ways that pushed each other away because neither wanted to feel the full impact of the hurt of losing their sibling again so soon after coming together.

Therapeutic Care recognises the importance of siblings as relational resources for children in out-of-home care. As yet, it has not developed and articulated a nuanced approach to making these relationships available and effective for children. There is a need to develop ways to assess the quality of sibling relationships and siblings' experience of living together and/or having contact when they are separated. It is incumbent on the network of relationships around children to determine the conditions that need to be organised for siblings to experience each other in ways that are most helpful, enjoyable and strengthening of their individual needs together.

We need to become more sophisticated about the dynamics of collaboration in networks of people around children in out-of-home care

It is increasingly clear that the effectiveness of interagency and cross-system collaboration can lead to improved outcomes for children and families in the child protection system (Nwabuzor Ogbonnaya and Keeney, 2018). Of course, this is not a new finding. However, the subtle dynamics that affect how well groups of professionals can work together continues to elude practice in our experience. The qualities of the deliberations and connectedness that occur in Therapeutic Care Teams require attention to be given to the dynamics that emerge between and with those in relationship with children and carers.

The work of Anne Edwards from the Department of Education at the University of Oxford may offer a way forward that can reshape the landscape of collaboration. Instead of personal agency, she has defined a new quality and competency that a resourceful practitioner should possess – relational agency, which is

> the capacity to align one's thoughts and actions with those of others in order to interpret problems of practice and to respond to those interpretations. (Edwards, 2005, pp.169–170)

More specifically, she describes relational agency as an enhanced version of personal agency in that it is the capacity of individuals to

> work with others to expand the object that one is working on and trying to transform by recognising and accessing the resources that others bring to bear as they interpret and respond to the object. It is a capacity which involves recognising that another person may be a resource and that work needs to be done to elicit, recognise and negotiate the use of that resource in order to align oneself in joint action on the object. (p.172)

This concept of relational agency is clearly applicable in Therapeutic Care. The common project (object) is the focus of the collective efforts of the Therapeutic Care Team, which is affirmed by Edwards (2011) as needing to reach beyond their own individual institutional contexts and align themselves with the shared goals and ambitions of the team as defined by the needs of children and the carers who support them.

For Edwards, relational expertise is

> based on confident engagement with the knowledge that underpins one's own specialist practice, as well as a capacity to recognise and respond to what others might offer in local systems of distributed expertise. (p.33)

The Therapeutic Care Team is an example of a network of distributed intelligence with individual and relational forms of expertise. This network interacts at the boundaries where practice intersects and common knowledge emerges. Common knowledge itself comes to be mobilised in the way that the team members use it. The positioning of the child's needs, the clarity with which the child's trauma experiences is always aligned to explanations about their behaviour, the understanding of the nature of the interaction between children and their relational and sensory environment, the collective commitment to compassionate inquiry are experiences that are all negotiated at the boundaries of practice. Citing Hartley (2007), these are the 'inter' spaces that bring together multiple inter-subjectivities and create the opportunities for new solutions to be created for the child.

It is in these spaces that pay attention to organisational boundaries that the dynamics of individuals working together meet and set the parameters about what is possible, how much change can be allowed and how the experience of plans and decisions are felt.

> Boundaries...are places where practices are alerted to changes which may affect actors' relative power, their resources and identities. Working relationally at organisational boundaries, therefore, involves the personal challenges of negotiating expertise in settings where one may not be able to manipulate practices, and where the practices that were being protected by the boundary may themselves be destabilised by your actions... [O]rganisational boundaries can be uncomfortable places. (Edwards, 2011, p.35)

Not only the Therapeutic Specialist but all members of the Therapeutic Care Team, as Macnamara has observed in his earlier chapter, work horizontally across boundaries between organisations. This task needs cooperative effort and cannot be easily imposed by organisations through policy and procedural edict. All members of the team act more as 'gardeners' (Christiensen and Laegreid, 2007, as cited in Edwards, 2011) tending to the growth of new emergent properties of the collaboration.

Examples of the innovation in thinking when this occurs is evidenced by the recent research reported by Biggart *et al.* (2017) which highlights the commonality of experience that can occur when teams work together, resulting in the experience of availability, acceptance, cooperation and belonging – all the qualities acting as a secure base for practitioners in their day-to-day experiences.

This is the form of praxis that will deliver reconstituted understandings of how planning and decision-making about children, with children and their carers, can be optimised for the benefit of children. The evolution of Therapeutic Care will be promoted by the inclusion and exploration of knowledge about the microlevel negotiations that enable collective practice to feature even more resolutely as part of its system of organisation.

We need to work with sensitivity and commitment to integrate a focus on children's cultural heritage for their well-being

Western approaches to understanding and responding to the needs of children in care dominate, yet the data tells us children from minority groups and diverse cultural backgrounds constitute significant populations of children in the care system. In the United States, of the 273,539 children who entered foster care during 2016, 53% identified from a minority cultural background including African-American (21%), Hispanic (20%) and other races or multiracial (10%) (Child Welfare Information Gateway, 2017). In England, 25% of children in foster care come from other cultural backgrounds than that described as 'white', with this percentage increasing over time (Department of Education, 2018). As Glenda Kickett and colleagues noted in their earlier chapter, although they only make up 5.5% of all children aged 0–17 years in Australia (Australian Institute of Health and Welfare (AIHW), 2018), Aboriginal and Torres Strait Islander children are almost ten times more likely than non-Indigenous children to be placed in out-of-home care, making up 36.9% of all children in care (AIHW, 2018).

> Knowing one's family and being a part of one's community are both vital aspects of the child/young person's cultural identity and both

> need support if the child or young person is going to be culturally cared for. Cultural care/support plans need to be living documents, rather than records which are updated from time to time, because cultural identity is formed out of ongoing experiences. (Libesman, 2011, p.12)

A critical barrier to appropriate cultural care and culturally strong Therapeutic Care is often the lack of meaningful understanding about the significance of cultural care and how it impacts on all aspects of a child's well-being (Libesman, 2011). This is not surprising given that child welfare practice has its roots in social work, a largely Western discipline in its origins and teachings. The need for culturally sensitive approaches to the provision of Therapeutic Care for children from diverse cultural backgrounds is imperative. The achievement of this vision will take time, careful consideration and a willingness to critically appraise the assumptions underpinning service and system design in the development and delivery of Therapeutic Care. Gray and her colleagues (2013) refer to the need to 'decolonise practice' and seek locally developed, culturally relevant forms of practice and research. Decolonising practice

> recognizes and credits the strengths and contributions of Indigenous knowledges, traditions and practices, and supports Indigenous Peoples' cultural survival and Indigenous rights. It means recognizing that the cultural knowledges and practices of Indigenous Peoples serve as an important counterweight to Western ways of thinking and behaving. (Gray *et al.*, 2013, p.28)

Acknowledging the enormity of this challenge, Gray *et al.* (2013) noted the difficulty for

> practitioners working with Indigenous Peoples or in non-Western contexts, or even with cultures other than their own in Western contexts, to make mainstream social work practice models fit these contexts. This difficulty reflects the tension within social work concerning what constitutes professional social work practice and what can be appropriately transported to other cultures. (p.30)

In the face of the globalisation of knowledge and evidence-based models of practice in Therapeutic Care, these words are a timely and critical call to action in the future development of practice, research and knowledge building in the field.

We need a sustained commitment to undertake reform that embeds Therapeutic Care into the systems of child protection and out-of-home care

Many systems internationally have undergone numerous reviews of out-of-home care. As far back as 2008, Mitchell identified a decade of review after review in Australia with very little actual reform being achieved. The issues facing out-of-home care have changed little in more than 20 years. The number of children coming into care has increased significantly. The needs of the children coming into care have become more complex and their behaviour more challenging. Placement stability remains elusive. The number of carers willing and able to look after children in these circumstances is on the decline. The number of children who are being placed with relatives or kin is increasing. Carers, of all types, are seeking additional and intensive levels of support to be able to respond to and manage the needs of children in their care. The financial support offered to carers rarely meets the full cost of looking after children in out-of-home care. The coordination of services for children is beleaguered by interagency and interdisciplinary issues and tensions. Systems struggle to consistently implement adequate planning processes for children in care. The developmental, education and social outcomes for children in out-of-home care are often not resourced effectively.

These are concerns that Therapeutic Care has the chance to remedy. It matches the complexity of the issues facing the system with a complex and integrated set of strategies. At its core, it finds its resources in the actions of relationships which are critical in the lives of children in out-of-home care.

As a paradigm of practice, it is greater than any specific model or approach. In its consilience, it draws from the lessons of those making the effort to combine therapeutic intent into the ways that children experience the micro-opportunities for healing that relationships offer them. Therapeutic Care is the expression of a system of care that has the capacity to coordinate and co-organise the multiple dimensions of these children's lives into a helix of experiences whose sum total is stability, love and transformation.

Therapeutic Care needs a sustained commitment so that it becomes embedded into the systems of out-of-home care provided to children who have suffered from the trauma of violation and neglect.

Therapeutic Care is a reform. It is also a realisation of our collective hope for our most vulnerable children.

Although there is still much to learn and much that can be improved, we should not lose sight of the difference we are already making in the field of Therapeutic Care. Shining a light on this are the words of a child who experienced the TrACK Program:

> I never thought anyone would care about me. Everyone thought I was too hard to deal with, getting aggro and stuff. I'm not sure what happens, I just know it's been there for a long time. I tried hurting myself to get the anger out but it just made things worse. Everyone seemed even more frightened of me. No one seemed to be able to deal with me. They meant well, I guess. I felt like I didn't deserve anyone caring about me. What if I let them down? What if they stopped caring? It all changed when I came here to live with Andrew and Cathy. That was four years ago. It's the longest I have lived anywhere. Things have changed a lot. I know I will never be able to live with my Mum and Dad but I still see them. They are still my family. But so are Cathy and Andrew...they support me and care about me and stuff. I feel like a normal kid now. I don't blow up like I used to. Don't need to any more.

It is what children in out-of-home care need and deserve.

References

Affronti, M., Rittner, B. and Semanchin Jones, A.M. (2015). Functional adaptation to foster care: Former foster youth speak out. *Journal of Public Child Welfare*, 9(1), 1–21.

Albert, V.N. and King, W.C. (2008). Survival analyses of the dynamics of sibling experiences in foster care. *Families in Society*, 89(4), 535–541.

Australian Institute of Health and Welfare (2018). *Child Protection Australia 2016–17*. Supplementary Data Tables. Canberra: AIHW.

Barth, R.P., Lloyd, E.C., Green, R.L., James, S., Leslie, L.R. and Landsverk, J. (2007). Predictors of placement moves among children with and without emotional and behavioural disorders. *Journal of Emotional and Behavioural Disorders*, 15(1), 45–55.

Biggart, L., Ward, E., Cool, L. and Schofield, G. (2017). The team as a secure base: Promoting resilience and competence in child and family social work. *Children and Youth Services Review*, 83, 119–130.

Bolin, A. (2016). Children's agency in interprofessional collaborative meetings in child welfare work. *Child and Family Social Work*, 21(4), 502–511.

Child Welfare Information Gateway (2017). *Foster Care Statistics 2016*. Washington, DC: US Department of Health and Human Services, Children's Bureau.

Christiensen, T. and Laegreid, P. (2007). The whole of government approach to public service reform. *Public Administration Review*, November/December, 1059–1066.

Cossar, J., Brandon, M. and Jordan, P. (2014). 'You've got to trust her and she's got to trust you': Children's views on participation in the child protection system. *Child and Family Social Work*, 21(1), 103–112.

Department of Education (2018). Children looked after in England (including adoption), year ending 31 March 2018. Accessed on 8/1/2019 at https://assets.publishing.service.gov.uk/government/uploads/system/uploads/attachment_data/file/756232/Children_looked_after_in_England_2018_Text.pdf.

Edwards, A. (2005). Relational agency: Learning to be a resourceful practitioner. *International Journal of Educational Research*, 43(3), 168–182.

Edwards, A. (2011). Building common knowledge at the boundaries between professional practices: Relational agency and relational expertise in systems of distributed expertise. *International Journal of Educational Research*, 50(1), 33–39.

Gray, M., Coates, J., Yellow Bird, M. and Hetherington, T. (2013). Scoping the Terrain of Decolonisation. In M. Gray, J. Coates, M. Yellow Bird and T. Hetherington (eds), *Decolonising Social Work*. Farnham: Ashgate.

Hartley, D. (2007). Education policy and the 'inter'-regnum. *Journal of Education Policy*, 22(6), 695–708.

Hegar, R.L. (2005). Sibling placement in foster care and adoption: An overview of international research. Special Issue: Siblings in Foster Care and Adoption. *Children and Youth Services Review*, 27(7), 717–739.

Hegar, R.L. and Rosenthal, J.A. (2009). Kinship care and sibling placement: Child behaviour, family relationships and school outcomes. *Children and Youth Services Review*, 31(6), 670–679.

Hegar, R.L. and Rosenthal, J.A. (2011). Foster children placed with or separated from siblings: Outcomes based on a national sample. *Children and Youth Services Review*, 33(7), 1245–1253.

Hojholt, C. and Kousholt, D. (2015). Children Participating and Developing Agency in and across Various Social Practices. In M. Fleer and B.V. Oers (eds), *International Handbook on Early Childhood Education*. Dordrecht: Springer.

Knezevic, Z. (2017). Amoral, im/moral and dis/loyal: Children's moral status in child welfare. *Childhood*, 24(4), 470–484.

Kosher, H. (2018). What children and parents think about children's right to participation. *International Journal of Children's Rights*, 26(2), 295–328.

Kucynski, L., Harach, L. and Bernardini, C.S. (1999). Psychology's Child Meets Sociology's Child: Agency, Influence and Power in Parent–Child Relationships. In F.M. Berardo and C.L. Shehan (eds), *Through the Eyes of the Child: Re-Visioning Children as Active Agents in Family Life, Vol 1, Contemporary Perspective on Families*. Stamford, CT: JAI Press.

Leathers, S.J. (2005). Separation from siblings: Associations with placement adaptation and outcomes among adolescents in long-term foster care. *Children and Youth Services Review*, 27(7), 793–819.

Libesman, T. (2011). Cultural Care for Aboriginal and Torres Strait Islander Children in Out of Home Care. Secretariat of National Aboriginal and Islander Children in Care (SNAICC) and Barnardos, Melbourne.

McCormick, A. (2010). Siblings in foster care: An overview of research, policy and practice. *Journal of Public Child Welfare*, 4(2), 198–218.

Miron, D., Sujan, A. and Middleton, M. (2013). Considering the best interests of infants in foster care placed separately from their siblings. *Children and Youth Services Review*, 35(9), 1385–1392.

Mitchell, J. (2008). A case study in attempted reform in out of home care: A preliminary examination of the introduction of the Circle Therapeutic Foster Care Program in Victoria. Unpublished Masters Thesis, Monash University, Victoria.

Nwabuzor Ogbonnaya, I. and Keeney, A.J. (2018). A systematic review of the effectiveness of interagency and cross system collaborations in the United States to improve child welfare outcomes. *Children and Youth Services Review*, 94, 225–245.

Schwartz, I. (2017). Putting the child at the centre of inter-professional cooperation in out of home care. *Child and Family Social Work*, 22, 992–999.

Stevenson Wojciak, A. (2017). 'It's complicated.' Exploring the meaning of sibling relationships of youth in foster care. *Child and Family Social Work*, 22(2), 1283–1291.

Stevenson Wojciak, A., McWey, L.M. and Waid, J. (2018). Sibling relationships of youth in foster care: A predictor of resilience. *Children and Youth Services Review*, 84, 247–254.

Thomas, N. and O'Kane, C. (1998). When children's wishes and feelings clash with their best interests. *International Journal of Children's Rights*, 6(2), 137–154.

Trieschman, A.E., Whittaker, J.K. and Brendtro, L.K. (1969). *The Other 23 Hours*. Chicago, IL: Aldine Publishing.

Author Biographies

Jon Baylin, Clinical Psychologist, Delaware, USA
Jon Baylin began developing a brain-based model of trauma-focused treatment twenty years ago. For the past ten years, he has collaborated with Dan Hughes, leading to the publication of *Brain-based Parenting*, 2012 and *The Neurobiology of Attachment-focused Therapy*, 2016. Dan and Jon continue to refine their integrative model and to present it to professionals internationally.

Shaun Chandran, Program Manager, Australian Childhood Foundation, Western Australia
Shaun Chandran has worked as a psychologist with children, young people and their families in a range of settings, including out of home care, education and youth homelessness. He has led the development and delivery of a number of therapeutic care programs and practice frameworks in partnership with the government and community sector.

Elaine Farmer, Emeritus Professor of Child and Family Studies, School for Policy Studies, Bristol, UK
Elaine Farmer worked as a social worker in England and Australia. After doing this for a number of years, she led many large-scale government-funded research studies and has published widely on child protection, reunification, kinship and foster care.

Kathomi Gatwiri, PhD, Southern Cross University, Australia
Dr. Kathomi Gatwiri is the author of *African Womanhood and Incontinent Bodies*. She is a social worker and psychotherapist, and holds a Master's in Counselling and Psychotherapy from the Cairnmillar Institute in Melbourne, and a PhD from Flinders University in South Australia.

Kim S. Golding, Clinical Psychologist, Kim S Golding Ltd, Worcestershire, UK

Kim Golding is a clinical psychologist specialising in helping children in care or adopted from care. She is a DDP consultant and trainer. Kim is a board member of DDPI and director of DDP Connects UK. Kim is the author of books and programmes written for parents, educational staff and practitioners supporting children with experience of developmental trauma.

Dan Hughes, Clinical Psychologist, Founder of Dyadic Developmental Psychotherapy (DDP), South Portland, Maine, USA

Dan has developed a model of therapy (DDP) for abused children and their foster or adoptive families. DDP has evolved as an attachment-based model of family therapy. He has written many books and articles and has spoken professionally and trained therapists in his model of treatment all over the world for the past 20 years. His most comprehensive book, written with two colleagues is titled *Healing Relational Trauma with Attachment-Focused Interventions.*

Glenda Kickett, Social Worker, Lecturer in Social Work and Social Policy, University of South Wales, Manager for Aboriginal Therapeutic Services, Australian Childhood Foundation, Australia

Glenda Kickett is a determined Whadjuk and Ballardong Noongar woman who has worked tirelessly for more than 30 years in Aboriginal-related areas of policy, management and community services. She is a social worker by profession and lectures in social work and social policy at the University of Western Australia.

Meredith Kiraly, Research Fellow, University of Melbourne, Australia

Meredith Kiraly is a psychologist with extensive practice experience in out-of-home care. She is a Research Fellow at University of Melbourne, and has a small consultancy in human services. Her specialty research area is kinship care on which topic she has published extensively and engaged in advocacy for better support.

Noel Macnamara, Executive Manager Policy and Research Australian Childhood Foundation, Australia
Noel has been a social worker and manager for over 30 years in a variety of settings in Australia and the UK. These have included: Therapeutic community for children, child protection, Family & Couple Counselling and the Family Court of Australia. He worked as an Executive Officer in the DHS, Victoria before taking up his current position as Executive Manager at ACF. Noel is the co-author of: *Supervising Child Protection Practice: What Works?*

Lynne McPherson, BSW, MSW, M.AASW, Ph.D. (Churchill Fellow), Australia
Dr McPherson is a senior lecturer in social work at Southern Cross University, Australia. Lynne has more than 25 years as a social work manager and practice leader in child protection. Her research interests include therapeutic approaches in out of home care and supervision and leadership.

Cathy Malchiodi, PhD, Executive Director, Trauma-Informed Practices and Expressive Arts Therapy, Louisville, USA
Cathy Malchiodi has over 30 years of experience working with traumatized children, adolescents, adults, families and communities and has expanding the range of understanding the arts therapies through 20 books, 50 chapters and over 500 invited presentations.

Janise Mitchell MSW, Deputy CEO, Australian Childhood Foundation and Director, Centre for Excellence in Therapeutic Care, Camberwell, Australia
Janise Mitchell has pioneered the development of therapeutic foster, kinship and residential care programs in Australia. She has worked in the fields of child protection, public policy and therapeutic intervention for three decades.

Orgilmaa Munkhbaatar, Harvard University Student, Massachusetts, USA
Orgilmaa Munkhbaatar is a senior at Harvard University, graduating with a degree in Neurobiology under the Mind, Brain, & Behavior track. She conducted her undergraduate thesis exploring the impacts of postpartum depression and childhood maltreatment on maternal neurobiology under the guidance of Dr. Martin Teicher at McLean Hospital.

Bruce D. Perry, M.D., Ph.D., Senior Fellow, The Child Trauma Academy, Adjunct Professor, Department of Psychiatry & Behavioral Sciences, Feinberg School of Medicine, Northwestern University, Chicago IL & School of Allied Health, College of Science, Health and Engineering, La Trobe University, Melbourne, Victoria
Dr. Bruce Perry is a researcher, clinician and teacher in the areas of child development, traumatology and maltreatment for more than 30 years. His work has been instrumental in translation of concepts from the neurosciences into clinical practice, programs and policy.

Allan Schore, Clinical Faculty Member, UCLA David Geffen School of Medicine, California, USA
Allan Schore is the author of six seminal volumes, most recently *Right Brain Psychotherapy*, and *The Development of the Unconscious Mind*, as well as numerous articles and chapters. He has had a private practice in psychotherapy for five decades.

Martin H. Teicher, Director Developmental Biopsychiatry Research Program, McLean Hospital, Associate Professor of Psychiatry, Harvard Medical School, Massachusetts, USA
Martin pioneered research into the effects of childhood maltreatment on trajectories of brain development and risk for psychopathology. He has identified sensitive exposure periods when brain regions are most vulnerable and is exploring the neurobiological basis of resilience. He is a PhD Experimental Psychologist and an MD Psychiatrist.

Joe Tucci, PhD, CEO of the Australian Childhood Foundation, Richmond, Australia
Joe Tucci is the CEO of the Australian Childhood Foundation, a major not for profit organisation providing therapeutic support to children and young people who have experienced abuse related trauma. He has combined his experience in child protection, trauma therapy and advocacy for children across his career over the past 30 years.

Ed Tronick, PhD, Developmental Neuroscientist and Clinical Psychologist, Boston, USA

Dr. Ed Tronick is a University Distinguished Professor of Developmental Brain Science at the University of Massachusetts Boston and a Research Associate in the Department of Newborn, Medicine Harvard Medical School. He is internationally recognized for his research on infant neurobehavior and infant face-to-face infant interactions. He formulated that Still-Face paradigm, and the Mutual Regulation Model with its reparation-mismatch theory of interactions and therapeutic interactions.

Subject Index

Author Index